ESSENTIALITY OF WORK

RESEARCH IN THE SOCIOLOGY OF WORK

Editor-in-Chief: Rick Delbridge

Associate Editors: Markus Helfen, Andreas (Andi) Pekarek, Gretchen Purser

Recent Volumes:

Volume 1:	Class Consciousness
Volume 2:	Peripheral Workers
Volume 3:	Unemployment
Volume 4:	High Tech Work
Volume 5:	The Meaning of Work
Volume 6:	The Globalization of Work
Volume 7:	Work and Family
Volume 8:	Deviance in the Workplace
Volume 9:	Marginal Employment
Volume 10:	Transformation of Work
Volume 11:	Labor Revitalization: Global Perspectives and New Initiatives
Volume 12:	The Sociology of Job Training
Volume 13:	Globalism/Localism at Work
Volume 14:	Diversity in the Workforce
Volume 15:	Entrepreneurship
Volume 16:	Worker Participation: Current Research and Future Trends
Volume 17:	Work Place Temporalities
Volume 18:	Economic Sociology of Work
Volume 19:	Work and Organizations in China after Thirty Years of Transition
Volume 20:	Gender and Sexuality in the Workplace
Volume 21:	Institutions and Entrepreneurship
Volume 22:	Part 1: Comparing European Workers Part A
	Part 2: Comparing European Workers Part B: Policies and Institutions
Volume 23:	Religion, Work, and Inequality
Volume 24:	Networks, Work and Inequality
Volume 25:	Adolescent Experiences and Adult Work Outcomes: Connections and Causes
Volume 26:	Work and Family in the New Economy
Volume 27:	Immigration and Work
Volume 28:	A Gedenkschrift to Randy Hodson: Working with Dignity
Volume 29:	Research in the Sociology of Work
Volume 30:	Emerging Conceptions of Work, Management and the Labor Market
Volume 31:	Precarious Work
Volume 32:	Race, Identity and Work
Volume 33:	Work and Labor in the Digital Age
Volume 34:	Professional Work: Knowledge, Power and Social Inequalities
Volume 35:	Ethnographies of Work

EDITORIAL ADVISORY BOARD

Ifeoma Ajunwa
Cornell University, USA

Michel Anteby
Boston University, USA

Steve Barley
Stanford University, USA

David Courpasson
Emlyon Business School, France

Liz Gorman
University of Virginia, USA

Bill Harley
University of Melbourne, Australia

Josh Healy
The University of Newcastle, Australia

Heather Hofmeister
Goethe University, Germany

Hajo Holst
University of Osnabrück, Germany

Alexandra Kalev
Tel Aviv University, Israel

Arne Kalleberg
University of North Carolina, USA

Erin Kelly
Massachusetts Institute of Technology, USA

Kate Kellogg
Massachusetts Institute of Technology, USA

Julie Kmec
Washington State University, USA

Marek Korczynski
University of Nottingham, UK

Anne Kovalainen
University of Turku, Finland

Robin Leidner
University of Pennsylvania, USA

Steve Lopez
Ohio State University, USA

Irene Padavic
Florida State University, USA

Valeria Pulignano
Catholic University, Belgium

Lauren Rivera
Northwestern University, USA

Dee Royster
New York University, USA

Vinnie Roscigno
Ohio State University, USA

Jeff Sallaz
University of Arizona, USA

Ofer Sharone
University of Massachusetts Amherst, USA

Sheryl Skaggs
University of Texas Dallas, USA

Don Tomaskovic-Devey
University of Massachusetts Amherst, USA

Catherine Turco
Massachusetts Institute of Technology, USA

Steve Vallas
Northeastern University, USA

Geert Van Hootegem
Catholic University, Belgium

Matt Vidal
King's College London, UK

Chris Warhurst
University of Warwick, UK

Christine Williams
University of Texas Austin, USA

George Wilson
University of Miami, USA

Adia Wingfield
Washington University St Louis, USA

Patrizia Zanoni
Hasselt University, Belgium

RESEARCH IN THE SOCIOLOGY OF WORK, VOLUME 36

ESSENTIALITY OF WORK

Edited by

MARKUS HELFEN
Hertie School, Germany

RICK DELBRIDGE
Cardiff University, UK

ANDREAS (ANDI) PEKAREK
University of Melbourne, Australia

AND

GRETCHEN PURSER
Syracuse University, USA

United Kingdom – North America – Japan
India – Malaysia – China

Emerald Publishing Limited
Emerald Publishing, Floor 5, Northspring, 21-23 Wellington Street, Leeds LS1 4DL.

First edition 2024

Editorial matter and selection © 2024 Markus Helfen, Rick Delbridge,
Andreas (Andi) Pekarek and Gretchen Purser.
Individual chapters © 2024 The authors.
Published under exclusive licence by Emerald Publishing Limited.

Reprints and permissions service
Contact: www.copyright.com

No part of this book may be reproduced, stored in a retrieval system, transmitted in any form or by any means electronic, mechanical, photocopying, recording or otherwise without either the prior written permission of the publisher or a licence permitting restricted copying issued in the UK by The Copyright licencing Agency and in the USA by The Copyright Clearance Center. Any opinions expressed in the chapters are those of the authors. Whilst Emerald makes every effort to ensure the quality and accuracy of its content, Emerald makes no representation implied or otherwise, as to the chapters' suitability and application and disclaims any warranties, express or implied, to their use.

British Library Cataloguing in Publication Data
A catalogue record for this book is available from the British Library

ISBN: 978-1-83608-149-4 (Print)
ISBN: 978-1-83608-148-7 (Online)
ISBN: 978-1-83608-150-0 (Epub)

ISSN: 0277-2833 (Series)

Printed and bound by CPI Group (UK) Ltd, Croydon, CR0 4YY

INVESTOR IN PEOPLE

CONTENTS

About the Editors — ix

About the Contributors — xi

Chapter 1 Essential Work, Inessential Workers?
Markus Helfen, Rick Delbridge, Andreas (Andi) Pekarek and Gretchen Purser — 1

Chapter 2 Doing Essential 'Dirty Work': Making Visible the Emotion Management Skills in Gendered Care Work
Anna Milena Galazka and Sarah Jenkins — 11

Chapter 3 Defining Essential: How Custodial Labour Became Synonymous with Safety During the COVID-19 Pandemic
Annie J. Murphy — 39

Chapter 4 Fear and Professionalism on the Front Line: Emotion Management of Residential Care Workers Through the Lens of COVID-19 as a 'Breaching Experiment'
Valeria Pulignano, Mê-Linh Riemann, Carol Stephenson and Markieta Domecka — 57

Chapter 5 The Politics of Essentiality: Praise for Dirty Work During the COVID-19 Pandemic
Nancy Côté, Jean-Louis Denis, Steven Therrien and Flavia Sofia Ciafre — 81

Chapter 6 Essential Workers in the United States: An Intersectional Perspective
Caroline Hanley and Enobong Hannah Branch — 109

A Note from the Editors: Introducing 'Spotlight on Ethnography' — 143

Chapter 7 Floral Ethics and Aesthetics: Understanding Professional Expertise at Work
Isabelle Zinn — 145

**Chapter 8 Ethnographic Studies of Essential Work:
Jana Costas' 'Dramas of Dignity' and Peter Birke's
'Grenzen aus Glas' as Two German Exemplars**
Markus Helfen   *163*

**Chapter 9 'More Than a Slight Ache': On the Ethnographic
Sensibility and Enduring Relevance of Studs Terkel's *Working***
Gretchen Purser   *177*

Index   *189*

ABOUT THE EDITORS

Markus Helfen is a Senior Research Fellow in the Hertie School Berlin, Germany as well as a Private Lecturer at Freie Universität, Berlin. He is a member of the Advisory Boards of the *German Journal of Human Resource Management* and the journal *Industrielle Beziehungen – The German Journal of Industrial Relations*. He has been a regular Co-convenor at the European Group of Organization Studies annual colloquia with the international research group 'Organization Studies and Industrial Relations'. He publishes in leading management and industrial relations journals like *Organization Studies, Human Relations*, and the *British Journal of Industrial Relations*. He does research in the fields of organization theory and employment relations with a focus on collective action, institutional work, and sustainability. Current research topics and projects include the humanization of warehouse work in the digital transformation and global labour standards in supply chains.

Rick Delbridge is Professor of Organizational Analysis at Cardiff Business School and Co-convenor of the Centre for Innovation Policy Research, Cardiff University. He has research interests across various aspects of work, management, organization and innovation in both private and public sector organizations and has published widely on these. He also has a long-standing interest in Japanese business and management and is currently undertaking work on traditional Japanese craft firms. He has been awarded best paper prizes by Academy of Management Review and Organization Studies. He has been elected to Fellowships of the Academy of Social Sciences, British Academy of Management, and the Learned Society of Wales.

Andreas (Andi) Pekarek is a Senior Lecturer in the Department of Management and Marketing at the University of Melbourne, Australia. He is fascinated by how people work, and his research has focussed on how collective action by workers and their allies can steer the world of work in a more sustainable direction, towards fairness and social justice. His recent projects have centred on gig work in the platform economy, unions and industrial relations institutions, the HRM occupation, and interdisciplinary approaches to the study of work. He has published in such journals as *Industrial and Labor Relations Review, Organization, Human Resource Management Journal, British Journal of Industrial Relations*, and *New Technology, Work and Employment*. In addition to his role as Associate Editor for *Research in the Sociology of Work*, he serves on the editorial board of the *Journal of Industrial Relations* (Sage).

Gretchen Purser is an Associate Professor of Sociology at the Maxwell School of Citizenship and Public Affairs at Syracuse University. Her scholarship focusses broadly on the intersection between precarious work and the low-wage labor market and the reproduction and lived experience of urban poverty in the USA. She uses ethnographic and/or community-based research methods to explore the changing nature of work and workers' movements as well as the ground-level practices of neoliberal poverty management. Her articles have appeared in leading journal such as *Ethnography*, *Journal of Contemporary Ethnography*, *Critical Sociology*, *Social Service Review*, *Working USA*, and *Anthropology of Work Review*. She has received a wide variety of publication awards from the American Sociological Association and the Working Class Studies Association and serves as Associate Editor of both *Research in the Sociology of Work* and *Critical Sociology*.

ABOUT THE CONTRIBUTORS

Enobong Hannah Branch is a Professor of Sociology at Rutgers University-New Brunswick, USA. She specializes in race, gender, and labor inequality. Hanley and she are the co-authors of *Work in Black and White: Striving for the American Dream* (Russell Sage Foundation, 2022).

Flavia Sofia Ciafre completed her Bachelor of Laws (L.L.B.) from Université de Montréal, Canada in 2022, where her academic interests centred on the sociology of law, administrative law, and health law. As of fall of 2023, she is enrolled as a student at the Quebec Bar, pursuing further education and training to advance her career in the legal field.

Nancy Côté is an Associate Professor in the Department of Sociology at Université Laval (Québec, Canada) and a Researcher at the VITAM Research Centre in sustainable health, where she co-leads the research theme Environments: Living Environments and Work Environments. She holds a Canada Research Chair in the sociology of work and healthcare organizations. Her research program is situated at the crossroads of the sociology of work, professions, and organizations. Her works focusses on the transformations of healthcare and social care sectors, with particular interest in their impact on the work of professionals and managers. She is interested in social innovations, leadership, work engagement, new modes of collaboration, and redefinition of professional roles.

Jean-Louis Denis is Professor in Health Policy and Management at the Université de Montréal, Canada, School of Public Health, and Researcher on innovation and health system at the CRCHUM. He holds a Canada Research Chair on design and adaptation of health systems. His research program is located at the intersection of applied health services research, organizational studies, and policy research. His research aims at developing a comparative and transdisciplinary perspective on large-scale health reforms and on transformations and improvement in health systems and organizations. He is an elected Member of the Academy of Social Sciences of the Royal Society of Canada (2002) and Fellow of the Canadian Academy of Health Sciences (2009). In 2019, he was elected Fellow of the UK Academy of Social Sciences (2019) for his exceptional contribution to the field of health policy and management. He is Co-editor of the Organizational Behaviour in Healthcare series at Palgrave.

Markieta Domecka, a Senior Lecturer at the University of Roehampton, and a Research Fellow at the CESO, KU Leuven. Her research interests centre around sociology of work, unpaid labour, inequality and the meaning of work across social classes, genders, ethnicities, industries, and national contexts. Her most recent publications are: 'Working Hard for the Ones You Love and Care for Under COVID-19 Physical Distancing', *Work, Employment & Society*, with Valeria Pulignano and Lander Vermeerbergen, and 'How State Influence on Project Work Organization Both Drives and Mitigates Gendered Precarity in Cultural and Creative Industries', *British Journal of Industrial Relations*, with Valeria Pulignano, Deborah Dean, and L. Vermeerbergen.

Anna Milena Galazka is a Lecturer in Management, Employment, and Organization in the Management, Employment, and Organization section at Cardiff Business School, Cardiff University, UK. Her research interests include the transformative power of positive relationships, reflexivity, social innovation, emancipation, stigma, and dirty work. Much of her research has been conducted in the context of wound care provision. Her interdisciplinary work has appeared in *Work, Employment and Society, Sociology of Health & Illness, Journal of Critical Realism, International Journal of Management Reviews*, and *International Wound Journal*. Her current research interests include responsible social innovation in community care. She is member of the CARE Research Centre at Cardiff University.

Caroline Hanley is an Associate Professor of Sociology at William & Mary, USA. She specializes in earnings inequality, employment relations, and work.

Sarah Jenkins is a Professor in the Sociology of Work and Organization in the Management, Employment, and Organization section at Cardiff Business School, Cardiff University, UK. Her research interests examine contemporary working realities related to skills and emotions at work as well as the varied experiences of work linked to detailed case studies of work organizations. She has also studied lies and deception in organizations and has published in *Organization Studies, Organization Theory, Work, Employment and Society* and *Gender, Work and Organizations*. Her current research examines the nature of work in adult social care linked to cooperative organizational forms. She is a member of the CARE Research Centre at Cardiff University.

Annie J. Murphy is a Doctoral student in Sociology at the University of Texas at Austin. Her research focusses on the reproduction of class inequality within and through organizations.

Valeria Pulignano is Francqui Research Professor and Professor of Sociology of Work and Industrial Relations at CESO – KU Leuven, Belgium. She is Research Coordinator of RN17 Work, Employment and Industrial Relations at the European Sociological Association. She received PI ERC Advanced Grant ResPecTMe. Her research interests are comparative industrial (employment) relations, precarious work, inequality, job quality, working conditions, and collective voice at work. Her recent books: *Reconstructing Solidarity*, (with) van Hoyweghen and Meyers, Palgrave; *Labour Unions, Precarious Work, and the Politics of Institutional Change in Europe*, (with) Doellgast and Lillie, OUP.

About the Contributors

Mê-Linh Riemann is a Postdoctoral Researcher at CESO, KU Leuven, Belgium/ Europa-Universität Flensburg, Germany. Her research interests include sociology of work, biographical methods, precarity, and migration. Her most recent book is: *Leaving Spain: A Biographical Study of an Economic Crisis and New Beginnings*, Leuven University Press.

Carol Stephenson is Director of Education and Associate Professor in the Sociology of Work at Northumbria University. Her research approach shaped by interests in biographies of work and activism, with a focus on trade union and community resistance and gender and class inequalities in postindustrial contexts: see Brock A., Stephens-Griffin N., Stephenson C., and Wyatt T. (2022), *Sociological Research Online*.

Steven Therrien is a Master's student in Sociology at Université Laval, Québec, Canada. During his studies, he has developed a particular interest in the sociology of work and the professions, as well as in economic sociology, which are brought together in his recent work. As part of his thesis, he is attempting to define the contours of a new ethos prescribed in the training of stock market traders. In doing so, his current research, driven by a critical perspective, focusses on the new forms of self-employment that are developing in an increasingly democratized financial world.

Isabelle Zinn is a Tenure Track Professor at Bern University of Applied Sciences – Business School. Her research interests include qualitative methods, in particular ethnography, the transformation of work, and gender inequalities. She holds a joint PhD in Social Sciences from the University of Lausanne and EHESS, Paris and is currently Co-chair of the Swiss Sociological Association's Gender Studies Committee. She recently co-authored an article entitled 'Persistent Pandemic: The Unequal Impact of Covid Labor on Early Career Academics' with Edmée Ballif, published in the journal *Gender, Work & Organization*, https://onlinelibrary.wiley.com/doi/10.1111/gwao.13092.

CHAPTER 1

ESSENTIAL WORK, INESSENTIAL WORKERS?

Markus Helfen[a], Rick Delbridge[b], Andreas (Andi) Pekarek[c] and Gretchen Purser[d]

[a]*Hertie School, Germany*
[b]*Cardiff University, UK*
[c]*University of Melbourne, Australia*
[d]*Syracuse University, USA*

ABSTRACT

In this chapter, we introduce the topic of essentiality of work, exploring its implications for workers, labour markets, and public policy. The essentiality of work often corresponds in a dialectical way with the precarity of work, raising pressing questions about how societies value and, more pertinently, devalue various types of labour, thereby influencing life chances and societal integration. What we see in the contributions to this volume and the wider evidence is that essential work is typically performed by workers who are treated as expendable, or inessential. We proceed to outline the various contributions from the studies compiled in this volume. These present diverse perspectives on 'essentiality' and the experiences of essential workers. Offering a range of new empirical insights, the volume underlines the vitality and lasting relevance of essentiality – both as a concept and in the experience of workers – beyond the pandemic.

Keywords: Essential work; essentiality of work; emotional labour; care work; intersectionality; precarity and precarious work settings; inessential workers

INTRODUCTION

The COVID-19 pandemic prompted new reflections on the meanings of essential workers and essential work. As we compiled the call for chapters for this volume, the memory of the COVID-19 pandemic and its profound implications for work, workers, and workplaces – and yes, also for employers – was still fresh. The pandemic served as a 'critical juncture', an opportunity to examine and debate anew the poor state of work and labour markets for millions of workers, most of them in the service sector. Notably, debate about essential work extended beyond academia and into both popular media and legislative circles. Now as we compile this volume, just 18 months later, the signs and displays cherishing essential workers – in hospitals, grocery stores, and beyond – have long since vanished. Extra 'hazard pay', meant to incentivize and reward workers for working throughout the pandemic, has generally gone by the wayside. Now that the acute crisis has settled, what it means to be an 'essential' worker has been more clearly brought into relief. Society's clamour of gratitude has fallen silent; a silence that speaks volumes. It thus seems a good time to take stock and reflect further on what is meant by essentiality of work and how essential work continues to be experienced at the workplace.

As the contributions in this volume show, the 'essentiality' of work is a good entry point into a number of the most complex and profound problems of contemporary work and labour markets. However, it is difficult to pin down a singular meaning of the term. 'Essentiality' surfaces deeper considerations about the meaning and value of work in relation to the life world of workers and also in the context of what society needs and values. 'Essential work' as a term and as a phenomenon points towards hidden or forgotten realities because it does not fit squarely within the dominant beliefs about how labour markets work or should work for workers. For example, 'essential work' as a category cuts across taken-for-granted job demarcations and boundaries drawn around occupations and educational profiles often justifying pay differentials and disparate levels of recognition and reward. In short, there is an unresolved uneasiness about what has been called essential work, which is of a more general theoretical, empirical, as well as practical interest.

One of the most striking contradictions of essential work is this: On the one hand, the emphasis on essentiality indicates a rediscovery of the public value of work and the societal relevance of labour which is essential for societies to function properly (e.g. Boyer, 2022). On the other hand, looking more closely into the work and employment conditions in 'essential' jobs, essential work is often found to be precarious work (e.g. Loustaunau et al., 2021), that is, employment that is 'uncertain, unpredictable, and risky from the point of view of the worker' (Kalleberg, 2009, p. 2). One might be left with the conclusion that essential work is seen as important but those who undertake it are not and remain treated like they are 'inessential' workers.

For a short moment during the pandemic, the risks taken by 'essential' workers were visible to, and lauded by, all. As Jamie McCallum (2022) put it, 'the category of the essential worker became a synecdoche for our risk-intensive economy' (p. 5).

McCallum (2024) further notes the ambiguous status of essential workers who 'were called heroes when they left for work and treated like sacrificial lambs when they got there' (p. 5). In many countries, media reports were full of examples of mass infections in workplaces such as parcel delivery centres, meat processing and packaging plants, elderly care homes, hospitals, and schools. Indeed, worksites became what some have referred to as 'sacrifice zones' (Carrillo & Ipsen, 2021). The pandemic revealed that essential workplaces – in hospitals, janitorial services, agriculture and food-processing, construction sites, and retail, logistics, and transport – are filled with what are treated as 'inessential', or expendable, workers.

Of course, the pandemic also threw into sharp relief the inequalities in today's labour markets. In the shadow of socially constructing the category of 'essential' work also came the framing, at least implicitly, of 'inessential' work. We would not seek to deny the challenges and disruption that all experienced during the pandemic but there were clear degrees of difference in those experiences. Essential workers put their lives on the line, risking daily exposure, while others continued working remotely from the relative safety and security of their homes. For those with comparatively comfortable living conditions and at the 'higher quality' pole of the labour market, experiences were quite different and hardships were on a different scale. For many of those keeping their office jobs during the pandemic, the shift towards remote work not only offered a sense of security, albeit amidst a bewildering time, but also appears to have had a lasting effect in normalizing working from home; something many still seem to welcome. These egregious labour market disparities between those deemed 'essential' yet treated as expendable and everyone else even led a high-ranking business executive from Amazon to publicly resign. Tim Bray, vice-president at Amazon and distinguished engineer, left the company over what he saw as the mistreatment of warehouse workers during the pandemic (Bray, 2020).

This Janus-faced nature of 'essential work' reveals once more the social character of work – and the socially constructed discourses that shape and inform the economic valuation of work, the qualitative experiences of workers, and the public perception of these jobs. This rediscovery of essentiality alludes to the diverging societal relevance attached to various types of work, but also reminds us of the fact that many questions around the valuation and valorization of different activities as work are still unsettled and remain contested (e.g. Lamont, 2012). What has been exposed is the jarring disconnect between those whose roles have central significance to the functioning of society and everyday life and the 'value' that society places upon their work. Essential work is often invisible and forgotten in normal times; sometimes, essential workers are even expelled from visibility (Sassen, 2014) or subject to replacement and automation in polarized labour markets (Autor & Dorn, 2013). It takes place in locations and sites distant from sanitized office spaces. But during periods of crisis those activities come to the fore. Unfortunately, the pay, job status, and working conditions of many of those doing essential work – including care work, the work that makes all other work possible – are inferior compared to jobs and occupations implicitly recognized as 'inessential'. Indeed, and known long before COVID-19, most of this essential work is undertaken by those suffering the greatest societal and economic disadvantages, including women and immigrants (e.g. Acker, 2006; Vosko, 2010; Zanoni et al., 2010). We knew this before and a process of collective forgetting is once again well underway.

THE STRUGGLE CONTINUES? FROM RECOGNITION AND DIGNITY TO PUBLIC VALUE AND REWARD

We distinguish between three levels or spheres in which debate about essential work takes place: (1) a macro-level concerning support through public policy, society, and the state in reregulating the essential segments of the labour market, (2) the (inter-) organizational level of firms and industries in which management and unions negotiate about working conditions and employment standards under which essential work is performed, and (3) the micro-level that examines how individual workers reflect on and experience being 'essential' workers.

As for the regulatory macro-environment, new crises have swiftly followed the COVID-19 pandemic, leading to a state of affairs that some now call a 'polycrisis', that is, an ever more worrying co-occurrence of the climate crisis and the resurfacing of geopolitical rivalry and wars shackling post-pandemic labour markets globally (Tooze, 2022). At the same time, in the Global North, the dominant regulatory approach seems to have fallen back to pre-pandemic austerity measures. And in the Global South short-lived achievements in combating poverty, un- and underemployment as well as low-quality, precarious work have already been reverted (ILO – International Labour Office, 2023). This cumulation of crisis phenomena epitomizes more general trends that have affected the world of work in recent decades and throws their consequences for societal resilience in the face of polycrisis into sharp relief. In combination, it appears that the public and economic policy decisions shaping the development of economies in the decades before the pandemic have undermined the standing of exactly the work and workers necessary for the functioning of society, thereby jeopardizing and diminishing societies' crisis responsiveness.

Nevertheless, during the pandemic, policymakers and the media have made wide reference to 'essential work' and 'essential workers', shaping the ways in which governments have responded to the crisis. Keeping essential work running has been identified as the key to withstanding COVID-19 despite its disruptions and deadly risks. Keeping on with essential work was regarded as 'essential' for maintaining a functioning society, building up resilience, and overcoming the crisis. This widespread recognition of the value of essential work presented an opportunity to reflect on policy measures to improve the conditions essential workers (Behrens & Pekarek, 2023). The evidence, including that presented in Côté et al. (this volume, Chapter 5), is that any improvements have proven temporary at best in most cases.

The impact, or lack of it, that derives from the macro-level can be readily witnessed at the organizational and sectoral levels. For instance, the pandemic revealed the need to consider curbing subcontracting and even reversing privatization. It was not by historical coincidence that, at least in the case of Europe, many of the essential sectors were previously organized as public services provided by organizations in public ownership. Privatization now abounds in these segments and subcontracting and outsourcing have become widespread, often de facto excluding the workers in essential activities from voice and representation. Litwin et al. (2017), for example, show how subcontracted cleaning services contributed to the spread of infections in health care settings, already before the pandemic. However, it would be a false conclusion to see these things only happening in high-risk industries or in situations of crisis with high demands on security and safety. Rather, these cases pinpoint a general lack of labour inspection and a failure to maintain labour standards in what has been described as the fissured workplace (Weil, 2019), characterized by multi-employer relationships (Marchington et al., 2005). In private service industries, such as property and facility services, cleaning services, food and parcel delivery, catering or security, we find extensive subcontracting of various activities no longer considered to be in the 'core' of operations which then turned out to be essential after all. Business and government have both been slow to recognize this, failing to reverse mistaken decisions. More broadly there has been considerable reluctance to revisit ideologically driven outsourcing decisions that fail tests of efficiency and effectiveness. Indeed, the lack of positive regulatory impact from the macro-level has fueled growing concern that the frustration of essential workers may jeopardize societal integration and drive right-wing populism (Altreiter et al., 2022).

At the micro-level – in Hirschman's (1970) terms – this regulatory landscape shifts workers' responses towards exit from essential work roles and jobs. 'Quitting' this world of precarious employment in essential jobs has become a widely discussed option for workers in the last four years; 'labour shortage' has become a widely reported reality in many industries in which employment has not recovered to pre-pandemic levels. In Germany, for example, there was a lot of media talk about people quitting care work, in all its varieties from hospitals to aged care, during and after the pandemic, exactly because of the harsh experiences suffered by workers during the pandemic. But the spotlight on essential work also showed the endurance, solidarity, dignity, and work ethic of those engaged in such work, especially in some of the most affected sectors during the pandemic. We see evidence reported of employees working in the face of tremendous adversity, even beyond the point of individual exhaustion (see, e.g., Pulignano et al., this volume, Chapter 4).

Both the stagnation in crisis-ridden economic and labour policy, as well as the individual level responses, point towards the shadow of the more 'instrumental' aspects of essential work, the interests of essential workers in particular, and how these are negotiated in industrial relations. Returning to the meso-level, despite differences in the type of essential work, between say retail work in a supermarket and care work in a hospital, we observe a disproportionate share of part-time and fixed-term contracts, and various subcontracting arrangements like posted work or temporary agency work. Further, in many essential job markets, we find a predominantly female and/or migrant workforce. These jobs are low-paying and deemed 'low skilled', despite high stress levels and high physical performance requirements. In some countries, like Germany, a part of these jobs is referred to as a 'mini job'.

Frequently, and as already known before the pandemic, the protections of collective bargaining agreements, unions and shopfloor representation is often absent or ineffective in these workplaces (e.g. Behrens & Pekarek, 2023; Bosch, 2015).

All in all, one may be tempted to conclude that the more a job has been classified as being essential during the pandemic, the lower both the pay and labour standards. Unsurprisingly, such conditions are bracketed with such jobs having less scope for formal industrial relations and collective bargaining arrangements; the rare case such as the strike activity of UK doctors orchestrated by the British Medical Association proving very much the exception rather than the rule. This pinpoints the important question about whether and how workers and their allies (e.g. unions) can mobilize positive public sentiment towards essential work in campaigns for better pay and working conditions. We plan to explore such issues in an upcoming volume of Research in the Sociology of Work on worker organizing.

AN OVERVIEW OF THE CHAPTERS

This volume curates a selection of qualitative and quantitative research undertaken from various theoretical perspectives. It constitutes a rich collection that sheds light on both enduring and newly emerging questions concerning the essentiality of work. By delineating the meaning and use of 'essentiality', the contributions also reveal the processes via which work is categorized, evaluated, and valued given persistent labour market structures and institutionalized norms. Notably, three contributions foreground the experiences of essential workers in a diverse array of care work settings in the USA, the UK, Canada, and Germany, thereby revealing commonalities and differences across contexts. Employing a varied set of theories, the chapters reveal the rich reality of essential care work as involving both 'dirty' work and emotion management, but also expose profound inequalities stemming from devaluation and institutionalized segmentation in health care systems. These three contributions, along with those on custodial work and an analysis of various segments of essential work in the USA, draw upon a variety of methods: quantitative data analysis, critical discourse analysis, qualitative case studies, and ethnographic fieldwork.

The various contributions to this volume can be grouped into two broader streams or questions that examine different aspects of the essentiality of work: (1) What is it like to do essential work, that is, how is it rewarded, how is it performed, and how do workers cope with it? and (2) How is 'essential work' constructed discursively in the political and public sphere and how does this designation shape policy responses? In addressing these two questions the chapters engage to varying degrees and in a variety of ways with the three levels of essentiality of work outlined above.

The second chapter by Anna Milena Galazka and Sarah Jenkins connects to the first question by showing how essential 'dirty work' is performed, with a particular focus on the emotion management skills in gendered care work. Drawing on interviews with two types of essential care workers – wound clinicians and care workers – the chapter examines stigma management in dirty work through the lens of emotion management and gender studies. First, the chapter shows how emotion management skills emanate from the deep relational work with clients rather than through occupational communities. Second, the chapter extends the literature on dirty work by identifying how emotion management skills are central to two features of stigma management in relation to undertaking physically dirty bodywork while caring for socially stigmatized clients: how the dirty work 'is done' and the 'end purpose' of work. By comparing two occupations with different contexts and conditions of work, the authors illustrate how complex emotion management skills are gendered in care work. They argue that by focussing on the concept of emotion management, the hidden skills of dirty work in gendered care work are illuminated, contributing to contemporary debates about how stigma might be overcome by focussing on context and conditions of work.

The third chapter asks the important question 'essential for whom?', linking to the second of our questions about the regulatory constructions of essential work as laid out above. Using the case of custodial labour at a large public university in the USA, the chapter by Annie J. Murphy examines the construction of essential labour during the early months of the COVID-19 pandemic. The chapter also explores the impact of government policies on the differentiation between essential and non-essential work, and the consequences of that demarcation for workers. In her case study of custodial service employees, Murphy examines the federal, state, and municipal guidelines about COVID-19 safety and critical infrastructure in order to understand the policy landscape under which custodial work was formally deemed essential. The result was that these workers were sacrificed in order to reassure others of a sanitized workplace and the campus' safe reopening.

In the fourth chapter, Valeria Pulignano, Mê-Linh Riemann, Carol Stephenson, and Markieta Domecka turn their attention to the individual responses of essential workers. In their comparative examination of residential care work in the UK and Germany, they interpret the COVID-19 pandemic as an ethnomethodological 'breaching experiment' (Garfinkel, 1967) and discuss the disruptions caused by the pandemic to the 'emotion management' practices of residential care workers in these two countries. They examine the influence of professional feeling rules on workers, emphasizing the prescribed importance of displaying affective, empathetic concern for residents' health and well-being. Findings demonstrate that authenticity and adherence to professional feeling rules are not mutually exclusive in managing emotions. The authors highlight how adherence to professional feeling rules contributed to upholding authentic care by reinforcing a professional ethos. Ultimately, the study showcases how a professional ethos substantiates altruistic motivations, guiding proficient emotion management practices among care workers. In doing so, essential workers draw upon their personal understanding and experiences to determine the appropriate emotions to be expressed while providing care for residents amid the unprecedented challenges of the pandemic. Perhaps surprisingly, the UK–Germany comparison reveals substantial similarity in care workers' responses 'on the ground', shedding light on the relevance of different institutions, in this instance 'professional values'.

The fifth chapter explicitly explores the macro- and meso-level politics of essentiality, building on the widely held impression that the praise for heroic essential workers during the COVID-19 pandemic quickly receded into ignorance, silence, and even scorn after the pandemic. The chapter by Nancy Côté, Jean-Louis Denis, Steven Therrien, and Flavia Sofia Ciafre looks at how the discourse surrounding the essentiality of care aides emerged and developed in Quebec during the COVID-19 pandemic, but ultimately failed to have a sustained impact on care aides' working conditions, because the underlying institutions and organizational structures working to their disadvantage remained unchanged. The authors perform a critical discourse analysis on three main types of documents: scientific-scholarly works, documents from government, various associations and unions, and popular media reports published between February 2020 and July 2022. To explain this outcome, the chapter utilizes a framework of performativity. According to this framework, Canadian pandemic politics influenced the recognition, through discourses of essentiality, of low-status workers and more specifically of care aides as an occupational group that performs society's 'dirty', but 'essential' work. However, public recognition through political discourse alone is a necessary but insufficient condition for social change. While a discourse of essentiality at the highest level of politics is associated with rapid policy responses to value the work of care aides, it is embedded in a system that restrains the establishment of substantive policies of improving care aide work. The chapter contributes to the literature on performativity by demonstrating the importance of the institutionalization of competing logics in contemporary health and social care systems and how it limits the impact of discourse in promulgating new values and norms and engineering social change.

The sixth chapter in the essential work section of the volume takes a broader and quantitative view on essential work. Caroline Hanley and Enobong Hannah Branch employ an intersectional perspective to understand the wage gap for essential workers in the USA. They start by delineating how public health measures implemented early in the COVID-19 pandemic brought the idea of essential work into the public discourse, and what types of work have been formally defined as being essential for society to function. From there, they analyse the questions of who performs that work and how the labour of these essential workers is rewarded. Employing an intersectional lens on work that was officially deemed essential in 2020, the authors highlight longstanding patterns of devaluation among essential workers, including those undergirded by systemic racism in employment and labour law. Using data from the US Bureau of Labor Statistics' Current Population Survey to examine earnings differences between essential and non-essential workers, the authors find that patterns of valuation among essential workers cannot be explained by human capital or other standard labour market characteristics. Rather, intersectional wage inequalities in 2020 reflect historic patterns that are highly durable and did not abate in the first year of the global pandemic.

CONCLUSION

This volume dives deeply into the dialectics of essential work, showing a persistent struggle for recognition and dignity as well as for revaluing and materially rewarding essential work. Our contributors highlight the lived experience of essential workers at their workplaces. These essential workplaces have been rediscovered and were cherished as key to maintaining life and keeping society going during the global COVID-19 pandemic. This brought about renewed public attention to labour and employment standards in these often-neglected segments of the economy. However, our contributors also show how and why this attention has consistently failed to lead to sustained improvement in the standing and material circumstances of those undertaking essential work.

The accompanying struggles for recognition and reward are highly resonant with more general developments in the nature and experience of work under the current situation of ongoing polycrisis. Each of the chapters in the volume sheds light on aspects of essentiality and precarity showing essential work to be a Janus-faced phenomenon. Taking the dialectics of 'essentiality vs precarity' across these inter-related levels (i.e., the societal, the sectoral and organizational as well as the individual level) as a starting point, we hope the volume inspires new debates about the centrality of the work experience in modern life for those working as well as those benefiting from that work and raises new questions about the essence of work and its place in contemporary society.

REFERENCES

Acker, J. (2006). Inequality regimes: Gender, class, and race in organizations. *Gender and Society, 20*(4), 441–464. https://doi.org/10.1177/0891243206289499

Altreiter, C., Flecker, J., & Papouschek, U. (2022). Solidaritätsorientierungen und soziale Positionen. Klassenhabituelle Haltungen zu Sozialstaat und Geflüchteten in Österreich. *Berliner Journal für Soziologie, 32*, 317–348. https://doi.org/10.1007/s11609-022-00473-x

Autor, D. H., & Dorn, D. (2013). The growth of low-skill service jobs and the polarization of the US labor market. *American Economic Review, 103*(5), 1553–1597.

Behrens, M., & Pekarek, A. (2023). Delivering the goods? German industrial relations institutions during the COVID-19 crisis. *Industrial Relations: A Journal of Economy and Society, 62*(2), 126–144. https://doi.org/10.1111/irel.12319

Bosch, G. (2015). Shrinking collective bargaining coverage, increasing income inequality: A comparison of five EU countries. *International Labour Review, 154*(1), 57–66, https://doi.org/10.1111/j.1564-913X.2015.00226.x

Boyer, R. (2022). Développement anthropogénétique et reconnaissance de l'utilité social du travail. *Sociologie du Travail, 64*(1–2). https://die.org/10.4000/sdt.40685

Bray, T. (2020). *Bye, Amazon*. https://www.tbray.org/ongoing/When/202x/2020/04/29/Leaving-Amazon

Carrillo, I., & Ipsen, A. (2021). Worksites as sacrifice zones: Structural precarity and COVID-19 in U.S. meatpacking. *Sociological Perspectives, 64*(5), 726–746. https://doi.org/10.1177/07311214211012025

Garfinkel, H. (1967). *Studies in ethnomethodology*. Prentice Hall.

Hirschman, A. O. (1970). *Exit, voice, and loyalty. Responses to decline in firms, organizations, and states*. Harvard University Press.

ILO – International Labour Office. (2023). *World employment and social outlook: The value of essential work*. ILO.

Kalleberg, A. L. (2009). Precarious work, insecure workers: Employment relations in transition. *American Sociological Review, 74*, 1–22. https://doi.org/10.1177/000312240907400101.

Lamont, M. (2012). Toward a comparative sociology of valuation and evaluation. *Annual Review of Sociology, 38*, 210–221. https://doi.org/10.1146/annurev-soc-070308-120022

Litwin, A. S., Avgar, A. C., & Becker, E. R. (2017). Superbugs versus outsourced cleaners: Employment arrangements and the spread of health care-associated infections. *ILR Review, 70*(3), 610–641. https://doi.org/10.1177/0019793916654482

Loustaunau, L., Stepick, L., Scott, E., Petrucci, L., & Henifin, M. (2021). No choice but to be essential: Expanding dimensions of precarity during COVID-19. *Sociological Perspectives, 64*(5), 857–875. https://doi.org/10.1177/07311214211005491

Marchington, M., Grimshaw, D., Rubery, J., & Willmott, H. (Eds.). (2005). *Fragmenting work. Blurring organizational boundaries and disordering hierarchies*. Oxford University Press.

McCallum, J. (2022). *Essential: How the pandemic transformed the long fight for worker justice*. Basic Books.

Sassen, S. (2014). *Expulsions. Brutality and complexity in the global economy*. Harvard University Press.

Tooze, A. (2022, October 28). Welcome to the world of the polycrisis. *Financial Times*. https://www.ft.com/content/498398e7-11b1-494b-9cd3-6d669dc3de33

Vosko, L. F. (2010). *Managing the margins: Gender, citizenship, and the international regulation of precarious employment*. Oxford University Press.

Weil, D. (2019). Understanding the present and future of work in the fissured workplace context. *Russell Sage Foundation Journal of the Social Sciences, 5*(5), 147–165. https://doi.org/10.7758/RSF.2019.5.5.08

Zanoni, P., Janssens, M., Benschop, Y., & Nkomo, S. (2010). Unpacking diversity, grasping inequality: Rethinking difference through critical perspectives. *Organization, 17*, 9–29. https://doi.org/10.1177%2F1350508409350344

CHAPTER 2

DOING ESSENTIAL 'DIRTY WORK': MAKING VISIBLE THE EMOTION MANAGEMENT SKILLS IN GENDERED CARE WORK

Anna Milena Galazka and Sarah Jenkins

Cardiff Business School, UK

ABSTRACT

Drawing on interviews with two types of essential workers – wound clinicians and care workers – the chapter examines stigma management in dirty care work through the lens of emotion management. The study combines two dimensions of dirty work: physical taint in relation to bodywork and social taint linked to working in close proximity to socially stigmatized clients. Hence, stigma management extends to dealing with the physically and socially dirty features of essential care work. In addition, the authors' assessment of social stigma includes how essential care workers also sought to alleviate the social stigma encountered by their clients. In so doing, the authors extend the literature on dirty work to identify how emotion management skills are central to the stigma management strategies of the essential care workers in this study. The authors demonstrate how both groups deal with their stigma by emphasizing the emotion management skills in 'doing' dirty work and in the 'purpose' of this work, which includes acknowledging how the authors attempt to address the social taint encountered by their clients. Additionally, by comparing two occupations with different contexts and conditions of work, the authors show how complex emotion management skills are gendered in care work to expand the understanding of gender and stigma management. Furthermore, these emotion management skills emanate from the deep relational work with clients rather than through occupational communities. The authors argue that by focussing on emotion management, the hidden skills of dirty work in gendered care work are illuminated and contribute to contemporary debates about whether stigma can be overcome.

Keywords: Care work; dirty work; emotions; emotion management; skills; stigma; social care; wound care

INTRODUCTION

The chapter explores the relatively under-studied area of how dirty work is performed and stigma is managed in essential care work (for an exception, see Bolton, 2005b; Stacey, 2011). The concept of dirty work (Hughes, 1958) is used by sociologists of work to study how people in occupations considered 'dirty' by society manage stigma threats to their occupational identity. According to Ashforth and Kreiner (1999, p. 415), work can be physically dirty through its association with waste, bodily fluids, or physical danger. Social taint is associated with regular contact with individuals who are themselves stigmatized, such that workers become 'tainted by the reflected deficiencies of others' (Ashforth & Kreiner, 2014, p. 83). This includes the work of nurses and social care workers reported in this study who often work with socially stigmatized groups. Morally tainted work is 'sinful', 'dubious', 'deceptive', 'intrusive', or defying 'the norms of civility'. For example, this can include the work of counsellors on mental health prison wards and slaughterhouse workers (Press, 2021). Subsequent studies have shown that work can also be emotionally tainted when working with difficult emotions of service users (McMurray & Ward, 2014). Work can also be simultaneously tainted in multiple ways (Ashforth & Kreiner, 1999). In the study reported in this chapter, the two groups of essential care workers encounter both physical and social taint in relation to their own work as well as supporting their clients to manage the social taint they encounter.

The central focus within the dirty work literature is how occupational communities achieve societal affirmation when their work is stigmatized (Ashforth & Kreiner, 1999). Studies demonstrate that this is accomplished by symbolically elevating their status by appealing to discursive strategies within cohesive occupational communities, supported by workers' common values, and shared experiences (Ackroyd & Crowdy, 1990; Dick, 2005; Tracy & Scott, 2006). However, our research problem centres on whether taint can be overcome, in all cases, and whether essential care workers can achieve positive value from dirty work which combines physically dirty bodywork (Wolkowitz, 2007) on socially stigmatized clients, such that this work also includes supporting clients in dealing with social stigma. Stigma management thus includes two dimensions in this study of essential care workers. First, workers seek to manage the stigma of their work by infusing their work with 'admirable qualities' in how they 'do' dirty work by emphasizing their emotion management skills and second in relation to the 'end purpose' of their work (Deery et al., 2019) they reflect on how they support their socially stigmatized clients to alleviate the stigma they encounter. We compare two occupational groups, both distinguished by the UK Government as critical during the Covid-19 pandemic and each with different degrees of status and prestige, centring on wound care clinicians and care workers who undertake in-depth relational care work with socially stigmatized clients in varied care contexts. Both groups encounter stigma in their roles linked to the physical taint of their work and the social taint associated with their client groups. As Galazka (2021) has shown, wound clinicians' physical proximity to wounds, sometimes accompanied by gangrene infections, provokes strong visceral reactions in outsiders who consider this work as physically repellent. Such that the physical taint of wound healing and the nature of the clients they work with challenge clinicians' claims to a professional status. Within the medical profession wound healing tends to be seen as a 'Cinderella' service (see also Sandoz, 2016), with little insight into the complex skills required to care for the wounds on the bodies of distressed patients (Galazka, 2021). Likewise, care workers are often disregarded as low skilled workers. These perceptions are linked to the physically dirty work involved in intimate bodywork, whereas there is also a social stigma for care workers who support people with a physical and/or learning disability, some of whom display challenging behaviour in public. In this case, the complex skills involved in supporting clients are not acknowledged. For the two occupational groups in this study, the stigma of undertaking physically dirty work as well as the social taint involved in working closely with stigmatized clients arguably reinforces the under-recognition of their work as skilled. Consequently, stigma management strategies address these issues by emphasizing the skills in doing dirty work and in the wider purpose and value of their work for their clients. In these contexts, essential care workers manage the stigma they encountered and that which their clients endure by drawing on emotion management skills. In so doing, we advance four hitherto under-developed features of the dirty work literature.

First, we answer a recent call from Mikkelsen (2022) to better capture how workers actually 'do' dirty work. This call seeks to better attend to the material realities of dirty work (Hughes et al., 2017; Mikkelsen, 2022; Zulfiqar & Prasad, 2022) which means that stigma is not always easy to manage by drawing upon ideological techniques to symbolically reframe, refocus, and recalibrate job taints (Ashforth & Kreiner, 1999). These studies acknowledge that some dirt, like bodily waste, can cause visceral reactions which cannot be linguistically neutralized (Hughes et al., 2017; Wolkowitz, 2007). In addition, although there is more attention on the 'doing' of physically dirty work in the literature, there is much less focus on how workers deal with social stigma including that encountered by their socially stigmatized clients. This stigma both rubs off onto care workers, socially tainting the occupation and can include them supporting and attempting to alleviate the social stigma of their clients.

Consequently, our study finds that in relation with their clients, workers draw on complex and hitherto, often hidden emotion management skills to manage both physically and socially dirty work as well as reduce the intensity of their clients' negative experiences to social stigma. Hence, a second contribution identifies that for essential care workers, social relations within occupational groups may not be the main relational dimension for how dirty workers gain a sense of value and purpose. We contribute to recent scholarship which shows that stigma management can also be influenced by emotional considerations of direct contact with clients who can be the source of dirt and be stigmatized (Galazka & Wallace, 2023), as is the case in essential care work (Bolton, 2005b; Stacey, 2011). We extend this literature to delineate that in the context of care work, where relations with clients are deep, stigma management in how work is done and its purpose are configured around clients rather than relations with an occupational community, and these relations are under-pinned by emotion management skills.

Third, the literature on stigma management is dominated by analyses of male occupations mainly undertaking physically dirty jobs who draw on traditionally masculine qualities including physical strength, stamina, and heroism (Ackroyd & Crowdy, 1990; Deery et al., 2019; Tracy & Scott, 2006). Our study seeks to better capture stigma management in female dominated care work by extending the existing research on dirty work in gendered care (Bolton, 2005b; Stacey, 2005; Whiley & Grandy, 2022). Moreover, although emotions have appeared in recent studies on dirty work (Gunby & Carline, 2020; Malvini Redden & Scarduzio, 2018; McMurray & Ward, 2014; Mikkelsen, 2022; Rivera, 2015), there has not been a specific focus on emotion management skills (Bolton, 2005a) to emphasize how dirty workers use skills to regulate one's own and others' feelings while priding themselves on how the work is done and its purpose.

Finally, it is argued that the dirty work studies downplay the content and context of work (Deery et al., 2019). By comparing two types of essential care occupations, we demonstrate that care work is not homogenous in terms of the content of dirty work because of the depth of taint encountered (Ashforth & Kreiner, 2014). More recent work identifies how stigma management is greatly influenced by the content and context of work. Factors like the depth of taint encountered including the material realities of dirt (Hughes et al., 2017; Zulfiqar & Prasad, 2022), the gendered work features (Bolton, 2005b) and the significance of power relations relating to the status and prestige of occupations (Adams, 2012; Malvini Redden & Scarduzio, 2018; Tracy & Scott, 2006) can, for some, make stigma management difficult to achieve, if not impossible.

To address these features, the chapter examines how workers engage in stigma management by emphasizing the emotion management skills required to do essential dirty care work and the purpose of this work to improve the lives of stigmatized clients. To do so, we integrate the dirty work and emotion management literature to pay greater attention to the hidden nature of skills in gendered care work in stigma management.

GENDER AND EMOTION MANAGEMENT

Care work is highly gendered, classed, and racialized. Cain (2017, p. 345) states care work is not just gendered in terms of the predominance of women, but also in the way gender is accomplished in interactions which are influenced by broader social norms (West & Zimmerman, 1987) and infused within organizational structures of caring work (Acker, 1990, 1998). Acker's (1990, p. 146) view of gendered organizations means that 'advantage and disadvantage, exploitation and control, action and emotion, meaning and identity, are patterned through and in terms of a distinction between men and women, masculine and feminine' in how workplace behaviour is prescribed. As Husso and Hirvonen (2012, p. 30) elucidate, gendered stereotypes and constructions guide, justify, and legitimate gendered decisions and ways of organizing and dividing work in the labour market in both implicit and explicit ways. In particular, gendering plays out readily in how emotions are performed and experienced in organizations (Bolton, 2005a; Cain, 2017).

The expression of emotions is an implicit and integral feature of essential care work, where gender is woven into the fabric of work and shaping the expectations of workers' actions aligned to organizational norms. For example, Cain (2017, p. 346) identifies how healthcare professionals 'do gender' in both naturalistic and challenging ways through their professional performance in how they manage their emotions in interactions with colleagues and clients which is aligned to both their professional positions as well as sex. The advantage of this conception is that it aims to denaturalize the association of masculinity with men and femininity with women in emotion management; care workers also perform masculinity through activities presumed to be natural aptitudes for men: keeping calm under high-pressure situations and emotionally distancing oneself, demonstrating that feminine and masculine qualities are both enacted in caring work (Cain, 2017). As such, gender may be implicit in organizational structures (Acker, 1990) but feeling rules also influence definitions of appropriate emotion management responses for a given setting.

Bolton's (2005a) concept of 'emotion management' captures how for many groups, including care workers, emotions are not entirely controlled by organizations (Lopez, 2006). For Bolton (2005a, pp. 56–59) and Bolton and Boyd (2003) 'emotion management' includes how organizational actors determine what is appropriate within different organizational contexts and identifying different guiding feeling rules. This includes the suppression of emotions such as grief in neo-natal nursing (Lewis, 2005), developing empathetic relations with pupils (Jenkins & Conley, 2007) as well navigating varied feeling rules in call-centre work (Jenkins et al., 2010). For example, professional feeling rules can exert normative notions of appropriate professional behaviour, organization feeling rules attempt to identify the emotional norms required in a specific organizational context, while social feeling rules are based on the everyday rules of social interaction. For Bolton, groups engaging in skilled emotion management juggle these different feeling rules using their discretion to deploy the appropriate emotions in a given situation (Bolton, 2001).

Bolton's (2005a) model develops the 4Ps to link different forms of emotion work and varied feeling rules. *Pecuniary* emotion work is aligned to emotional labour and is based on the deployment of emotions underscored by commercial feeling rules imposed by the organization. *Prescriptive* emotion management is often determined via membership of a professional body or organization. In this case, there is a degree of prescription involved as the emotion display is controlled or influenced by the professional or organizational feeling rules. *Presentational* emotion management is influenced by social feeling rules such that social actors can manage their emotions to fit into the accepted 'conventions of feeling' (Bolton, 2005a, p. 133). Finally, *philanthropic* emotion management is considered by Bolton (2005a, p. 139) to be a 'special case' as 'it denotes extra effort has been invested into offering a sincere performance as a gift to those around us'. This form of emotion work is defined as representing the 'everyday humanity in the workplace' (Bolton, 2005a, p. 140).

In this way, the lens of emotion management captures the often-hidden skills involved in care work. Arguably, the depth and degree of emotion management skills are often rendered invisible in care work. This under-recognition of skills is a crucial dimension in discussions of the 'essential' nature of care work (Stacey, 2011; Wolkowitz, 2002) because gender is implicit to care work which adds to the invisibility of skill (Daniels, 1987). Therefore, focussing on emotion management demonstrates how care workers are capable of wide-ranging emotional dexterity, including the deployment of a range of complex skills related to discretion and autonomy (Jenkins et al., 2010) within different care labour processes to help differentiate between skill levels. For example, Lewis (2005, p. 568) indicates how neo-natal nurses navigate the gendered nature of the prescriptive emotion management, dominated by professional values such as emotional detachment, expertise and self-discipline, and philanthropic emotion management which highlights rapport, supportiveness, and empathy. For Lewis (2005, pp. 573–574) 'nurses are highly skilled and active emotion managers – demonstrating significant agency in their ability to move between different forms of emotion management'.

However, both care occupations and professions face a 'care penalty' (England & Folbre, 1999) resulting from a combination of factors. Historically, the implicit assumption that care and emotion work is 'natural' to women, emanating from a familial ideology (Palmer & Eveline, 2012) which aligns paid care to women's unpaid care in the domestic sphere (Bolton & Wibberley, 2014; Hayes, 2017). Hence, social constructions of skill perceive this work as linked to women's innate talents rather than as 'learnt skills' (James, 1989; Phillips & Taylor, 1980). Finally, as England and Folbre (1999) observe, there is no market mechanism for care workers to charge a price that reflects their value and skills; they are reliant on the political will of the State, and in the context in the UK this has served to sustain care as low paid work (see Meagher et al., 2016). In many ways, emphasizing emotion work involved in care work tends to undermine attempts to classify this work as skilled. Therefore, we seek to reclaim the skills involved in emotion management in care work.

DIRTY WORK

The invisibility of emotion skills can also be augmented by the dirty nature of some gendered care jobs (Bolton, 2005b). The gendered dimensions of dirty work emerge most clearly in the study of stigma management where workers seek to secure positive identities through *reframing, refocusing,* and *recalibrating* their work. Reframing represents the most powerful technique because it transforms the meaning attached to the occupation thus *infusing* work with a positive value by emphasizing how the 'work is done' or the 'ends (the purpose) of the job'

(Ashforth & Kreiner, 1999; Deery et al., 2019) and presenting it as a badge of honour or by *neutralizing* negative values (Ashforth & Kreiner, 1999). Here, most dirty work literature emphasizes how male-dominated occupational groups manage the stigma of physically dirty work by infusing their work with 'admirable qualities' (Deery et al., 2019) linked to physical strength, stamina, and heroism as evident in studies of slaughtermen (Ackroyd & Crowdy, 1990), butchers (Simpson et al., 2014), firefighters (Tracy & Scott, 2006), and cleaners (Deery et al., 2019). Hence, popular societal discourses for legitimating dirty work include self-sacrifice and heroism, performing a critical service, achievement and excellence, and attaining rewards (Ashforth & Kreiner, 2013). Moreover, Purser's (2009) comparative ethnography of immigrant day workers shows that in pursuit of self-worth cultural constructions of masculinity are perceived as dignified whereas femininity is considered submissive to demonstrate how gendered values reframed work as honourable and valuable. In contrast, studies of women performing dirty work in care settings reveal that women workers emphasize the skills involved in performing intimate dirty work. For example, Stacey's (2005) home care aids demonstrate pride in accomplishing dirty activities which are mastered through intimate professional practice. Bolton's (2005b) study of gynaecology nurses also viewed their work as 'significant and honourable' requiring 'special skills'. As Ashforth and Kreiner (2014, p. 88) concede, the same ideologies of masculine heroism are not available to women performing dirty work. Thus, appeals to femininity as a rationale for dirty work do not have the same weighting in most social settings.

Furthermore, care workers often must deal with the combined stigma of undertaking physically dirty work (physical taint) and working with socially stigmatized clients (social taint). As Tracy and Scott (2006, p. 32) identify, social taint, emanating from stigmatized clients, can be more difficult to manage when 'the "dirt" has human agency'. In this context, reframing strategies often centre on the critical service workers perform (Galazka & Wallace, 2023). Socially stigmatized occupations tend to be populated by women (Ashforth & Kreiner, 2014, p. 88), whose emotional nurturing skills are naturalized by sociocultural ideologies of femininity. Listening, empathizing, and truly caring (Cain, 2017) are considered as natural, more to women than to men (Daniels, 1987), which renders women's emotion work in dirty work invisible (Simpson et al., 2012). Few studies focus on how workers deal with the social stigma of their clients (for an exception, see Olvera, 2017; Torelli & Puddephatt, 2021). Therefore, there is limited assessment in the dirty work literature of how care workers often deal with both physical taint and social taint of their job, as well as the impact of social stigma on their clients which transfers into and spills into worker–client interactions.

Gender is also a potential barrier for stigma management in terms of how power and occupational prestige can constrain reframing strategies (see Zulfiqar & Prasad, 2022). Hence, an important feature of assessments of stigma management is whether some care workers, for example, professional groups, can draw on a 'status shield' (Hochschild, 1983, p. 174) to insulate themselves from the stigma of dirty work. Although healthcare professionals did enjoy a status shield from the 'Clap for Our Carers' applauses during the Covid-19-related lockdowns, other dirty care workers like domestic aids (Stacey, 2005) lacked, and still lack, such symbolic tools to bolster their occupational identity and manage taint (Tracy & Scott, 2006). Ashforth and Kreiner (2014, p. 84) suggest that 'most physically and socially tainted jobs – independent of prestige – enjoy a "necessity shield", a protection against stigmatization threats based on the assertion that their jobs are *necessary* for society'. Therefore, the doing and reframing of dirty care work through emotion management skills, whether benefitting from a status shield or a mere necessity shield, is an area that required investigation.

To address the gaps in the literature, we examine how two groups of essential care workers whose work combines physical taint around intimate body work and social taint from close contact with stigmatized clients reframe the stigma of this work. Our research problem centres on whether stigma can be managed or overcome in the context of essential care work by considering the influence of gender, power, and occupational status in reframing strategies. We ask the following research questions: How do dirty workers in two types of care settings 'do' dirty care work to deal with both physical and social taint of 'dirty' care work? How do the groups manage the stigma of their work and what is the connection to emotion management? Did the groups invoke a 'status' or 'necessity' shield in managing stigma?

METHODS

As in prior comparative research (Malvini Redden & Scarduzio, 2018; Tracy & Scott, 2006), the qualitative data for this chapter were collected independently from two separate research projects to examine the content and context of work in care. Although neither study had an explicit focus on dirty work, several serendipitous conversations about our emergent findings indicated the similarities in our data sets. Through discussions, we identified the significance of understanding the range of skills employed in different care contexts. This also provided an opportunity to examine how different types of care workers undertake dirty work through a comparative analysis to illuminate the intersections with emotion management and gender (cf. Tracy & Scott, 2006).

Data Collection

The first project was based on a qualitative case study of social care support workers in CareCoop – a large social care cooperative provider which supports adults with physical and learning disabilities to lead independent lives in the community. The organizational values emphasized person-centred support focussed on coproduction. The care workers worked in supported living houses in the community which included two 'sleep-ins' a week in the clients' homes. Furthermore, clients and support workers were often together for several years. The data included in-depth semi-structured interviews with 27 care workers and managers, which lasted between 45 minutes and one hour. The sample of care workers was divided between 20 female and 7 male participants. The interviews focussed on a detailed discussion of the nature of work and skills involved in this type of care work.

The second project was an exploratory ethnography of wound healing, which aimed to develop an understanding of compassion in clinician-patient relations. It involved 120 hours of observations of clinician-patient interactions in a specialist, outpatient wound healing clinic, where consultations were run by nurses and podiatrists (all female), with male and female doctors visiting individual consultation rooms to offer advice on complex wounds. In addition to fieldnotes from non-participant observations, the study involved 51 interviews with patients, nurses, podiatrists, and doctors from wound healing and affiliated specialties. For meaningful comparison with the first project, only the interviews with 12 clinicians working in wound care were used in preparing this chapter.

All interviews were digitally recorded and transcribed verbatim. Pseudonyms and additional information on the participants are used to refer to the participants, whose profiles are shown in Table 2.1.

Table 2.1. Participants' Pseudonyms and Profiles.

Pseudonym	Wound Clinic
Ella	Research podiatrist, 18 months
Amanda	District nurse, 15 years
Eva	Acute care nurse, 15 months
Mary	Community nurse, 20 years
Christina	Psychiatric and general nurse, 2 years
Claire	Community nurse, 10 years
Deborah	Community nurse, 3 years
Sam	Advanced podiatrist, 7 years
Megan	Surgical nurse, 7 years
Helen	Podiatrist, 14 years
Catherine	Diabetic nurse
Pauline	District nurse
	Care Coop
David	Service manager, 10 years
Julie	Care worker, 5 years
Suzy	Care worker, 2 years
Ellie	Assistant manager and care, 6 years
Frances	Service manager, 25 years
Mia	Care worker, 6 years
Cynthia	Service manager, 13 years
Katrina	Care worker, 9 months
Ray	Care worker, 5 years
Ellen	Assistant manager and care worker, 11 years
Jenny	Service manager, 4 years
Zoe	Service manager, 16 years
Rose	Care worker, 4 years
Yasmin	Care worker, 4 years
Fiona	Assistant manager and care worker, 14 years
Bruce	Assistant manager and care worker, 5 years
Evan	Care worker, 18 years
Susan	Care worker, 15 years
Pat	Care worker, 8 years
Tracy	Care worker, 3 years
Phil	Care worker, 14 years
Lilly	Assistant manager and care worker, 4 years
Oliver	Assistant manager and care worker, 14 years
Robin	Care worker, 7 years
Helen	Care worker, 11 years
Bill	Area manager, 15 years
Carl	Assistant manager and are worker, 2 years

Source: Author created.

Data Analysis

Data analysis followed an interpretive and iterative process. We held multiple conversations about the content of dirty work and how stigma was managed. Using Glaser and Strauss (1967) constant comparative method, we repeatedly re-read our data sets to assess the similarities and differences between the groups in our study. This allowed us to identify the ways in which emotion management skills and gendered considerations were a feature of both occupations in how they performed dirty work, as well comparing how each group drew on different feeling rules. Our iterative coding resulted in first-level codes related to social, physical, and emotional taints, as well as contextual features concerning organizational context and occupational status. Our second-level codes related to emotion work, emotion management skills, feeling rules and gendered work. This meant that we compared and contrasted our findings to identify patterns as well as differences. This included identifying similarities in the way both groups undertook physically dirty bodywork, managed the social taint of their work and addressed the stigma encountered by clients by drawing on emotion management skills, as well as the different types of feeling rules which influenced these approaches. For example, the clinicians drew on professional feeling rules while the care workers drew on organizational and social feeling rules in interactions with clients. Additionally, there were similarities between the ways both groups were exposed to gendered forms of emotion management associated with care work, although both groups also transgressed gendered norms. Moreover, stigma management was influenced by the context of work, as clinicians were able to benefit from a 'status shield' (Hochschild, 1983) aligned to the profession of nursing, in ways in which care workers were not, because they were tainted by society's undervaluation of their work.

Like Tracy and Scott (2006) and Andrews and Shahrokni (2014), we found that collaboration between two researchers supported more detailed inspection and comparison of the data through mutual sharing and questioning of ideas, which individual researchers cannot easily benefit from. We held ongoing discussions of the emerging findings and the links to the existing literature on dirty work. By constantly comparing the data we were able to delineate the relevance of contextual features in discussions of how dirty work is undertaken as well as how stigma is managed by linking to themes such as occupational prestige and 'status' and 'necessity' shields (Ashforth & Kreiner, 2014). As such, the explanatory framing of the study was based on an iterative process between engagement with the data and drawing on the literature to sharpen our conceptual contribution.

MANAGING STIGMA

Both groups undertook in-depth relational care work which involved physically 'dirty' bodywork (Wolkowitz, 2002) on socially stigmatized clients and worked in organizational contexts which extolled the importance of person-centred, holistic care. However, there were also differences in their work contexts. Wound clinicians worked in a leading-edge out-patient clinic attached to a university research-centre such that clinicians enjoyed the prestige of the setting and the professional status of work. In contrast, care workers primarily worked in supported living contexts in the community and did not enjoy professional status. These features are relevant when considering how stigma management was attempted. In the 'Findings' section, we divide the two refocusing strategies in relation to: how workers 'do' dirty work and the 'end purpose' of their work. By emphasizing the skills involved in 'doing' dirty work, workers sought to alleviate the physical and social taint of their work being under-valued, whereas, emphasizing the 'purpose' of their work allowed them to identify how they supported their clients to manage the social stigma they encountered and hence, improve their lives.

Doing Dirty Work

Wound Clinicians

Physically dirty bodywork was a core feature of clinicians' work which involved caring for wounds that were chronic, deep, large, wet or smelly, and deemed embarrassing:

> It's not like when you fall over as a child, cut your leg and pick the scab .... If you've never seen a wound, it can be quite horrific. (Mary)

As Mary further explained below, patients were often physically repulsed by their own wounds, which made them feel 'dirty' and excluded them from social life. Clients often carried these feelings into their interactions with clinicians, who then had to look after them both physically and emotionally in how they spoke to them:

> [...] she was wild in the waiting room .... And she was so upset ... she was going to her son's wedding, and she felt she couldn't go cause she had this dripping leg ... I also said to her, 'You've got to work with me' .... Somebody's got to look after them. (Mary)

Therefore, clinicians had to be understanding and empathetic to patients' distressed states. Although they would sometimes tell of their bodily reactions to wounds – feeling 'physically sick', 'gagging', or having their 'stomach flipping', clinicians had to use emotion management skills of suppressing disgust not to reinforce social stigma by showing an emotional concern for patients' bodily comfort:

> You've got to learn not to show. You can't stand there wincing. You've got to stand there and reassure ... are you comfortable? ... You can't give any cues away as to how awful you think it is. (Catherine)

> [...] I suppose it comes with the job, doesn't it. You know you're gonna smell horrible things. And you know that if you point that out you are gonna make that person feel awful, so you just swallow it. (Eva)

Despite this normalization, the feeling of disgust did not disappear completely. So as not to upset the patient further, clinicians appeared viscerally detached while emotionally working to imagine the abhorrence felt by patients. Therefore, clinicians maintained a professional face (Bolton, 2001) to help patients deal with the wounds on their bodies, which the society publicly rejected as a material threat to safety:

> [...] this gentleman had a cancer in his ear. But when you looked at it, cause he's lost an ear, and he is a heavy drinker, he'd gone out. But there was no dressing, he took the dressing off. So

the police picked him up and they thought, somebody shot his ear off. Cause it looked raw and horrible and extensive ... where the wound was covered, it had been exposed, so it frightened a lot of people around him. (Claire)

For patients, the society's reaction to wounds excluded them from community life:

There was a little old man the other day, he'd come into the clinic on the bus, and his legs were quite smelly. And he said to me, 'Amanda, are these smelling?' And I said, 'Oh, a little bit'. He said, 'Oh', he said, 'there was a little boy on the bus and he was staring at me'. And I thought, 'Isn't that just dreadful?' He said, 'I don't think I will go on the bus again'. (Amanda)

Clinicians spoke of their own emotional distress on hearing patients' stories of wound stigma, which, 'caused people a lot of problems, a lot of pain, anxiety, embarrassment' and 'stopped them going out' (Pauline). In extreme cases, patients self-mutilated in order to remain under the care of wound clinicians who would see them even when the society wanted them hidden:

A lot of our patients are elderly and so they very often live very solitary lifestyles ... getting to clinic every week, or every fortnight, is possibly their only chance of seeing someone. So, their fear is, if they heal their wound, they're never going to see anybody again. Whereas actually if they ... keep picking on their wound so to say, or they keep tampering, that means it will keep them in clinic. And they will get seen. (Sam)

Frequently, patients' needs were physical, social, emotional, and psychological. Doing physically dirty work for such clients required 'special type of person' (Ella) able to meet all these needs. In explaining what she meant, Ella elaborated that people often commented that they could never do a job that involved bodily contact with ill patients. This would suggest that being a wound clinician came with innate skills, not skills acquired through education and training (cf. Cain, 2017). Such a description, however, took for granted and masked the complexity of emotion management skills deployed in combining physical stamina to dirt, objective scientific knowledge and soft communication skills of translating this knowledge to reassure, comfort, and empathize with individuals dealing with the 'emotional aspects of having a stinky, smelly horrible wound' (Helen). For example, Megan identified the importance of clear communication:

[...] you're honest with them and you say, 'today it is smelling, but don't worry we'll see whether it's infected and if we can treat it, or if we can use a charcoal dressing to sort of get rid of the smell'.

Although clinicians spoke of helping to manage the emotions of their clients by being 'careful with the language' (Christina), this contrasted with the brutal honesty that nurses reported male doctors used:

[...] some patients' lives are hard. As the consultant said, 'life is s***', he regularly says that life for some patients is 's***'. Dreadful. They've got to go through so much and we've got to appreciate that. And just be kind and patient. (Amanda)

Female clinicians often felt uncomfortable with this approach, as Christina admitted in a corridor conversation, she would not use such words herself. Crucially, both male and female clinicians displayed a sincere care for patients, but did it in different ways that, for nurses and podiatrists, spoke to feminine ideas of care and kindness, while male doctors demonstrated masculine views of being stern and no-nonsense (cf. Cain, 2017).

Regardless of gendered differences in communications, all clinicians were aided in asking patients about their dirty wounds by their association with medicine, which gave them a status shield that made it less likely patients would challenge them:

> I think when you're in a uniform as well it's much easier because you're seen as that professional status. (Eva)

The uniform set the foundation for building a collaborative clinician-patient relation, but the details of how such relations were further developed were less clear from clinicians' accounts. When asked how they do it, they admitted that it came natural to them:

> It's tricky, I don't think, I always do! (Christina)

> I think I just do what I do and it comes naturally .... As a nurse, you should be approachable. (Eva)

The above quotes show that nurses have internalized an image of their occupation as founded on feminine qualities of kindness and helpfulness such that they do not stop and think about the emotion management skills in the doing of their dirty work. They become specialists in intrapersonal interactions as there is an expectation that the emotion skills needed for the job are naturalized (Daniels, 1987). Therefore, socio-cultural ideologies of gender write expectations of approachability into the job description making invisible the skill involved (Hatton, 2017). Interestingly, it was nurses' accounts of patients who acted out of line or could not be helped that alluded to the complex emotion skills and feeling rules that framed dirty work of wound care as skilled emotion work:

> [...] it's also important to make sure you've got that line so that the patients don't feel overfamiliar with you as well. Because sometimes they can feel that your relationship maybe sometimes goes past that nurse-patient ... sometimes [a patient] can say things which you really don't have an answer for because you're like: 'Awww ... oh' and you just smile, smile politely and go, 'Awww, you shouldn't really be saying that. (Eva)

Above, Eva emphasizes the complex emotion work of navigating between gendered expectations of what a nurse should be and the gentle way in which they should manage the boundaries following professional rules of conduct; and authentic embodied emotions expressed through body language illustrated the enactment of Bolton's (2005a) emotion management feeling rules. Here, humour is offered to alleviate the awkward tension and get through the consultation (Bolton, 2000), while maintaining the connection with the feminine image of nursing and not giving in to own emotions.

Yet, clinicians sometimes had to draw a line as the long nature of patient contact meant patients saw clinicians as their friends. For example, Amanda explained that clinicians would often receive invitations to personal celebrations. However, she would not attend. This generated tensions in managing stigma for patients because although clinicians acknowledged patients as whole persons, they also remained distanced following professional display rules. Below, Amanda explains how she managed this tension by exercising discretion to draw a line at offering the emotion gift (Bolton, 2000) of assisting with grief, evident of philanthropic emotion management (Bolton, 2001):

> It's a fine line between being patient-friendly in the clinic and then starting to go to social engagements ... certainly, in the NMC [Nursing and Midwifery Council] you are encouraged not to have a social relationship with patients .... The only situation where I would go as a district nurse I used to go to lots of funerals ... in my mind, it was a way of saying to the family: 'We're here for you after'.

Finally, Christina explained the emotion work that went into intentionally adopting a non-judgemental attitude towards patients whose behaviours they did not approve of.

> I don't like the way they speak to me, I don't like their approach. I don't like, perhaps, the way they speak to their carers or their loved ones, or their ... sometimes, you call that an inappropriate relationship, because I don't like them and I'm sure there are patients who don't like me. And sometimes you have to be professional. (Christine, nurse)

The examples above confirm that sometimes nurses may feel judgemental or feel their personal boundaries are being crossed, but have to withdraw these feelings or know how to assert their boundaries in a patient-focussed and caring way (Bolton, 2000). Clinicians are aware of the negative consequences of the stigma of wounds for patients' social and familial lives. Thus, skilled emotion work enables them to steer the interaction with a patient in a way that will validate patients' feelings of upset and distress, give them a safe space in which to express these emotions, but also offer them a sense of relief from the stigma by making them feel accepted, welcome and non-judged. The emotion skill lies in the ability to suppress one's dislike and maintain a professional face – something that clinicians are aided in by the professional 'status shield' (Hochschild, 1983) of codes of conduct of healthcare professionals. Thus, the physical and social stigma wound clinicians encounter and which undermines the recognition of skills required for this work is managed by emphasizing the complex skills of 'doing' dirty work. Clinicians are therefore provided with a sense of professional fulfilment that shields them from the stigma of their work.

Care Workers

Like the wound clinic, at CareCoop, the organizational value system also extolled a person-centred, holistic approach to support disabled adults to live independently in the community. As Rose reflects, the values were based on:

> Respecting individuals, user-focused, person-centred care and valuing people. (Rose)

In this setting, emotion management feeling rules were influenced by the organizational context. However, care staff exercised a high level of discretion in how these values were enacted. As most care workers were based in supported living houses whereby typically four clients lived together in the local community, they either worked alongside other support workers or worked alone and had limited contact with the formal organization. The work integrated a range of roles including domestic duties such as shopping, cooking, and cleaning to 'manage the home', intimate personal care and administering medication, dealing with personal finance as well as accompanying clients on different activities in the community. Additionally, care workers spent two nights a week on 'sleep-ins' within these homes. There are two notable features of this type of care work; it is often 'hidden' in plain sight within the community and as such, the skills are also associated within the domestic sphere, and it is marked by in-depth relations with clients as care workers had supported their clients over many years.

In this setting, dirty work primarily focussed on supporting socially stigmatized clients and engaging in physical dirty bodywork. Care workers reflected that being able to deal with intimate bodily care including toileting and washing clients was initially considered challenge which they did not know they would be able to overcome. However, most conceded that proficiency in intimate bodywork was a 'specialised skill' (see also Bolton, 2005b; Stacey, 2011) based on managing both their own and their clients' emotions. First, the care workers noted they had to sensitively conceal any innate disgust to remain 'professional':

> I thought the only problem I'm going to have is personal care, because I'd never done that. And I thought I really don't want to be unprofessional, when I do it for the first time. But ... it doesn't bother me at all. It's not for everybody. My husband will always say to me, 'I couldn't do your job'. (Suzy)

'Professional' in this context, like the wound clinic also meant suppressing felt emotions. Second, they also emphasized managing their clients' emotions in these intimate interactions by 'bonding' with them first (Katrina). As Yasmin explained, making these connections allowed care workers to deal with their initial nervousness by communicating with her clients for mutual reassurance:

> I talk to them all the way through it. I know some of the people we look after haven't got the capability to understand everything, but I still talk them through it. I do it like my child, 'Come on then, socks on now ... we'll do your top now'. I talk them through everything and that makes me feel better and they're understanding what I'm doing as well. (Yasmin)

As Stacey (2005) indicated this centred on the reciprocal exchange between receiver and giver. However, as well as drawing on emotion management skills, staff also acknowledged the material challenges of intimate care with clients who had complex needs which also could make physical stigma difficult to manage:

> It's also very challenging ... My user had diarrhoea and it was very difficult because he was moving all the time when we were trying to clean him. (Ray)

The pride developed from mastering intimate bodywork, the uniqueness of these skills, was also reinforced socially by family and friends' reactions:

> A lot of my friends have said 'I have no idea how you can do that?' ... some of my friends say, 'How can you do it, how can you do personal care with adults?' I said, 'Well, I've done it with, looked after children that way so I just turn a blind eye, just get on with it because they need the help more than, you know, they need it. (Suzy)

For most care workers, dealing with dirty physical work was an intrinsic part of essential care work. However, mastering the material realities of intimate body work was considered a skill which required care staff to manage their clients' emotions through reassurance and communication as well as their own emotions in suppressing visceral reactions. However, it was also acknowledged that in some cases, the material realities of this work were not easily overcome (see Hughes et al., 2017). Compared to the wound clinicians who drew on medical professional feeling rules to manage physically dirty work, the support workers were more likely to utilize a range of feeling rules. For example, although some training was provided by the organization, workers' emotion management was often informed by peer relations to manage intimate bodywork as well as those emanating from their own experiences of care in the private sphere based on social feeling rules as indicated above by Suzy.

As well as physically dirty work, a more significant feature of this work involved confronting the social stigma encountered by the client group. The range of clients' needs and capacities varied greatly; some had physical disabilities while others had complex learning abilities and some had spent a large proportion of their lives in long-term medicalized institutions and were experiencing independent living for the first time. As such, individual support workers assisted clients with everyday activities as well as ensuring their clients engaged in hobbies, sports, and social events to lead fulfilled lives. Depending on the client, the nature of work varied, for example, some clients displayed challenging behaviour including being physically violent. For workers accompanying clients in the community, they were aware how the public's reaction stigmatized their clients. Suzy noted that after one bad experience:

> The next day (the client) he'll be like 'no I don't want to go out' and may show behaviours because of the reaction that they get from some members of the public.

On another occasion, a care worker noted how the Christmas cards clients sent their neighbours had been returned. To address the social stigma clients encountered, care workers used relationship building and emotion management to calm patients to avoid behavioural outbursts which could further stigmatize clients. Phil noted how, after 12 years with his client, he was better able to pre-empt physical attacks:

> I'd worked with him for twelve years, and he was extremely challenging. Extremely challenging, physically violent, you know? But we built up a relationship ... I got to learn his triggers, what would set the behaviours off ... I could see when he was coming off baseline, you know? I could see; I could tell; I could feel it. (Phil)

This work required a high level of emotion skills to learn to appreciate and anticipate the emotion cues which could trigger clients. Care workers also conceded that managing stigmatized clients with threatening behaviour was not easily overcome. This was especially apparent when the female care workers spoke of their visceral fear of some clients. Patricia stated that one client would frequently 'slam support workers' heads into the wall' and Tracy noted how another user 'would bite and scram her till she bled'. For many of the female care workers interviewed there was also heightened anxiety especially when they stayed overnight in supported hours and took users with unpredictable behaviour out in the community. Workers who supported these clients as well as managed their clients' emotions to reduce anxiety also managed their own emotions to suppress fear and anxiety:

> I'm quite a stern person. Whereas like other people, I just see them coming in and you can see that they're afraid of them (clients). You can't show that like. They do know, and they will play on it. Whereas I'm quite strict with them, and now they don't ... I don't take no messing, basically. And if you're too soft, they are going to hurt you then, you know? (Tracy)

Within this context, gendered norms of care work became realized. Although not openly discussed in the organization, care workers conceded that the most challenging and violent clients tended to be supported by male workers. As Patricia noted that after she was physically attacked by a client, she asked to be moved out of the supported living house, she reflected:

> There are a lot of men there now.
>
> Interviewer: Does he hit the men in the same way?
>
> He tries. But obviously, he doesn't get as far with them ... they handle it.

When dealing with the most challenging, physically violent clients, male staff were used predominantly to manage these clients.

At CareCoop the predominant gendered emotion management skills focussed on feminized qualities of being caring, supporting and empathetic which were influenced by both the feeling rules encouraged by the organization's person-centred care approach as well as care workers' own social values. However, as Cain (2017, p. 347) identified, workers also perform masculinity through activities presumed to be natural aptitudes for men as exemplified by Tracy's emotion management performance. Hence, 'doing' essential dirty work included both feminine and masculine qualities evident in emotion management. As Cain (2017) identified, emotion management is gendered through social definitions, this was exemplified in the way physically violent clients were supported by mainly male care workers.

This section demonstrates how both clinicians and care workers reframed their work to emphasize the complex emotion management skills 'to do' dirty work which includes attempting to manage the stigma of physically dirty bodywork as well as working with socially stigmatized clients. By focusing on skills to overcome the stigma of their work, these two types of gendered essential dirty workers sought to contest the social undervaluation of skills in this work. However, the type of stigma and ensuing stigma management strategies differed for the two occupations; clinicians work focussed more on physical dirty work and care workers dealt with the social taint from socially stigmatized clients. Gender was a feature of emotion management in doing dirty care work as both groups drew of feminine qualities of caring including patience, understanding, reassurance, kindness, and support. However, these roles were not exclusively feminine; clinicians' emotion management was moderated by professional feeling rules of benign emotional detachment from clients to manage boundaries. Hence, stigma management in this context was aided by invoking a 'status shield' (Hochschild, 1983) by appealing to a professional status. Whereas, some care workers resorted to traditional masculine emotional performances to suppress the fear when dealing with violent clients, in the main the organization resorted to gendered organizational solutions (Acker, 1990) by selecting male workers to support the most physically challenging clients. These emanated from social feeling rules as there was limited training or recognition of skills involved in supporting clients with complex needs.

Purpose of Work

In addition to demonstrating the emotion management skills involved in 'doing' dirty care work, both groups also engaged in reframing around the 'end purpose' of their roles. They gained a sense of purpose and value from emphasizing how they improved the lives of their clients by acknowledging the social stigma their clients confronted and, through emotion management skills demonstrated how they helped them deal with, and potentially alleviate their stigma to lead better quality lives.

Wound Clinicians – Health-related Quality of Life

Wound clinicians emphasized that their end purpose was through medical interventions, to 'clean' dirty wounds to reduce the social stigma which their patients experienced from unsightly and malodorous wounds by emphasizing their role as health focussed professionals by drawing on emotion management skills. One way through which clinicians did this was by refocusing on patient-centred outcomes aimed at alleviating the 'dirt' that gave rise to social stigma; directing attention from own visceral emotions and focussing on the healing intervention to improve patient's quality of life, affected by the wound and its stigma:

> [...] whether [smell] makes you feel right or not it doesn't matter, because all that is telling you is extra information that you've got of the wound to choose treatment. (Sam)

Reframing dirty work in a patient-centred way included using emotion management skills to make the patient feel comfortable to talk about their wounds. Eva explained that creating this safe environment required them to build a relationship with the patient to encourage clients' emotional disclosures without judgement.

> [...] making them feel more positive about their wound [so that] hopefully, you might help. (Eva)

The sense of acceptance was reinforced by clinicians' emotion management performance which involved putting on a professional face motivated by relationship building:

> Maybe the family will go, 'Oh your leg smells, don't show me the dressings, don't show me your legs'. And to have somebody just be nonchalant about it: 'Yeah, it is a bit smelly, but it's not too bad'. Putting the dressing up in the face to have a sniff. It makes them think 'It can't be that bad, everybody at home thinks it's horrible'. (Ella, podiatrist)

The skill here was to manage their clients' emotions by being honest in their assessment but also compassionate and thoughtful by adopting a holistic approach as a 'whole person', reflecting also organizational feeling rules. As explained by Christina:

> [...] when the patient isn't healing, people (clinicians) try and change the dressing. Whereas, in fact, they need to go back and look at the individual to say why they are not healing?

This way of working authentically with the clients was one where the genuine emotions of sympathy were translated into practical solutions that made a difference to patients' lives:

> [Patient] opened up to me that he used to drink 24 cans of beer a day ... I never prompted him on it, but he then just started saying, you know, all the problems he'd had with losing the feeling in his feet ... his wife has left him ... and he said to me, 'I'm much better now. I drink about 10 ... I know I have to cut down because I am not looking after myself'. And then we started talking and he said he was in a new relationship, and he was happy .... And I felt quite privileged that he had shared that with me, but maybe it helped him understand that maybe some of them problems he was having with recurrent infection were high because of his problem, the alcohol, the drinking. (Ella)

In the above account, Ella used her empathy and listening skills to withhold judgement. However, the questioning was framed as indirect advice in a respectful manner, designed to make the patient feel comfortable yet guide the patient to learn to make positive healthy choices. It facilitated the patient to discuss difficult emotions. It also provided an opportunity for the clinicians to reflect on the value of in-depth relational care work, which stretched beyond the technical skill of wound care.

In fact, sometimes, clinicians had to acknowledge the contested emotions of having to accept and communicate the limits of medical practice. This was the case with some patients for whom healing was never an option. The inability to help patients frustrated clinicians, who would reframe their work to concentrate on symptom control, by adopting a holistic approach:

> I try and refocus .... Sometimes when the patient is just too physically ill ... you have to accept that [the wound]'s not a priority .... But I always try and look for some positive steps for me and the patient. So, if I can stop the smell, if I can contain the exudate, if I can relieve the pain, if I can prevent wound infection, I can feel like I'm doing something that contributes to their well-being even if their healing is never going to be an option. (Christina)

With practice, Christina also acquired an ability to limit her involvement when she could not help any more and disassociate by shutting down her emotions. In so doing, she was demonstrating her agency in opting for the conscious suppression of naturally felt powerful emotions (Lewis, 2005) to protect herself and to focus on the execution of the professional tasks:

> We've got this description in nursing called professional blunting when, because you know you can't make a difference and it's so disheartening that you go in, do the dressing, go out, because you don't want to engage, because you know you can't help so people will do that as a defence mechanism, sometimes. (Christina)

Above, Christina explains professional blunting as a technique for curtailing her own emotional investment by limiting her emotional bonding with the patient to simply doing what she is expected to do; an example where a professional status shield is used as a tactic to neutralize any accusations of being unempathetic (Dick, 2005). Knowing when to draw the boundaries allowed clinicians to care to the highest professional standard informed by objective, scientific medical decisions, protecting themselves from burnout. In other words, these relations were closely bound by professional feeling rules based on a degree of benign detachment (Fineman, 1993).

Care Workers – Enabling Independency and Advocacy

Care staff also acknowledged how their 'end purpose' was to help alleviate, where possible, the experience and consequences of social stigma their clients encountered by supporting them to lead more independent and fulfilled lives in the community. Refocusing in this context emphasized the emotion management skills which built relations over time to qualitatively improve their clients' lives.

All the workers noted how their support contributed to improving their clients' lives:

> We enable them ... independence is the main thing. Their own choice, freedom and being valued. (Jenny)

Care workers offered examples of how through developing lasting and trusting relations with clients they helped them to integrate into the community to become more independent which also could relieve the social stigma they had previously encountered. Mia noted how one woman had progressed and thrived over time:

> Just watching her grow, that's been amazing, from not leaving the room to now, she's grown so much in confidence that she is now asking about supporting one of the others. [clients]

Most care workers recounted with ease and pride the way they had supported clients to become active citizens, as Bill noted:

> I supported this guy who was living with his mother. Then he said he wanted to move out and we helped him with that .... He is now living in a flat alone and he loves his life. Everyone thought that he wouldn't cope .... But the team really worked for him, and he is happy, he has developed himself and he is loved by his neighbours, he's a real respected member of the community.

To do so, workers invested emotion management skills, based on patience, perseverance and reassurance. In some cases, this involved considerable time and effort, often in workers' private time to research and locate suitable activities as reflective philanthropic emotion management (Bolton, 2005b). In these cases, by investing in time by managing the emotions of their clients through empathy and understanding, they could witness qualitative improvements in clients' lives. In some cases, this involved learning to understand the emotion needs of clients who were non-verbal:

> [Client] is non-verbal, and she has her own ways of .... She will rub your hand, and she will grab your hand, and it's like she's happy then .... Another lady, and she does happy hands when she's happy with you. It's like you get to know ... it's nice. (Katrina)

Staff explained how over-time they learnt how to anticipate when clients were happy or distressed which gave them a sense of value:

> Once you get to know somebody, it's fantastic, because you get to know their little ways, their behaviours and helping them manage their behaviours so their anxiety levels don't go off the scale. (Jenny)

Staff also noted how clients with previously challenging behaviour had improved over time by helping them manage their own emotions, which in turn alleviated the social stigma clients encountered in the community:

> He could never leave his flat, years ago. He's got challenging behaviour and he would be at least four times a day and he wouldn't socialise, he wouldn't talk to anybody .... Now, he can go out and about and he loves going out and very rarely has challenging behaviour now. It's the way we supported him then doing little bits at a time and we could see the improvement coming on .... He has a much more sociable existence than he used to .... That's the real reward of the job. (Zoe)

The narratives above signify that essential care workers gained pride and value by refocusing on the purpose of their work which emanated from making a material difference to the socially stigmatized clients they supported. Emotion management skills were central to how, through long-term relationship building, they were able to support some clients to address social stigma by encouraging them to lead independent lives in the community. There were no discernible differences in the emotion management between male and female staff as the organizational feeling rules extolled person-centred support such that male and female care workers reported the rewarding purpose of their work.

A further extension of their enabling role was to act as guardians and advocates for their clients' interests based on acknowledging the social stigma which their clients confronted:

> People kind of look at them and think they've got a learning disability, they can't do that ... so there is still a big stigma ... but being valued and having them go out there and have the opportunities that they get is one of our main things, you know? (Jenny)

Care workers were often fiercely determined to extol the rights of socially stigmatized clients by representing the interests of 'invisible' clients to become visible and heard because they understood their clients' needs better than others (see also Stacey, 2005):

> We're their voice so we've got to speak up for them and if we think something's not right, it's down to us, we're the ones who look after them and it's down to us to speak on their behalf and make sure they get the right care and the right things they need. (Rose)

This advocacy role was most evident in relation to giving a voice to clients who did not want to attend local authority day-care centres. Rose reported that some clients 'cried the whole time' when they were at the day-centre. Katrina described the day centres as 'a holding pen for people' Jenny referred to them as a return to 'institutionalised' care, which contradicted the values of person-centred care extoled by CareCoop. As Jenny stated:

> Just because the service user has got a learning disability, doesn't mean they need to be stuck in a day centre. Obviously, this lady ... she's got a voice ... she did start to display behaviours and the day centre was starting to say it's not the right place for her. I did say that it was sad it had to get to that .... For them to listen. Because they won't give us any hours, you know .... Obviously, they've got their restrictions, which are passed on to us ... I go home at night thinking, I could've done so much more.

In response, some staff established an alternative community centre for their clients to attend which was more flexible. Workers used their emotion management skills to better advocate for their clients by appealing to the depth of relations which gave them a better insight into their clients' emotions. However, the role of advocate could also present tensions between organizational feeling rules which extoled emotion management centred on valuing person-centred support, and the broader institutional context of an under-funded social care system. Within this context, workers and their managers recounted the struggle for resources and the negotiations they had with local authorities to 'fight' for more hours to support their clients.

Although refocusing centred on their contribution to improving the lives of clients, it was also evident that care workers did not feel society conceived their work as valuable:

> You feel you are not appreciated because you are on rubbish money, you've got to work all the time .... We don't get paid enough for what we do. (Tracy)

Care workers believed the low social value attributed to these activities reflected the lack of public understanding of the skills entailed in care work:

> People on the outside have a limited understanding of the work ... many people don't realise what it entails and what you've got to do, the policies and procedure and you've got to follow regulations and I think some people have a shock when they come in. (Lilly)

Contrary to Ashforth and Kreiner's (2014) argument that a 'necessity shield' can insulate workers from stigma by emphasizing the essentiality of this work, in the context of under-valued care work it was difficult to invoke a 'necessity shield' with regard to the essentiality of this work to the public. Instead, care workers focussed on the necessity of their role to their clients as the primary source of affirmation to manage the stigma of this work.

Both cases emphasize that stigma management revolved around refocusing the stigmatized features of their work by extolling the purpose of their work which contributed to qualitatively improving the lives of their stigmatized clients. In so doing, the two groups acknowledged the nature of the social stigma faced by their clients and sought to alleviate and, where possible, help them overcome social taint. Clinicians achieved this by emphasizing both their medical and emotion management skills to deliver health-related quality of life outcomes. In contrast, care workers identified how through the in-depth relational work in managing the emotions of their clients they were able to reduce social stigma while their advocacy sought to give voice to seldomly heard clients in order to resist the social stigma they encountered. While the clinicians were able to draw on a 'status shield' (Hochschild, 1983) to highlight their prestige as medical professionals, the care workers were not able to invoke a 'necessity shield' (Ashforth & Kreiner, 2014) because their work and skills were deemed invisible to society. For this reason, care workers gained affirmation from their relations with clients.

DISCUSSION

This chapter has shown that emotion management skills are central to stigma management by 'dirty' essential care workers. These skills are exemplified in the way dirty workers navigate their own and their clients' emotions in relation to exposure to bodily dirt and proximity to stigmatized groups, as well as in helping to address aspects of the social stigma their clients' encounter. In so doing, stigma management in these contexts includes attending to the gendered expectations of care work which includes nurturing deep relations with clients, navigating various feelings rules applicable in each context, and recognizing how power and occupational prestige matters for assessing whether stigma can be overcome.

We make several contributions to the literature on dirty work. First, our analysis extends the existing literature (Bolton, 2005b; Galazka & Wallace, 2023; Stacey, 2011) to show that in these types of dirty care work, client-focussed interactions are both the source of occupational stigma (through proximity to physical and social taint as the very essence of the jobs) and a resource which informs how workers then seek to manage the stigma by emphasizing the skills in how the work is done and its purpose to better the lives of their stigmatized clients. By drawing on the emotion management literature we shine a light on how these features influence how dirty work and its stigma is managed in different contexts. Predominantly, it was the relations with clients rather than their occupational communities (Ashforth & Kreiner, 1999; Tracy & Scott, 2006) which were the primary source of stigma and affirmation at the same time. This focus on client relations has been a neglected dimension of dirty work scholarship (Galazka & Wallace, 2023). In this study, the 'purpose' of this work emphasized how both groups were able to improve the lives of their stigmatized clients by acknowledging the social stigma faced by their clients and in attempting to alleviate social taint. Wound clinicians did so by 'cleaning' dirty wounds and by focussing on their contribution as health professionals. Care workers focussed on enabling clients to live independent, active lives in the community as well as in their advocacy to resist the social stigma encountered by their clients.

The lens of emotion management also underscores the second contribution of this study which is to illuminate the hidden skills of essential care work by acknowledging and detailing how emotion management was also central to managing the stigma faced by the clients, at least within the realm of worker–client interactions. Both groups used emotion management to perform the physically dirty work features of intimate bodywork in how they suppressed their own 'real' feelings and in how they managed the emotions of clients through reassurance, patience, and understanding. Additionally, both groups also dealt with the stigma encountered by clients based on in-depth relational work. Wound clinicians emphasized how their emotion management skills drew on 'professional feeling rules' (Bolton, 2005a) to enact 'boundaried emotional interactions' with patients, whereas care workers were more likely to emphasize the significance of in-depth relational work by drawing on peer informed and social feeling rules to manage both physical dirty work and clients' social stigma. In this way, it was more difficult for care workers to manage the emotion boundaries as these became blurred based on the work being undertaken in the private sphere of the home.

Third, as emotion management is gendered in the context of care work it also informs how stigma is managed. With few exceptions (Adams, 2012), physically dirty work in the client-facing care sector tends not to be considered skilled work, but something premised on innate, taken-for-granted and therefore invisible natural capacity of predominantly female workers to care. By explicitly comparing how two groups of essential care workers do dirty work and address the social stigma of their clients, we have made visible the gendered skills of emotion management in dirty care work. Gendered emotion management was significant for understanding how stigma was managed by emphasizing the importance of in-depth relations which involved a complex mix of managing their own as well as their clients' emotions. Hence, the feminine qualities of care work included building relations with clients based on patience, understanding, reassurance, kindness, and support. However, at times, emotion management also transgressed gendered norms, for example, clinicians drawing on 'emotional blunting' to manage professional boundaries to deal with the tensions between gendered expectations such as the ideal of the approachable nurse, while also trying to be professionally detached (see Lewis, 2005). Whereas female care workers used their individual discretion to resort to stern emotion management performances to conceal their fear of violent clients, the organization adopted gendered solutions to deal with the most extreme forms of challenging behaviour. Hence, gender emotion management was enacted in ways which drew on feminine as well as, in some cases, masculine qualities (Cain, 2017). Navigating the gendered expectations of care work as well as noting how these sometimes transgressed professional and social feeling rules illuminates the skilled nature of emotion management in different care contexts as well as how it informs stigma management.

Finally, linking to more recent dirty work scholarship, it is also important to acknowledge that stigma management cannot always overcome the taint of dirty work (Hughes et al., 2017; Zulfiqar & Prasad, 2022). This refers to both managing the material realities of dirty work as well as its stigmatizing features. In line with the speculation of Ashforth and Kreiner (2014) this study identifies that some forms of dirty work are more difficult to manage than others. For example, Tracy and Scott (2006, p. 32) identify, social taint, emanating from stigmatized clients, can be more difficult to deal with when 'the "dirt" has human agency'. Furthermore, occupational status and prestige can significantly influence attempts to manage stigma. For example, wound clinicians emphasized that when healing wounds was no longer an option, they used their professional 'status shield' as nurses (Hochschild, 1983) to support clients deal with the social stigma of their wound. This was also supported by the context of work as clinicians were based within the Wound Clinic, a medical setting which provided the infrastructure to support professional nursing work. However, as Tracy and Scott (2006) observe, embodied forms of taint are particularly difficult to manage when occupational members do not possess a status shield. Hence, Ashforth and Kreiner (2014) hypothesize that 'most physically and socially tainted jobs – independent of prestige – enjoy a necessity shield' as a protection against stigmatization threats based on the assertion that their jobs are necessary for society. We found that there was a less clear impact of a 'necessity shield' in this context as care workers acknowledged society's undervalued perceptions of their work. Arguably, this undervaluation is linked to the hidden nature of gendered care work. Consequently care workers did not think society viewed their work as necessary, although they gained affirmation from conceiving this work as necessary for their clients. We would suggest that in this way, gender influenced how stigma was managed because of the links to power and prestige at the occupational level as well as in the way society recognizes worth and value. In line with other dirty work studies which recognize the importance of context in examining how dirt and stigma is managed (Hughes et al., 2017; Zulfiqar & Prasad, 2022), we would caution claims about whether stigma can be overcome in all contexts.

CONCLUSION

Our research sought to address how the stigma of dirty work can be managed and overcome in essential care work. Through integrating the literatures on dirty work, gendered care work, and emotion management we have sought to contribute to the dirty work literature by making visible the centrality of complex emotion management skills involved in managing the stigma of essential care work. By comparing how two occupational groups undertook dirty work and focussed on the purpose of their work, we have illustrated how emotion management skills are used to reframe this work as valuable and worthy. Examining these features enabled us to show that undertaking dirty essential care work and managing the combined stigma of physical and social taint required skilled emotion management. To this extent our contribution shines a light on an under-explored dimension of the dirty work literature and seeks to reveal the often 'invisible' skills of essential care work.

Our focus on essential care work has also provided further insight into two relatively under-developed features relating to the significance of social relations beyond the occupational group in the dirty work literature. First, within the literature, the focus on social stigma encountered by the clients of dirty workers and how this is managed by workers is relatively under-developed compared to other forms of taint. Our work explores how care workers in our study were able to do this through managing the emotions of their clients to help them deal with, although not necessarily overcome, the social stigma encountered in their lives. Second, we illustrate how client relations were central to the ways in which care workers managed their own stigma in relation to appealing to skills involved in both 'doing' dirty work and in terms of the purpose of their work. This was based on affirmation from their clients not just their occupational communities. Hence, we would question the premise in the dirty work literature that the occupational group is the primary domain for stigma management as well as suggesting that future research could explore further the interactions between dirty work and socially stigmatized clients.

Furthermore, the existing work on stigma management has often identified how gender can be used as resource by male physically dirty workers to overcome stigma by emphasizing 'heroic' masculine values (Ackroyd & Crowdy, 1990; Tracy & Scott, 2006). As Ashforth and Kreiner (2013) acknowledge, the relationship between gender and stigma management in feminine occupations can be more problematic. Although feminized occupations are protected by a 'status shield' (Hochschild, 1983), such as the clinicians in this study, there was evidence of worth and value emanating from their professional prestige. Ashforth and

Kreiner's (2014) speculation of a 'necessity shield' to offer protection for workers in the absence of status shield was not apparent from the case of care workers who were aware that society did not value and recognize the skills of their work. Our study confirms that the relationship between stigma management and feminized occupations is a more fragile accomplishment because of power relations and the lower social valuation of feminine qualities such as caring. Hence, we contribute to recent scholarship within the dirty work literature which adopts a more critical reading of whether stigma can be managed by discursive resources without recognizing both the material conditions of dirty work and the contextual framing including wider power relations in society (Hughes et al., 2017; Zulfiqar & Prasad, 2022). We recommend future research to further explore the connections between dirty work and stigma management in female-dominated occupations and professions.

As we have identified, contextual features are relevant for this study, and these influence our conclusions. As such, it is important to note that the two groups of essential workers were not 'typical' of all care work, as their work is marked by in-depth and in some cases enduring relations with their client group and they enjoy relatively high levels of discretion and autonomy to do their work. Hence, the lens of emotion management illuminates that essential care work is not a homogenous category but is influenced by various feeling rules and skill content depending on the care labour process. Consequently, we suggest further research on different types of essential care work would provide a more rounded assessment of the range of skills involved in this work and how this informs stigma management in dirty work.

REFERENCES

Acker, J. (1990). Hierarchies, jobs, bodies: A theory of gendered organizations. *Gender & Society, 4*(2), 139–158. https://doi.org/10.1177/089124390004002002

Acker, J. (1998). The future of 'gender and organizations': Connections and boundaries. *Gender, Work & Organization, 5*(4), 195–206. https://doi.org/10.1111/1468-0432.00057

Ackroyd, S., & Crowdy, P. A. (1990). Can culture be managed? Working with "raw" material: the case of the English slaughtermen. *Personnel Review, 19*(5), 3–13. https://doi.org/10.1108/00483489010142655

Adams, J. (2012). Cleaning up the dirty work: Professionalization and the management of stigma in the cosmetic surgery and tattoo industries. *Deviant Behavior, 33*(3), 149–167. https://doi.org/10.1080/01639625.2010.548297

Andrews, A., & Shahrokni, N. (2014). Patriarchal accommodations: Women's mobility and policies of gender difference from urban Iran to migrant Mexico. *Journal of Contemporary Ethnography, 43*(2), 148–175.

Ashforth, B. E., & Kreiner, G. E. (1999). "How can you do it?": Dirty work and the challenge of constructing a positive identity. *Academy of Management Review, 24*(3), 413–434. https://doi.org/10.5465/AMR.1999.2202129

Ashforth, B. E., & Kreiner, G. E. (2013). Profane or profound? Finding meaning in dirty work. In B. J. Dik, Z. S. Byrne, & M. F. Steger (Eds.), *Purpose and meaning in the workplace* (pp. 127–150). American Psychological Association.

Ashforth, B. E., & Kreiner, G. E. (2014). Dirty work and dirtier work: Differences in countering physical, social, and moral stigma. *Management and Organization Review, 10*(1), 81–108. https://doi.org/10.1111/more.12044

Bolton, S. (2000). Who cares? Offering emotion work as a 'gift' in the nursing labour process. *Journal of Advanced Nursing, 32*(3), 580–586. https://doi.org/10.1046/j.1365-2648.2000.01516.x

Bolton, S. (2001). Changing faces: Nurses as emotional jugglers. *Sociology of Health & Illness*, *23*(1), 85–100. https://doi.org/10.1111/1467-9566.00242

Bolton, S. (2005a). *Emotion management in the workplace*. Palgrave MacMillan.

Bolton, S. (2005b). Women's work, dirty work: The gynaecology nurse as 'other'. *Gender, Work & Organization*, *12*(2), 169–186. https://doi.org/10.1111/j.1468-0432.2005.00268.x

Bolton, S., & Boyd, C. (2003). Trolley Dolly or skilled emotion manager? Moving on from Hochschild's managed heart. *Work, Employment and Society*, *17*(2), 289–308. https://doi.org/10.1177/0950017003017002004

Bolton, S., & Wibberley, G. (2014). Domiciliary care: The formal and informal labour process. *Sociology*, *48*(4), 682–697.

Cain, C. L. (2017). Boundaried caring and gendered emotion management in hospice work. *Gender, Work & Organization*, *24*(4), 345–359. https://doi.org/10.1111/gwao.12166

Daniels, A. K. (1987). Invisible work. *Social Problems*, *34*(5), 403–415.

Deery, S., Kolar, D., & Walsh, J. (2019). Can dirty work be satisfying? A mixed method study of workers doing dirty jobs. *Work, Employment and Society*, *33*(4), 631–647. https://doi.org/10.1177/0950017018817307

Dick, P. (2005). Dirty work designations: How police officers account for their use of coercive force. *Human Relations*, *58*(11), 1363–1390. https://doi.org/10.1177/0018726705060242

England, P., & Folbre, N. (1999). The cost of caring. *The Annals of the American Academy of Political and Social Science*, *561*(1), 39–51.

Fineman, S. (1993). *Emotion in organizations*. Sage.

Galazka, A. M. (2021). From 'dirty wound care' to 'woundology': A professional project for wound healing clinicians. *Sociology of Health & Illness*, *43*(1), 99–115.

Galazka, A. M., & Wallace, J. (2023). Challenging the 'dirty worker'—'Clean client' dichotomy: Conceptualizing worker–client relations in dirty work. *International Journal of Management Reviews*, *25*(4), 707–724. https://doi.org/10.1111/ijmr.12330

Glaser, B., & Strauss, A. (1967). *Discovery of grounded theory: Strategies for qualitative research*. Routledge.

Gunby, C., & Carline, A. (2020). The emotional particulars of working on rape cases: Doing dirty work, managing emotional dirt and conceptualizing 'tempered indifference'. *The British Journal of Criminology*, *60*(2), 343–362.

Hatton, E. (2017). Mechanisms of invisibility: Rethinking the concept of invisible work. *Work, Employment and Society*, *31*(2), 336–351. https://doi.org/10.1177/0950017016674894

Hayes, L. J. B. (2017). *Stories of care: A labour of law: Gender and class at work*. Springer.

Hochschild, A. R. (1983). *The managed heart: Commercialization of human feeling*. University of California Press.

Hughes, E. C. (1958). *Men and their work*. Free Press.

Hughes, J., Simpson, R., Slutskaya, N., Simpson, A., & Hughes, K. (2017). Beyond the symbolic: A relational approach to dirty work through a study of refuse collectors and street cleaners. *Work, Employment and Society*, *31*(1), 106–122. https://doi.org/10.1177/0950017016658438

Husso, M., & Hirvonen, H. (2012). Gendered agency and emotions in the field of care work. *Gender, Work & Organization*, *19*(1), 29–51. https://doi.org/10.1111/j.1468-0432.2011.00565.x

James, N. (1989). Emotional labour: Skill and work in the social regulation of feelings. *The Sociological Review*, *37*(1), 15–42. https://doi.org/10.1111/j.1467-954X.1989.tb00019.x

Jenkins, S., & Conley, H. (2007). Living with the contradictions of modernization? Emotional management in the teaching profession. *Public Administration*, *85*(4), 979–1001. https://doi.org/10.1111/j.1467-9299.2007.00675.x

Jenkins, S., Delbridge, R., & Roberts, A. (2010). Emotional management in a mass customised call centre: Examining skill and knowledgeability in interactive service work. *Work, Employment and Society*, *24*(3), 546–564. https://doi.org/10.1177/0950017010371665

Lewis, P. (2005). Suppression or expression: An exploration of emotion management in a special care baby unit. *Work, Employment and Society*, *19*(3), 565–581. https://doi.org/10.1177/0950017005055673

Lopez, S. H. (2006). Emotional labour and organized emotional care: Conceptualizing nursing home care. *Work, Work and Occupations*, *33*(2), 133–160.

Malvini Redden, S., & Scarduzio, J. A. (2018). A different type of dirty work: Hidden taint, intersectionality, and emotion management in bureaucratic organizations. *Communication Monographs*, *85*(2), 224–244.

McMurray, R., & Ward, J. (2014). 'Why would you want to do that?': Defining emotional dirty work. *Human Relations, 67*(9), 1123–1143. https://doi.org/10.1177/0018726714525975

Meagher, G., Szebehely, M., & Mears, J. (2016). How institutions matter for job characteristics, quality and experiences: A comparison of home care work for older people in Australia and Sweden. *Work, Employment and Society, 30*(5), 731–749.

Mikkelsen, E. N. (2022). Looking over your shoulder: Embodied responses to contamination in the emotional dirty work of prison officers. *Human Relations, 75*(9), 1770–1797. https://doi.org/10.1177/00187267211019378

Olvera, J. (2017). Managing the "dirty work" of illegality. *Sociology of Race and Ethnicity, 3*(2), 253–267.

Palmer, E., & Eveline, J. (2012). Sustaining low pay in aged care work. *Gender, Work & Organization, 19*(3), 254–275. https://doi.org/10.1111/j.1468-0432.2010.00512.x

Phillips, A., & Taylor, B. (1980). Sex and skill: Notes towards a feminist economics. *Feminist Review, 6*(1), 79–88. https://doi.org/10.1057/fr.1980.20

Press, E. (2021). *Dirty work: Essential jobs and the hidden toll of inequality in America*. Farrar, Straus and Giroux.

Purser, G. (2009). The dignity of job-seeking men: Boundary work among immigrant day laborers. *Journal of Contemporary Ethnography, 38*(1), 117–139.

Rivera, K. D. (2015). Emotional taint: Making sense of emotional dirty work at the U.S. border patrol. *Management Communication Quarterly, 29*(2), 198–228. https://doi.org/10.1177/0893318914554090

Sandoz, H. (2016). *Under pressure: Why it's time to heal these wounds*. Retrieved January 9, 2018, from http://www.healthawareness.co.uk/wound-care/under-pressure-why-its-time-to-heal-these-wounds

Simpson, R., Hughes, J., Slutskaya, N., & Balta, M. (2014). Sacrifice and distinction in dirty work: Men's construction of meaning in the butcher trade. *Work, Employment and Society, 28*(5), 754–770. https://doi.org/10.1177/0950017013510759

Simpson, R., Slutskaya, N., Lewis, P., Simpson, R., Slutskaya, N., Lewis, P., & Höpfl, H. (Eds.). (2012). *Dirty work: concepts and identities*. Palgrave Macmillan.

Stacey, C. L. (2005). Finding dignity in dirty work: The constraints and rewards of low-wage home care labour. *Sociology of Health & Illness, 27*(6), 831–854. https://doi.org/10.1111/j.1467-9566.2005.00476.x

Stacey, C. L. (2011). *The caring self: The work experiences of home care aides*. Cornell University Press.

Torelli, J., & Puddephatt, A. (2021). Reframing "dirty work": The case of homeless shelter workers. *Symbolic Interaction, 44*(2), 310–338. https://doi.org/10.1002/symb.495

Tracy, S. J., & Scott, C. (2006). Sexuality, masculinity, and taint management among firefighters and correctional officers: getting down and dirty with "America's heroes" and the "scum of law enforcement". *Management Communication Quarterly, 20*(1), 6–38. https://doi.org/10.1177/0893318906287898

West, C., & Zimmerman, D. H. (1987). Doing gender. *Gender and Society, 1*(2), 125–151.

Whiley, L. A., & Grandy, G. (2022). The ethics of service work in a neoliberal healthcare context: Doing embodied and 'dirty' emotional labor. *Qualitative Research in Organizations and Management: An International Journal, 17*(1), 136–157.

Wolkowitz, C. (2002). The social relations of body work. *Work, Employment and Society, 16*(3), 497–510.

Wolkowitz, C. (2007). Linguistic leakiness or really dirty: Dirt in social theory. In B. Campkin & R. Cox (Eds.), *Dirt: New geographies of dirt and contamination* (pp. 15–24). I B Tauris.

Zulfiqar, G., & Prasad, A. (2022). EXPRESS: How is social inequality maintained in the Global South? Critiquing the concept of dirty work. *Human Relations, 75*(11), 2160–2186. https://doi.org/10.1177/00187267221097937

CHAPTER 3

DEFINING ESSENTIAL: HOW CUSTODIAL LABOUR BECAME SYNONYMOUS WITH SAFETY DURING THE COVID-19 PANDEMIC

Annie J. Murphy

The University of Texas at Austin, USA

ABSTRACT

This study examines the construction of essential labour during the early months of the COVID-19 pandemic in the United States. Research questions include: (1) How have government policies shaped designations of essential versus non-essential labour? (2) What are the consequences of these designations for essential workers? To address these questions, the author employs a case study of custodial services employees at Prairie University, a large public university in a major Texas city (Prairietown). The author begins with an examination of federal, state, and municipal guidelines about COVID-19 safety and critical infrastructure in order to understand the policy landscape within which custodial employees at Prairie University were formally deemed essential. Drawing on theories of non-nurturant care work, the author shows how government guidelines for essential work released during the early period of the COVID-19 pandemic discursively invisibilized cleaning labourers. The author then demonstrates how this invisibilization contributed to Prairie University custodial services staff members' exposure to COVID-19.

The author concludes by considering the implications of the findings for future research on care work and the construction of essential labour.

Keywords: Essentiality; essential work; care work; COVID-19; inequality

INTRODUCTION

In a span of only a few weeks, the 'essential worker' emerged as something of a capitalist hero. Beginning in March 2020, news media outlets across the country called for better pay and more recognition for those working on the 'front lines', and essential workers were valorized for putting their lives at stake in the national fight against COVID-19 (Pearl, 2020; Williams, 2021). Journalists and news anchors discussed essential work as though it were ontologically real, a form of labour that was naturally and uniquely necessary for the continued functioning of local and global economies. There was some truth in this; essential workers were performing labour without which survival would be imperiled (e.g. food delivery, sanitation, medical services). Yet, like all divisions of labour, essential work is first and foremost a social construction (Berger & Luckmann, 1967; Martin, 2000). This chapter examines the construction of essential labour during the early months of the COVID-19 pandemic in the United States. Specifically, I ask: (1) How have government policies shaped designations of essential versus non-essential labour? (2) What are the consequences of these designations for essential workers?

To address these questions, I employ a case study of custodial services employees at Prairie University, a large public university located in a major Texas city (Prairietown).[1] I choose to focus on custodial staff for two reasons. First, the custodial services employees at Prairie University were initially designated as non-essential employees and then later redesignated as essential. Prairie University thus represents a compelling site within which to examine the social construction of essential labour as well as the consequences of an essential designation for employees. Second, custodial labour sits at the intersection of a larger debate about the valuation and treatment of essential workers. On the one hand, custodians have been celebrated as 'COVID-19's heroes' who 'risk their lives to stop the spread of COVID' (Pinho, 2020). On the other hand, custodial workers themselves have claimed that they are not treated like heroes in practice, and that they have been denied access to hazard pay, safe work environments, and even proper recognition from their employers (Schnell, 2020). Thus, an examination of custodial labour speaks to pressing questions about the experiences and valuation of essential workers in the United States.

I begin my analysis by considering the policy landscape within which custodial employees at Prairie University were formally deemed essential. Through an examination of federal, state, and municipal guidelines about essential work and critical infrastructure, I find that, unlike many other front-line workers (e.g. nurses, doctors, or food service employees) custodial labour itself is largely excluded from explicit designations of essential work – these documents mostly refer to 'cleaning' and 'sanitization' rather than to the labourers actually performing these tasks. Additionally, the government guidelines I analysed make a clear connection between cleaning and safety: in order to have safe workspaces for essential employees, these workspaces must be cleaned and sanitized regularly.[2] But what does this mean for the workers doing the cleaning? How are they meant to stay safe?

Drawing on theories of non-nurturant care work and invisibilization, I show that there is a long history of devaluing custodial workers – disproportionately people of colour and immigrants – in the United States (Duffy, 2011; England, 2005; Glenn, 1992; Roberts, 2015). I contend that the guidelines around essential work and critical infrastructure released during the early period of the COVID-19 pandemic reproduce this legacy of devaluation: by mandating that workplaces be sanitized without stipulating how the people doing the sanitizing will stay safe, these guidelines equate custodial services staff with their labour and thus discursively invisibilize them.

To understand the material consequences of this discursive invisibilization, I turn to an analysis of custodial services employees at Prairie University. I find that, between 15 March 2020 and 31 May 2020, claims to workplace safety at Prairie were achieved in part by capitalizing on the *unsafety* of custodial services staff. Although these custodial employees were not immediately designated essential employees by Prairie University's administration, they were called back to work one month earlier than other Prairie University staff members who had originally been deemed 'non-essential' in March. This meant that, unlike other initially non-essential staff at Prairie, custodial staff were denied access to paid time off during the month of May under Prairie University's emergency leave policy. Consistent with federal, state, and municipal guidelines on essential work and critical infrastructure, Prairie's administration brought custodial workers back to full-time rotation on 1 May in an attempt to make campus safe – that is, clean – for those students, faculty, and staff who would be returning to work on 1 June. However, this desire for safety created a paradox for custodial services staff: these employees were expected to work in an unsafe environment in which they were exposed to COVID-19 in order to generate safety for others. Thus, the discursive invisibilization of cleaning workers in essential work and critical infrastructure guidelines helped facilitate the exposure of custodial services employees at Prairie University – mostly Black and Latino/a people of colour – to COVID-19.

CARE WORK AND INVISIBILIZATION: THE DEVALUED LABOUR OF CLEANING

Feminist scholars have long been interested in the essential, everyday labour that people do to sustain and nurture our society: care work. Defined here as 'a species activity that includes everything we do to maintain, continue, and repair our "world" so that we can live in it as well as possible' (Tronto & Fisher, 1990, p. 52), care work is closely related to yet conceptually distinct from essential labour; essential work is a legally constructed category of paid labour within the formal economy, whereas care work is a theoretically defined form of labour that can be paid or unpaid, formal or informal. Yet, within the context of the COVID-19 pandemic, scholarship on care work offers key insights into the valuation, visibility, and overall treatment of the workers tasked with maintaining essential services.

Care work is a distinctly gendered – that is, feminized – form of labour. In one of the first edited collections on care labour, feminist scholars from a variety of disciplines presented their research on the experiences of women caregivers in contexts ranging from the nuclear family to nursing homes to hospitals (Abel & Nelson, 1990). While the essays in this collection demonstrate the immense social importance of care work and care workers, they also reveal the tendency for care labour to be exploited (un- or underpaid, minimized as 'women's work', etc.) and show how care work is linked to the reproduction of gender inequality.

In an effort to explain this link, scholars have since developed what sociologist Paula England (2005) calls the 'devaluation' perspective. According to this framework,

> cultural ideas deprecate women and thus, by cognitive association, devalue work typically done by women. This association leads to cognitive errors in which decision makers underestimate the contribution of female jobs to organizational goals, including profits. (England, 2005, p. 382)

In a vicious cycle, the symbolic devaluation of women contributes to the simultaneous material and symbolic devaluation of their work, which in turn contributes to women's material and symbolic inequality. Further, 'the devaluation perspective argues that care work is badly rewarded because the jobs are filled with women, *and* because care is associated with the quintessentially gendered role of mothering [emphasis added]' (England, 2005, p. 395). Thus, the devaluation of carework – rather than the more general 'women's work' – contributes to gender inequality precisely because care is a uniquely feminized (and thus devalued) skill associated with women and, more specifically, motherhood (see also Cancian & Oliker, 2000; Collins, 2008; England et al., 2002; England & Folbre, 1999; Hondagneu-Sotelo, 2007).

Of course, to speak of 'women' and 'care work' as universal concepts is to imply a false sense of homogeneity where, in reality, a myriad of experiences exists. In fact, care work in the United States is heavily stratified along lines of race and class as well as gender (Collins, 2008; Duffy, 2011; Glenn, 1992; Roberts, 2015). Historically, women of colour – particularly poor and/or immigrant women of colour – have been siloed into what Dorothy Roberts (2015) calls 'menial' care labour: the 'heavy, dirty, "back room" chores of cooking and serving food in restaurants and cafeterias, cleaning rooms in hotels and office buildings, and caring for the elderly and ill in hospitals and nursing homes, changing bed pans, and preparing food' (Glenn, 1992, p. 20). In contrast, white women are more often concentrated into what Roberts calls 'spiritual' care labour, which includes paid professions like nursing, social work, or counselling (Glenn, 1992) as well as unpaid domestic labour related to 'the moral upbringing of children' (Roberts 2015, p. 51).

In *Making Care Count*, sociologist Mignon Duffy (2011) proposes a related yet distinct binary between forms of care labour: nurturant versus non-nurturant.

Nurturant care work refers to paid labour that has an inherently relational component. 'The core labour of nurturant care workers', writes Duffy, 'involves intimate and face-to-face relationships with the people they are caring for' (2011, p. 6). Non-nurturant care work, on the other hand, does not necessarily include a relational component: 'these workers perform labour that is out of sight or at least does not involve an explicit relationship with those being cared for' (Duffy, 2011, p. 6). When compared with nurturant care work, non-nurturant care labour is typically compensated at a lower rate and tends to provide fewer workplace benefits (Duffy, 2011; Folbre, 2012). Further, because it lacks an explicit relational component and because it is typically performed by immigrants and/or women of colour, non-nurturant care work is subject to invisibilization as well as devaluation, meaning its importance for day-to-day social functioning is obscured and badly rewarded (Armenia, 2018; England, 2005). The division between nurturant and non-nurturant care work thus reinforces and perpetuates race, class, and gender inequality in the United States.

Neither the spiritual/menial nor the nurturant/non-nurturant division of care work are inevitable conclusions or natural outcomes. The continued race and class stratification within care-based markets is rooted in histories of slavery, settler colonialism, and restrictive US immigration policies, and the un- or underpaid care work performed by women of colour has always been crucial to the survival of white families in the United States (Collins, 2008; Hondagneu-Sotelo, 2007; Glenn, 1992, 2010, 2015; Dill, 1988). Of course, the spiritual/menial and nurturant/non-nurturant binaries are analytical rather than ontological – the work that people do in their day-to-day lives does not always fit neatly into either one or the other form of care labour (Duffy, 2011; Hondagneu-Sotelo, 2007). Yet, the fact remains that the 'ideological divisions within reproductive [i.e., care] labor are crucial to understanding the intersecting constructions of gender, racial-ethnic, and class inequalities' (Duffy, 2011, p. 17).

Existing literature on care labour provides important context for the social valuation and treatment of essential workers. As this work will show, federal, state, and municipal-level essential worker guidelines discursively invisibilize non-nurturant care workers like custodial services employees. While the construction of 'essential' as a prominent category of labour is relatively new, the race, gender, and class-based logics that render cleaning labour invisible are not. This chapter thus contributes to existing literature on care work by showing how guidelines about essential and critical infrastructure actively reproduce a discourse of devaluation that has long characterized non-nurturant care labour in the United States.

Custodial Work as Care Labour

Unlike domestic cleaning labour, custodial work is not always categorized as a form of care labour. According to Duffy (2011), this is partially due to the specific historical trajectory of cleaning labour in the United States. While domestic and custodial sanitation work share similar occupational tasks (e.g. sweeping, mopping, dusting, emptying trash) custodial labour itself is masculinized due to the higher concentration of men in these jobs and the location of custodial work (buildings and offices vs private homes). Yet, despite these differences, Duffy (2011) argues that custodial labour is still a form of non-nurturant care labour, albeit a masculinized one:

> While the nature of the tasks involved in cleaning an office building, apartment house, hotel, hospital, or school are similar in many ways, these jobs are constructed quite differently based on their location. By contrast, many nurturant care occupations are strongly feminized whether that labor takes place in a private home or in a public institution. For example, child care is numerically dominated by women and culturally associated with the feminine whether it occurs in a private home, in a family daycare setting, or in a more institutional child-care center or school. While there are gender-typed differences in cleaning tasks, the most visible differences are based on context rather than on the content of the labor. (p. 119)

Following Duffy's analysis, I conceptualize custodial labour as a form of masculinized care work. That is, I contend that custodial labour is structured by logics of devaluation and invisibilization that mirror those of other non-nurturant care labourers. Existing research on the day-to-day experiences of custodial services staff supports this claim; in his study of custodians working on college campuses, Peter Magolda (2016, p. 7) argues that 'campus custodians are an invisible, marginalized, and powerless campus subculture'. Like other non-nurturant care labourers, custodial workers are disproportionately people of colour and immigrants (Duffy, 2011; Magolda, 2016). This nationwide trend is reflected at Prairie University, where, as of 2020, 88.5 per cent of custodial services staff were people of colour (see Figs. 3.1 and 3.2). Thus, as with other forms of non-nurturant care

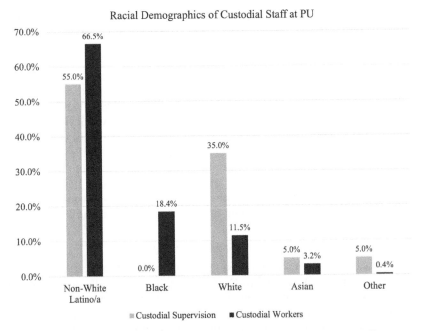

Fig. 3.1. Demographic Data on Race of Custodial Services Staff at Prairie University.

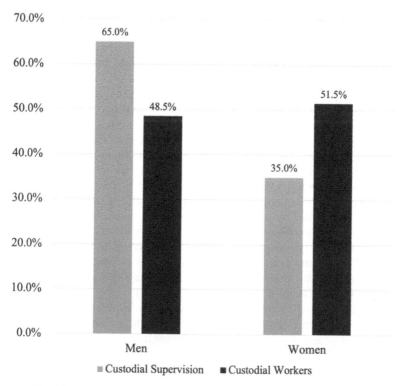

Fig. 3.2. Demographic Data on Gender of Custodial Services Staff at Prairie University.

work, custodial labour is closely associated with the reproduction of race and class-based inequalities.

METHODOLOGY AND RESEARCH DESIGN

To address my research questions, I carry out two phases of research. First, I analyse federal, state, and municipal guidelines on essential critical infrastructure and COVID-19 safety in order to understand the policy landscape within which custodial services employees at Prairie University were deemed essential. Importantly, much of the federal and state-level COVID-19 guidance released during the early pandemic was non-compulsory, meaning that tasks like defining essentiality and enforcing worker-safety policies were largely left up to the discretion of local governments in Texas. Although some US states did have centralized, state-wide policies and procedures, many others did not (National Conference of State Legislatures, 2021). Thus, although both state and federal guidance on COVID-19 was issued by conservative, Republican-led governments, final decision-making power during the early period of the COVID-19 pandemic was largely left up to Prairietown's progressive and Democrat-led municipal government.

At the federal level, I examine two versions of the Cybersecurity and Infrastructure Security Agency's (CISA) 'Memoranda on Essential Critical Infrastructure' as well as official Center for Disease Control (CDC) and Occupational Safety and Health Administration (OSHA) guidelines on workplace safety for essential workers. At the state level, I examine five executive orders issued by Texas Governor Greg Abbott: No. GA-08, No. GA-14, No. GA-18, No. GA-21, and No. GA-23. I also examine *Texans Helping Texans: The Governor's Report to Open Texas*, a document issued by Governor Abbott that outlines health and safety protocols for essential businesses. Finally, at the municipal level, I focus on Prairietown's 21 March 2020 'Stay Home – Work Safe' Order, which outlines essential critical infrastructure for Prairietown during the COVID-19 pandemic. To understand the construction of essentiality, I use content analysis – a form of sociological discourse analysis (Ruiz, 2009) – to examine the 'common sense' meanings embedded within federal, state, and municipal-level COVID-19 safety and critical infrastructure guidelines. Specifically, I employ a conventional content analysis wherein 'coding categories are derived directly from the text data' (Hsieh & Shannon, 2005, p. 1277).

After determining the policy landscape within which essentiality is constructed, I turn to the second phase of my research: a case study of custodial services employees at Prairie University. Prairie University is a large public university located in Prairietown, Texas. As discussed in the introduction, I choose to focus on custodial services staff at Prairie for two primary reasons: (1) these employees were initially designated as non-essential and then later redesignated as essential, making Prairie an ideal site for examining the construction of essentiality and (2) custodial labour sits at the intersection of contemporary debates around the valuation of essential workers in the United States. It is also worth noting that most members of the custodial services staff at Prairie University were eligible to join the Texas State Employees' Union; the majority of Prairie's custodial staff members were employed by Prairie University directly rather than contracted through another company. Of course, Texas is a 'Right-to-Work' state, meaning unions in the state are highly limited in the types of labour-organizing they can legally engage in (Shermer, 2009). Still, the fact that custodial services employees had the option to unionize is an important factor to consider when interpreting the construction of essentiality at Prairie University.

I focus my analysis on the period between 15 March 2020 and 31 May 2020. I choose this time period because it represents the first few months of the pandemic, a time when the reorganization of labour into essential versus non-essential was occurring most rapidly (Stevano et al., 2020). In terms of data, I rely on primary source material produced within Prairie University. These data largely take the form of internal emails, meeting minutes, and formal university guidance on COVID-19, and all of it was obtained through an open records request of the university. I use the primary source material obtained from Prairie University to reconstruct the events that lead to custodial services employees being redesignated as essential employees. That is, rather than studying the meaning embedded within the Prairie University emails, meeting minutes, and internal memoranda, I use these documents to understand what happened at the university in the period from 15 March to 31 May 2020.

DEFINING ESSENTIAL: THE POLICY CONSTRUCTION OF CUSTODIAL WORK AS ESSENTIAL LABOUR

On 17 March 2020, administrators at Prairie issued a statement that the university would be closing for the remainder of the spring semester and ordered all non-essential personnel – including custodial services employees – to vacate the campus. Less than two months later, the university formally redesignated custodial services staff as essential and asked them to return to in-person work at Prairie. In order to understand why custodial services staff were converted from non-essential to essential personnel, it is necessary to consider the policy landscape within which 'essentiality' is constructed. I thus begin my analysis by considering several federal, state, and municipal-level essential worker guidelines published between 15 March and 31 May 2020.

Federal Definitions – The United States

On 19 March 2020, the CISA of the United States Department of Homeland Security released an advisory memorandum outlining 'essential critical infrastructure' in the United States (U.S. Department of Homeland Security, 2020a). The memorandum covers 16 different critical infrastructure sectors – ranging from financial services to transportation and logistics – and lays out a specific set of workers who are considered essential for the continued operation of each sector. Custodial services staff are explicitly mentioned as essential workers only once in the document under the broader sector of Information Technology. Although an additional four sectors (Public Works, Food and Agriculture, and Chemical and Hazardous Materials) note the essential nature of workers who 'sanitize' or 'clean', custodial work is largely absent from the federal government's explicit definitions of critical infrastructure (U.S. Department of Homeland Security, 2020a).

Yet absent is not the same as being altogether excluded. While there are few explicit references to the importance of cleaning and custodial staff for critical infrastructures to function, this initial CISA memorandum relies heavily on non-specific and open-ended language that leaves open to interpretation whether or not custodial workers should be deemed essential. Take, for instance, the direction that 'workers supporting groceries, pharmacies and other retail that sells food and beverage products' are essential to the Food and Agriculture sector (U.S. Department of Homeland Security, 2020a, p. 6). Though no direct mention is made here to cleaning, custodial staff, or sanitization, a significant portion of food retailers and pharmacies – particularly major retailers – employ custodial services employees. Similarly, 'hospital and laboratory personnel' and 'workers in other medical facilities' are both listed as essential to the Healthcare sector, and custodial services staff could potentially be included within either of those categories (U.S. Department of Homeland Security, 2020a, p. 5). Thus, while explicit mentions of custodial labour as essential are limited in the 19th March CISA memorandum, there is also little in the memo to suggest that custodial services employees are *non-essential,* or that their labour is not also necessary in order to support critical infrastructure.

On 28 March 2020, CISA released an updated version of the advisory memorandum. As in the 19 March CISA memo, the language used to codify essential operations is flexible and non-specific; custodial labour cannot be discounted as non-essential for any of the 16 sectors listed. Additionally, in the updated 28 March version, custodial services employees are referenced more often and more explicitly. Janitorial and/or custodial staff are listed as essential personnel for the Hygiene and Products Services sector and the Transportation and Logistics sector (although there is no longer an explicit mention of custodial services employees in the Information and Technology sector). Further, the tasks of 'cleaning', 'promoting hygiene', and 'sanitizing' are mentioned as essential to 8 of the 16 critical infrastructure sectors in the updated memorandum (U.S. Department of Homeland Security, 2020b). Thus, although only 2 out of 16 sectors list custodial workers as essential, fully half of these sectors list the *labour* performed by custodial and other cleaning staff as essential.

OSHA and CDC guidelines released at the onset of the pandemic also associate cleaning labour with essentiality. Although neither of these guidelines make any formal distinction between essential and non-essential labour, they do lay out a series of 'steps all employers can take to reduce workers' risk of exposure to SARS-CoV-2' (Occupational Safety and Health Administration, 2020, p. 7). Many of these measures refer to individualized steps employees can take to protect themselves from COVID-19, such as handwashing, staying home when sick, and wearing PPE. However, the guidelines also encourage employers to 'maintain regular housekeeping practices, including routine cleaning and disinfecting of surfaces, equipment, and other elements of the work environment' (Occupational Safety and Health Administration, 2020, p. 9). As in the 28 March CISA memorandum, there is no mention of which workers will actually *perform* this cleaning duty, but the CDC and OSHA guidelines make clear that a crucial part of safely operating a business during COVID-19 is ensuring that workspaces are regularly cleaned and sanitized. 'Reducing the risk of exposure to COVID-19 by cleaning and disinfection', state the CDC guidelines, 'is an important part of reopening public spaces' (Center for Disease Control, 2020, p. 1). The essentiality of custodial and other cleaning labour is thus written into federal COVID-19 guidelines even where explicit mentions of custodial employees are absent. Further, the link between cleaning and safety outlined in these guidelines does not address how workers performing cleaning tasks are to be kept safe.

State Definitions – Texas

At the state level, the Texas government largely declined to codify formal designations between essential and non-essential labour, instead leaving that decision up to individual municipal governments. While Texas Governor Greg Abbott did

Defining Essential

make clear that 'all critical infrastructure will remain operational' in his 19 March 2020 Executive Order No. GA-08, he did not define this critical infrastructure or which employees were necessary to maintain it (Abbott, 2020a, p. 3). In terms of explicit definitions of essential work, there is little to glean from Texas state laws or guidelines. Still, an analysis of five executive orders issued by Governor Abbott in the period from 15 March to 31 May reveals how the importance of sanitation is written into state-level understandings of essential business operations. In his 27 April 2020 Executive Order No. GA-18, for instance, Governor Abbott notes that 'in providing or obtaining essential services or reopened services, people and businesses should follow the minimum standard health protocols ... and practice good hygiene, environmental cleanliness, and sanitation' (Abbott, 2020c, p. 5). Similar to the federal guidelines, custodial labour is implicitly written into Texas law as essential even when custodial labourers themselves are not explicitly mentioned.

In March, the state of Texas' Department of State Health Services (DSHS) released an advisory document titled *Texans Helping Texans: The Governor's Report to Open Texas*. The purpose of this document was to outline 'new protocols, guidance, and recommendations' for reopening as well as 'Open Texas Checklists that outline DSHS' minimum standard health protocols for all Texans' (Texas Department of State Health Services, 2020, p. 3). Similar to the CDC and OSHA guidelines, Texas' advisory memorandum reinforces the connection between cleaning labour and COVID-19 safety. Under the heading of 'Health Protocols for Your Facilities', for example, the document states that employers should 'regularly and frequently clean and disinfect any regularly touched surfaces, such as doorknobs, tables, chairs, and restrooms' as well as 'place readily visible signage at the business to remind everyone of best hygiene practices' (Texas Department of State Health Services, 2020, p. 7). Here again, there is no explicit mention of how the workers performing this labour will be kept safe; the basic assumption is that clean spaces will make work safe for essential employees.

Municipal Definitions of Essential Work – Prairietown, Texas

On 21 March 2020, Prairietown's Mayor issued a 'Stay Home – Work Safe' order that laid out which businesses and employees were considered essential in Prairietown.[3] The definition of critical infrastructure presented in the order is largely consistent with the 19 March CISA advisory memorandum. One important exception, however, is that the 'Stay Home – Work Safe' order explicitly mentions 'sanitation services' as critical infrastructure – cleaning here is formally codified as its own sector. Yet, despite the explicit mention of sanitation services in the order, there is little in the document to indicate which specific employees fall under the category and how the safety of these employees will be accounted for. Rather, the designation of sanitation services as a form of critical infrastructure upholds the idea that cleaning is an essential service, one intimately linked to safety.

Prairietown's 21 March 'Stay Home – Work Safe' order also states that 'educational institutions – including public and private K-12 schools, colleges, and universities' – shall be considered essential businesses insofar as they need to remain open 'for purposes of facilitating distance learning, performing critical research, or performing other essential functions, provided that social distancing of six-feet per person is maintained to the greatest extent possible' (Prairietown Mayor, 2020, p. 7). In combination with the link between workplace safety and workplace sanitization present throughout essential worker guidelines, the decision to include educational institutions under the heading 'essential businesses' all but necessitated the essentiality of custodial labour at Prairie University; federal, state, and municipal delineations between essential and non-essential labour made clear that, were Prairie University's administrators to choose to remain open or continue some operations, they would need to have cleaning staff continue to come in to maintain a 'safe' and 'hygienic' work environment.

Taken together, the government COVID-19 safety and essential worker guidelines I analysed discursively invisibilize cleaning staff like custodial workers. The majority of these documents do not list sanitation work as critical or essential infrastructure. At the same time, all three levels of government closely associate workplace safety with cleaning, implicitly marking custodial labour as essential even where custodial workers themselves are absent from formal designations of critical infrastructure. Even in the few cases where cleaning labour is explicitly listed as essential, safety guidelines do not address how people doing sanitation work are meant to be kept safe – these labourers are tasked with maintaining a clean workplace but, in order to accomplish this, they must enter spaces that are unclean and thus presumably unsafe. In order to understand the lived impact of this discursive invisibilization, I now turn to my case: custodial services staff at Prairie University.

SAFETY FOR WHO? CUSTODIAL SERVICES STAFF AT PRAIRIE UNIVERSITY

Becoming Essential

On 17 March 2020 – four days before Prairetown's Mayor issued the first 'Stay Home – Work Safe Order' – Prairie University announced that it would be closing for the remainder of the spring semester and that all classes would be taking place online (see Fig. 3.3). While essential employees were told to continue coming to campus, the majority of Prairie's faculty and staff were sent home to either work remotely or take paid time off under the university's emergency leave policy. About 150 custodial staff were asked to come to campus the night of 17 March to collect trash and disinfect restrooms and high-use-touch-point surfaces, and a small percentage of custodial employees continued working throughout the months of March and April to clean a handful of operational buildings (e.g. medical school, UHS clinic, law library) and 'support essential areas'. However, the majority of Prairie University's custodial services employees were granted a combination of paid emergency leave and work-from-home hours (mostly used to complete online trainings) through March and the first half of April. In March, a total of 363 custodial services employees used 16,349 hours

Defining Essential 51

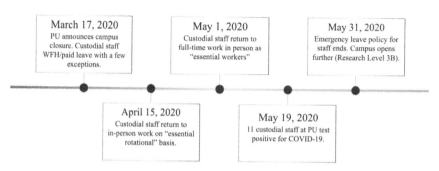

Fig. 3.3. Timeline of Events at Prairie University.

of emergency leave over 17 days. Similarly, in April, 270 employees used 27,413 hours of emergency leave over 30 days. With campus operations largely shut down and classes moved online, the need for custodial services at Prairie had declined significantly. That is, while cleaning was still needed in certain buildings, Prairie's administration had not declared custodial labour to be universally essential.

Beginning in mid-April, however, things started to shift. On 13 April 2020, all Building Attendants (custodial staff members who engage directly in cleaning, i.e. non-managerial staff) were called back to work and labelled 'essential rotational' employees. This meant that custodial staff were expected to begin cleaning campus buildings on a part-time basis on rotating schedules, the hope being that this would maximize the extent to which staff could socially distance while at work. Then, two weeks later, custodial staff were universally declared essential employees and told to return to work full-time starting 1 May 2020. 'We have permission to bring essential personnel to work full time starting 5/1/20', wrote the Associate Director of Custodial Services in an email to staff. 'Employees who are working from home (management and admins) will continue to do so'. This return to work under the designation of 'essential employees' meant that custodial services staff were no longer eligible to receive paid emergency leave as so many of them had in the months of March and April. Thus, custodial workers' salaries were now contingent on their ability to return to work in-person on 1 May 2020. As of 1 May, nothing substantial had changed about the university's operational status. There was no major influx of students, faculty, or staff returning to campus and no significant increase in the number of 'essential areas' that needed cleaning. Further, there were no changes to Prairie's emergency leave policy, which guaranteed staff paid time off through 31 May 2020. This raises an important question: why did Prairie University administrators designate custodial labour as essential on 1 May when they had the option of granting these employees another full month of paid time off under the university's emergency leave policy?

COVID-19 Safety and Cleaning Labour

In order to answer this question, it is first necessary to understand the economic and political climate at Prairie University more broadly. On 17 April 2020,

Texas Governor Greg Abbott announced a formal – and compulsory – plan to begin the process of reopening Texas businesses, meaning that administrators at Prairie University were facing state-level pressure to resume in-person operations (Abbott, 2020b). Further, as of 6 May 2020, Prairie had lost over $26 million in revenue as a result of the COVID-19 pandemic. While an initial round of budget cuts was made in April, Prairie President Jim Jones (pseudonym) announced in a 19 May 2020 email to faculty and staff that further 'mitigation plans will likely include furloughs or permanent reductions in force for staff members in ... units where revenues have declined'. The email also informed faculty and staff that the university's paid emergency leave would be ending on 31 May 2020 and that, starting 1 June, all employees who could not work from home would need to either use accrued paid leave or come into work in person. Thus, facing both political and economic pressure to reopen, Prairie's administrators decided to call hundreds of staff members back to campus.

Accordingly, 1 June marked a major change to Prairie's in-person operations. First, beginning in June, selected athletic teams were allowed to return to campus and begin practising for their upcoming seasons. This meant a further increase in the number of people – specifically student athletes and coaching staff – on campus as well as an increased number of facilities that needed cleaning. Second, and also beginning 1 June, the university shifted to Research Level 3B, meaning a number of research projects that had previously been halted due to the pandemic were allowed to resume. Research offices, labs, and libraries were partially reopened, and limited data collection and fieldwork recommenced. Research was also resumed in 'restart facilities where work [could not] be done remotely, with additional sanitization and distancing measures in place for common/shared equipment'. Here again, the resumption of campus operations is clearly linked to an increased need for custodial labour. Still, this relatively simple fact – that as more people returned to campus and more facilities were opened more custodial staff members were needed to clean those spaces – does not explain why custodial employees returned to in-person work on 1 May rather than 1 June.

To understand this decision, it is necessary to look closely at the logic used by university administration to justify Prairie's campus as a safe, COVID-19-free space in advance of the 1 June opening. Generally, official university documents as well as more informal addresses from Prairie's administrators reveal a pattern: the decision to partially reopen campus on 1 June and bring back hundreds of faculty, staff, and students was in part justified by the cleaning and sanitization-related measures that had taken place over the month of May. Prairie's campus was deemed safe for students and employees in part because of the work that custodial services staff had done prior to their arrival. In Prairie's official Research Restart Plan, for instance, one of the three main requirements for the university to shift from Research Level 4 to Research Level 3B (the shift that happened on 1 June) was that 'cleaning measures [were] understood and in place'. Beginning on 1 May, custodial services staff carried out increased levels of cleaning and sanitization and began working to ensure that 'safety signage [had] been placed in prominent locations through each zone/shop/work unit to reinforce physical distancing, hand washing, and face cover wearing'. Similarly, 'custodial services

Defining Essential 53

staff...established floor signs in the check-in areas indicating 6 feet distance where team members stand while check in/out' of work. In an announcement to staff, Prairie's Senior Vice President and Chief Financial Officer Dave Barnes (pseudonym) noted that there had been

> A heroic effort on the part of staff to respond to this situation [COVID-19] in ways that have really positioned the institution to continue to move forward .... I think in my own portfolio I think of some of the efforts from our custodial staff, who show up late at night—who have the same concerns as we do – who day after day show up to make sure this place is ready – is clean, is sanitary – for those folks who do come to campus to conduct their work every day. I feel really proud and appreciative of the outstanding work our staff have done.

Clearly, administrators at Prairie had made a connection between campus COVID-19 safety and custodial work. This logic mirrors the direct link between cleaning and safety made throughout federal, state, and municipal essential worker laws and guidelines. Without exception, formal guidance on essential workers and workplace openings strongly urged employers to make sure spaces were fully sanitized ahead of employees' return to work. Given this, I argue that, consistent with federal, state, and municipal essential worker laws and guidelines, Prairie's administrators brought custodial workers back to full-time rotation on 1 May in an attempt to make campus safe for those students, faculty, and staff who would be returning to work in June. The work that custodians did in April and May was later used to justify Prairie's campus as a COVID-19-free space in June.

But what did this promise of safety mean for custodial workers when they returned to work on 1 May? In practice, not much. On 19 May, the same day that Prairie's president announced the university's second round of budget cuts, Prairie University issued a message to the community which noted that 'a group of 11 custodial services employees had tested positive for COVID-19'. Up to that point, custodial employees had the highest rates of COVID-19 of any occupational group within the university community. Thus, the decision to bring custodial staff back to work on 1 May created an interesting paradox: it was only by placing custodial staff in an unsafe environment in which they were exposed to COVID-19 that Prairie University administrators deemed it safe to begin gradually opening campus to other students, faculty, and staff. Custodial staff were tasked with generating safety even as they themselves remained unable to access it. The discursive invisibilization of cleaning labour thus facilitated Prairie's decision to expose custodial services staff – overwhelmingly Black and Latino/a people of colour – to COVID-19.

CONCLUSION

In the beginning of this chapter, I proposed two research questions: (1) How have government policies shaped designations of essential versus non-essential labour? (2) What are the consequences of these designations for essential workers? My findings reveal how federal, state, and municipal-level COVID-19 safety and critical infrastructure guidelines discursively invisibilize cleaning labourers like custodial services staff. In the case of Prairie University, this invisibilization facilitated the exposure of custodial workers to COVID-19.

When put in conversation with feminist theories of care work, my findings demonstrate how essential worker policies and guidelines reproduce pre-existing logics of worker devaluation. Indeed, the central paradox highlighted by this case – that custodial workers were exposed to harm in order to create a safe environment for others – is in fact a predictable outcome in a society that consistently overlooks and invisibilizes non-nurturant care workers (Duffy, 2011; England, 2005; Glenn, 1992; Roberts, 2015). This chapter thus contributes to existing scholarship on care labour by demonstrating how COVID-19-era constructions of essentiality reinforce rather than challenge existing frameworks for valuing care labour. My findings also raise questions about the extent to which other logics of worker (de)valuation – for example, 'skilled' versus 'unskilled' – are reproduced by essential worker policies.

The federal, state, and municipal definitions of essential work that I analysed all unevenly account for the protection of people performing cleaning-based labour during the COVID-19 pandemic. In the case of custodial services staff at Prairie University, this uneven protection disproportionately resulted in people of colour – especially Black and Latino/a people – being exposed to COVID-19. This not only points to the tendency for essential worker policies to reproduce existing inequalities (in this case, race and class-based) but also to the heterogeneity inherent in the construction of 'essential labour' as a category of work. As my case demonstrates, not all essential workers are equally protected from the coronavirus. Thus, my findings suggest that future scholarship on the construction of essentiality should pay attention to variation within the broad category of essential labour.

The findings of this study are limited in three main ways. First, the nature of my data means that I cannot speak to the lived experiences of custodial services staff and other cleaning workers. While my analysis of government guidelines and primary source material from Prairie University allowed me to reconstruct the logics used to designate custodial workers as essential, future research should use interview or ethnographic methods to consider how such essential designations impact workers' day-to-day experiences. Second, I focus only on the period from 15 March to 31 May 2020. Further research is thus needed to determine whether and how the construction of essentiality has changed over the course of the COVID-19 pandemic. Finally, my case is focussed within a specific geographic and political context. As such, future research should examine how different federal, state, and/or municipal-level COVID-19 safety and critical infrastructure policies may differentially shape constructions of essential work. Further, future research should attend to the role of politics in shaping essential designations, paying close attention to the possibilities for unionization and worker activism to mold COVID-19-safety policies from the ground up and resist discursive invisibilization.

Moving forward, I believe my findings demonstrate the need to continue critically examining essential worker designations. Although the logics of devaluation and invisibilization written into the critical infrastructure and safety policies I examined aren't new or unique to COVID-19, they may still present an added challenge for workers and labour organizers long after the pandemic has ended. How will the essential worker definitions laid out during COVID-19 continue to unevenly impact worker safety after the pandemic? Will popular narratives about heroic essential workers continue to obscure the racialized, classed, and gendered logics of worker devaluation inherent in the labour categorization? These and other questions may be increasingly important to consider in the post-COVID-19 era. The coronavirus pandemic may not last, but situations that require the continued labour of certain 'essential' workers in dangerous conditions almost certainly will.

NOTES

1. Prairie University is a pseudonym, as are all municipal-level names and organizations presented in this chapter. Federal and state entities are not anonymized.
2. The extent to which cleaning and sanitization actually reduce the transmission of COVID-19 – an airborne disease – is debated. Because I am examining discourses, however, I do not take up questions related to the efficacy of cleaning measures in maintaining COVID-19 safety. Instead, I try to understand how cleaning has been discursively constructed as a means of mitigating the spread of the coronavirus. For more information on the spread of COVID-19 via surfaces (see Ghafoor et al., 2021; Lewis, 2021).
3. The 21 March 'Stay Home – Work Safe' Order was the first of many issued by Prairietown's Mayor during the period from 15 March to 31 May 2020. However, each of the successive orders defines essential work and critical essential infrastructure in effectively the same way, and thus an extended discussion of them in this chapter is not warranted.

REFERENCES

Abbott, G. (2020a). *Executive Order No. GA-08*. https://gov.texas.gov/uploads/files/press/EOGA_08_COVID-19_preparedness_and_mitigation_FINAL_03-19-2020_1.pdf

Abbott, G. (2020b). *Executive Order No. GA-17*. https://gov.texas.gov/uploads/files/press/EO-GA-17_Open_Texas_Strike_Force_COVID-19_IMAGE_04-17-2020.pdf

Abbott, G. (2020c). *Executive Order No. GA-18*. https://gov.texas.gov/uploads/files/press/EO-GA-18_expanded_reopening_of_services_COVID-19.pdf

Abel, E. K., & Nelson, M. K. (1990). *Circles of care: Work and identity in women's lives*. SUNY Press.

Armenia, A. (2018). Caring as work: Research and theory. In B. J. Risman, C. M. Froyum, & W. J. Scarborough (Eds.), *Handbook of the sociology of gender, handbooks of sociology and social research* (pp. 469–478). Springer International Publishing.

Berger, P. L., & Luckmann, T. (1967). *The social construction of reality: A treatise in the sociology of knowledge*. Anchor.

Cancian, F. M., & Oliker S. J. (2000). *Caring and gender*. Rowman & Littlefield.

Center for Disease Control. (2020, March). *Guidance for cleaning and disinfecting public spaces, workplaces, businesses, schools, and homes*. https://stacks.cdc.gov/view/cdc/87981

Collins, P. H. (2008). *Black feminist thought: Knowledge, consciousness, and the politics of empowerment* (1st ed.). Routledge.

Dill, B. T. (1988). Our mothers' grief: Racial ethnic women and the maintenance of families. *Journal of Family History*, *13*(4), 415–431. https://doi.org/10.1177/036319908801300404

Duffy, M. (2011). *Making care count: A century of gender, race, and paid care work*. Rutgers University Press.

England, P. (2005). Emerging theories of care work. *Annual Review of Sociology*, *31*(1), 381–399. https://doi.org/10.1146/annurev.soc.31.041304.122317

England, P., Budig M., & Folbre N. (2002). Wages of virtue: The relative pay of care work. *Social Problems*, *49*(4), 455–473. https://doi.org/10.1525/sp.2002.49.4.455

England, P., & Folbre N. (1999). The cost of caring. *The Annals of the American Academy of Political and Social Science*, *561*(1), 39–51. https://doi.org/10.1177/000271629956100103

Folbre, N. (2012). Should women care less? Intrinsic motivation and gender inequality. *British Journal of Industrial Relations*, *50*(4), 597–619. https://doi.org/10.1111/bjir.12000

Ghafoor, D., Khan Z., Khan A., Ualiyeva D., & Zaman N. (2021). Excessive use of disinfectants against COVID-19 posing a potential threat to living beings. *Current Research in Toxicology*, *2*, 159–168. https://doi.org/10.1016/j.crtox.2021.02.008

Glenn, E. N. (1992). From servitude to service work: Historical continuities in the racial division of paid reproductive labor. *Signs*, *18*(1), 1–43.

Glenn, E. N. (2010). *Forced to Care: Coercion and Caregiving in America*. Harvard University Press. https://doi.org/10.2307/j.ctv1p6hnw0

Glenn, E. N. (2015). Settler colonialism as structure: A framework for comparative studies of U.S. race and gender formation. *Sociology of Race and Ethnicity*, *1*(1), 52–72. https://doi.org/10.1177/2332649214560440.

Hondagneu-Sotelo, P. (2007). *Domestica: Immigrant workers cleaning and caring in the shadows of affluence* (1st ed). University of California Press.

Hsieh, H., & Shannon, S. E. (2005). Three approaches to qualitative content analysis. *Qualitative Health Research*, *15*(9), 1277–1288. https://doi.org/10.1177/1049732305276687

Lewis, D. (2021). COVID-19 rarely spreads through surfaces. So why are we still deep cleaning? *Nature*, *590*(7844), 26–28. https://doi.org/10.1038/d41586-021-00251-4.

Magolda, P. M. (2016). *The lives of campus custodians: Insights into corporatization and civic disengagement in the academy* (Reprint ed.). Stylus Publishing.

Martin, J. L. (2000). What do animals do all day? The division of labor, class bodies, and totemic thinking in the popular imagination. *Poetics*, *27*(2), 195–231. https://doi.org/10.1016/S0304-422X(99)00025-X

National Conference of State Legislatures. (2021). *COVID-19: Essential workers in the states*. https://www.ncsl.org/labor-and-employment/covid-19-essential-workers-in-the-states

Occupational Safety and Health Administration. (2020). *Guidance on preparing workplaces for COVID-19*. https://www.osha.gov/sites/default/files/publications/OSHA3990.pdf

Pearl, M. (2020, August 26). Essential workers are heroes; Pay them accordingly. *The Express*. https://www.lockhaven.com/opinion/columns/2020/08/essential-workers-are-heroes-paythem-accordingly/

Pinho, K. (2020, April 19). COVID-19 heroes: The essential workers keeping buildings clean. *Crain's Detriot*. https://www.crainsdetroit.com/covid-19-heroes/covid-19-heroes-essential-workers-keepingbuildings-clean

Roberts, D. (2015). Spiritual and menial housework. *Yale Journal of Law & Feminism*, *9*(1), 51–80.

Ruiz, J. R. (2009). Sociological discourse analysis: Methods and logic. *Forum Qualitative Sozialforschung/Forum: Qualitative Social Research*, *10*(2). https://doi.org/10.17169/fqs-10.2.1298

Schnell, L. (2020, June 12). 'We're heroes, too:' Hospital janitors risk lives to stop spread of COVID-19. *USA Today*. https://www.usatoday.com/story/news/nation/2020/06/12/essential-workers-includehospital-custodians-though-often-forgotten/5278789002/

Shermer, E. T. (2009). Counter-organizing the sunbelt: Right-to-work campaigns and anti-union conservatism, 1943–1958. *Pacific Historical Review*, *78*(1), 81–118. https://doi.org/10.1525/phr.2009.78.1.81

Stevano, S., Ali, R., & Jamieson, M. (2020). Essential for what? A global social reproduction view on the re-organisation of work during the COVID-19 pandemic. *Canadian Journal of Development Studies/Revue Canadienne d'études Du Développement*, *42*(1–2), 178–199. https://doi.org/10.1080/02255189.2020.1834362

Texas Department of State Health Services, Greg Abbott. (2020). *Texans helping Texans: The Governor's report to Open Texas*. State of Texas Government.

Tronto, J. C., & Fisher, B. (1990). Toward a feminist theory of caring. In E. Abel & M. Nelson (Eds.), *Circles of care* (pp. 36–54). SUNY Press.

U.S. Department of Homeland Security. (2020a). *Guidance on the essential critical infrastructure workforce: Ensuring community and national resilience in COVID-19 response*. https://www.cisa.gov/sites/default/files/publications/CISA-Guidance-on-Essential-Critical-Infrastructure-Workers-1-20-508c.pdf

U.S. Department of Homeland Security. (2020b). *Guidance on the essential critical infrastructure workforce: Ensuring community and national resilience in COVID-19 response*. https://static.carahsoft.com/concrete/files/6615/8620/0930/DHS_Guidance_on_Essential_Critical_Infrastructure_workers.pdf

Williams, C. L. (2021). Life support: The problems of working for a living. *American Sociological Review*, *86*(2), 191–200. https://doi.org/10.1177/0003122421997063

CHAPTER 4

FEAR AND PROFESSIONALISM ON THE FRONT LINE: EMOTION MANAGEMENT OF RESIDENTIAL CARE WORKERS THROUGH THE LENS OF COVID-19 AS A 'BREACHING EXPERIMENT'

Valeria Pulignano[a], Mê-Linh Riemann[a,b], Carol Stephenson[c] and Markieta Domecka[a,d]*

[a]KU Leuven, Belgium
[b]Europa-Universität Flensburg, Germany
[c]Northumbria University, UK
[d]University of Roehampton, UK

ABSTRACT

This study applies Garfinkel's (1967) concept of 'breaching experiment' to explore the impact of COVID-19-induced disruptions on the 'emotion management' practices of residential care workers in the United Kingdom and Germany. It examines the influence of professional feeling rules on workers, emphasizing the prescribed importance of displaying affective, empathetic concern for residents' health and well-being. Findings demonstrate that authenticity and adherence to professional feeling rules in relation to emotional management are not mutually exclusive. The authors underscore how adherence to professional

---

*'University of Roehampton, UK' is the first affiliation for Markieta Domecka. 'Europa-Universität Flensburg, Germany' is the first affiliation for Mê-Linh Riemann.

Essentiality of Work
Research in the Sociology of Work, Volume 36, 57–79
Copyright © 2024 by Valeria Pulignano, Mê-Linh Riemann, Carol Stephenson and Markieta Domecka
Published under exclusive licence by Emerald Publishing Limited
ISSN: 0277-2833/doi:10.1108/S0277-283320240000036004

feeling rules upholds authentic care by reinforcing a professional ethos, which acts as a cornerstone motivating residential care workers. Ultimately, the study showcases how a professional ethos substantiates altruistic motivations, guiding proficient emotion management practices among care workers. It highlights how these workers drew upon their personal understanding and experiences to determine the appropriate emotions to express while providing care for residents amid the unprecedented challenges of the pandemic.

Keywords: Breaching experiment; care work; COVID-19; emotion management; essentiality; professional ethos

INTRODUCTION

This chapter examines the emotion management of residential care workers in the United Kingdom and Germany during the COVID-19 pandemic. Care work is founded upon relationality and interdependence (Sevenhuijsen, 2003, p. 183) and is characterized by the ongoing interplay between the building and maintenance of relationships and the performing of tasks (see also Strauss et al., 1982 concept of 'trajectory work'). It encompasses a dynamic interconnection between nurturing relationships and fulfilling tasks, characterized by the nuanced orchestration of trust-building, proficient task execution, and emotional equilibrium by the workers (Lewis, 2005). The complexity of this interconnection is underscored by emotional management – the navigation by workers of their own emotions and that of others within relationships and practical provisions of care.

Scholars have explored how organizations, professions, and societies shape 'social feeling rules' that form the basis of the management of emotions in work settings through the establishment of codes of conduct and behaviour (Bolton, 2005; Bolton & Boyd, 2003; Hochschild, 1983). Bolton's (2005) typology of emotion management distinguishes between pecuniary and prescriptive emotion management. The former aligns with profit-driven instrumentalism, often combined with imposed identity, potentially fostering detrimental consequences on workers who find they are pressed into cynical emotional performance. Hochschild's (1983) early work in relation to emotional labour best exemplifies this pecuniary emotion management. By contrast, prescriptive emotion management widens the motivational basis of emotion management to altruistic and status-related reasons. This is the case with professional feeling rules that are not primarily imposed by the employer but learned and internalized during a secondary socialization into a profession (Omdahl & O'Donnell, 1999). These are unwritten rules or expectations about how individuals should express or manage their emotions that are not explicitly dictated by the organization but are learned by individuals as they become part of that professional environment through their socialization/immersion into the profession.

Bolton (2005) suggests that workers were able to express their 'authentic selves' within the context of what she called presentational and philanthropic emotional management. However in the context of a critical understanding of the challenges faced by care workers in contemporary settings, she saw diminished opportunities for workers to express their authentic selves in relation to the emotion management associated with professional feeling rules. This chapter leverages qualitative data from biographical narratives of care workers in the United Kingdom and Germany, conducted amid the unparalleled landscape brought about by the COVID-19 pandemic. Our inquiry focuses on how these workers reconcile their personal experiences within the established feeling rules during the COVID-19 pandemic. We aim to elucidate how adherence to professional feeling rules influences emotional management during this exceptional period. The pandemic, disrupting entrenched social norms and practices, exerted extraordinary pressure on those endeavouring to maintain stability in residential care settings. This study thus views the COVID-19 pandemic as a 'breaching experiment' (Garfinkel, 1967), offering a unique lens to unveil the unravelling of established structures amidst everyday activities.

The chapter makes two contributions to research on emotion management. First, we illustrate how professional feeling rules of care workers prescribed an affective, empathetic concern for the health and well-being of residents. We show how this emphasis relates to the genuine expression of authenticity in the residential care workers' emotional responses by illustrating, for example, how workers relied on their personal understanding and experiences to determine which emotions were appropriate to express, all while taking into consideration the perspectives of residents, their families, and their co-workers. We argue that the adherence to professional feeling rules is part of the authentic caring as a 'gift', and that emotions controlled by professional feeling rules can retain authenticity as these rules support the actor's emotional expression to care for the others. The chapter's empirical evidence showcases how care workers enact professional feeling rules by actively embodying them in their daily interactions within residential care homes, while also adhering to these rules by following established norms. In making such a claim, and this is the second contribution, this study underscores how the adherence to professional feeling rules retains authentic caring by reinforcing the importance of a professional ethos.

Care work is frequently viewed as not fitting within the realm of a profession, even within sociological discourses. Beyond the prevalent misconception that care work lacks the sophistication or recognition of a profession, our research delves into the profound intricacies and expertise underpinning this field. We highlight the often-overlooked dimension of care work: the cultivation of a professional ethos that impels residential care workers to navigate intricate 'feeling rules' – a web of emotional management, empathy, and adeptness in responding to varied needs and situations. Our findings therefore underscore the depth of expertise intrinsic to care work, dispelling the fallacy that it merely involves innate or intuitive abilities. Instead, we illuminate how care workers develop and employ an array of specialized skills, informed by a professional ethos, to navigate the complex emotional terrain inherent in care settings. These skills encompass not only technical competencies but also embrace the art of empathy, nuanced communication, and adaptive responses tailored to individual needs.

Professional work is 'specialized work [...] grounded in a body of theoretically based, discretionary knowledge and skill' (Freidson, 2001, p. 127). In the context of our study professional work seeks to comprehend and articulate the unique experiences of workers, involving their skills, during an unprecedented period marked by a shift in motivations behind emotion management.[1] We illuminate the symbiotic relationship between professional work and effective care provision by shedding light on how professional ethos as commitment affirms the inherent altruistic motivations that underlie the performance of effective emotion management. Residential care workers describe the professional work ethos they draw upon in order to carry out their work effectively by drawing upon a distinctly crafted professional work ethos, akin to that seen in recognized professions, to uphold standards of excellence and deliver quality care. This ethos is not merely a guideline but a cornerstone that elevates care work to a realm of skilled practice, demanding continuous learning, and refinement of techniques. Thus, the essentiality of – or the 'essential' in – care work fundamentally refers to the integration of skills, professionalism, and the management of emotions within care settings. It accentuates the pivotal role of a well-honed professional ethos in the delivery of compassionate, high-quality care – an ethos that is indispensable for meeting the diverse and intricate emotional needs of those under care.

Before delving into our findings and concluding discussion, we introduce the context of emotion-centred care work and outline our methodology.

CARE WORK AND THE MANAGEMENT OF EMOTIONS

Despite the essential nature of providing care to the elderly, sick, and vulnerable, this line of work is often marked by inadequate wages, unfavourable working conditions, and a lack of recognition as a professional occupation. Consequently, care work is largely undervalued, unrecognized, unrewarded, and unpaid (Duffy, 2011; Hatton, 2017; Pugh, 2015; Rubery, 2005). Nevertheless, care workers find their work meaningful and often report high levels of job satisfaction, despite dissatisfaction with pay (e.g. Hebson et al., 2015; Rakovski & Price-Glynn, 2010). In particular, Hebson et al. (2015) acknowledge that despite opportunity constraints, inadequate wages and working conditions, workers within the context of care work might genuinely develop attachment and altruistic motivations driven by emotions and feelings (p. 32).

Hochschild's (1983) classic definition of emotional labour associated the management of feelings and emotions with meeting job requirements in commercialized settings. Hochschild (1983) primarily focussed on short-term commercial interactions, as evidenced by her research on the work of flight attendants. However, that work involves vastly different work interactions and expectations to the long-term commitment and responsibilities associated with care work. Emotional labour in care settings encompasses 'the labour involved in handling other people's feelings' (James, 1989, p. 30). This definition highlights that emotional labour entails not only managing one's own emotions but also regulating the emotions of others within the work environment, which includes norms and expectations, comprising those influenced by gender. James (1989) highlights the intricate and multifaceted nature of emotional labour in caregiving, emphasizing its profound impact on both caregivers and the individuals they interact with, such as patients, clients, or residents. James (1989) concluded that caregivers derived a sense of fulfilment from their ability to positively influence the well-being of patients through the effective management of their emotions. These findings on the management of emotions align with earlier literature on 'sentimental work', as explored by Strauss et al. (1982) in hospital settings. Strauss's et al. (1982) research highlighted the active and agentic nature of emotional labour, emphasizing its role in establishing secure comfort, confidence, and trust: factors essential for making care both possible and tolerable.

Building on these ideas, Bolton and Boyd (2003) and Bolton (2005) developed a multidimensional analysis which is derived from abstract theorizing, essentially a typology, to elucidate the management of emotions. They propose that within the realm of emotional labour, workers have the opportunity 'to enact a prescribed performance' that aligns with 'organizationally imposed feeling rules' (Bolton, 2005, p. 93). In so doing, Bolton's work advances Hochschild's initial concepts of 'deep-acting' and 'surface acting', which respectively describe situations where workers' emotions either align with or diverge from the emotional performance required in their employment. In essence, Bolton (2005) goes beyond discussing terms from emotional labour – such as 'surface' and 'deep acting' – by introducing a broad typology of workplace emotions. The typology consists of pecuniary, prescriptive, presentational, and philanthropic forms of emotion management. Aligned to this typology are four categories of feeling rules: commercial, organizational, professional, and social. Commercial feeling rules govern 'pecuniary' emotion management, while organizational and professional feeling rules are associated with 'prescriptive' emotion management. In contrast, 'presentational' and 'philanthropic' emotion management are guided by non-institutional social feeling rules. Bolton's categorizing of emotion management lies in the differentiation between 'pecuniary' and 'prescriptive' emotion management (which aligns with an organization's-imposed feeling rules), and 'presentational' and 'philanthropic' emotion management (which is closely tied to 'the implicit traffic rules of social interaction') (Bolton, 2005, p. 133).

Bolton's (2005) typology highlights the significance of particular feeling rules within organizations, expanding our comprehension of motivation beyond commodified employment relationships. It elucidates how these feeling rules pertain to managing emotions based on financial considerations, often dictated by commercial feeling rules. This enables an exploration of the intricacies of organizational life by acknowledging the range of motivations associated with emotion management. Bolton's typology does not discount the parameters and constraints of employment and management expectations. Instead, it acknowledges the possibility that workers seek – and sometimes attain – the preservation of their sense of dignity, self-esteem, and control, ultimately preserving their individual identity (Bolton & Boyd, 2003). From this standpoint workers are viewed as highly adaptable, reflexive, and fundamentally human, actively seeking value and reward in their emotional labour, even in situations characterized by restraint and pressure: in other words, employees' behaviour is not solely driven by instrumental expectations for emotion management. Instead, individuals maintain their unique subjectivities and actively seek spaces within organizations to evade excessive managerial control. These spaces thus often become arenas for emotion management practices, and this chapter illustrates this in relation to the challenging circumstances presented by the COVID-19 pandemic.

The navigation of emotion management in the context of care work is intricately shaped by a complex interplay of social feeling rules derived from organizational and professional codes of behaviour, interactions with peers, and broader societal expectations. Care workers navigate intricate emotional dynamics within their roles, a nuanced process often best comprehended by an observer possessing a 'keen eye and an analytical perspective' (Strauss et al., 1982, p. 272). This multifaceted work unfolds in diverse forms within the context of care provisions, encompassing staff engagement with the personal histories of those they care for, the need to provide support in the aftermath of challenging medical and care interactions, the imperative of developing trust, and the influence of both professional and moral expectations. Bolton (2005) recognizes that workers can offer their 'authentic selves' but argues that this occurs only in relation to presentational and philanthropic emotion management which is offered as a 'gift' in accordance with social feeling rules that derive from basic socialization. Nevertheless, Bolton (2005) contends that there was a period when workers directly engaged with individuals who could benefit from positive emotional interactions (such as care workers, teachers, and medics) and had the opportunity to present their 'authentic selves' to patients, pupils, or clients. However, these opportunities have become limited (Bolton, 2005, p. 159). Bolton (2005, p. 160) further asserts that if these professionals were to diminish their philanthropic emotion management and merely engage in prescriptive emotion management half-heartedly, it would significantly impact the well-being of the consumer. According to Bolton (2005), professional feeling rules have a twofold protective function. They act as a shield that protects the worker's self from the emotional demands of the job, and they project the 'right' image or 'façade' of a professional. 'Keeping the face' as a professional can be both a burden and a benefit. Workers might become deeply attached to the professional image and its related benefits, to the extent that the effort required to maintain it is scarcely perceived as work. One consequence of this is that workers such as carers and nurses 'cannot truly share their feelings whilst at work as they must always maintain the professional face' (Bolton, 2005, p. 140) or offer 'the detached face of a professional carer' (Bolton, 2000, p. 584). This may suggest that the enactment of professional feeling rules is set against authentic caring which is given as a 'gift'.

Nevertheless, in emotion management research, motivations are seen as dynamic rather than rigid, as workers actively shape and adjust feeling rules in response to the circumstances they may encounter (Bolton, 2005, pp. 92–94). The onset of the COVID-19 pandemic provides a unique window for comprehensive empirical exploration into how adhering to established emotional guidelines within the realm of care work influences the way workers manage their emotions amidst the unparalleled challenges brought about by the pandemic. During the

COVID-19 pandemic, the conventional norms and routines governing care work and social interactions were disrupted, placing immense strain on relationships. These unprecedented circumstances compounded the already intricate challenges associated with managing emotions within residential care settings. The pressure to maintain a 'professional face' – as described by Bolton (2005, p. 140) – heightened the expectation for workers to potentially conceal their genuine or 'authentic' emotions.

This chapter is rooted in research conducted during the course of the breach of normal working practices to empirically investigate how care workers in residential settings in the United Kingdom and Germany navigated their personal experiences and emotions within the framework of feeling rules during the COVID-19 pandemic. In particular, it delves into how these workers managed their 'authentic' emotions, acknowledging the challenges posed by the suppression of such emotions during this time. The study thus delves into the implications of this emotional struggle, examining its effects on adherence to professional feeling rules and the underlying motivations guiding emotional management in this complex and uncertain work context.

RESEARCH STRATEGY AND METHODOLOGY

Focus

This chapter is centred on residential care in the United Kingdom and Germany, with a particular focus on the disruptions caused by the COVID-19 pandemic within our study's research framework. The pandemic served as an unprecedented external shock, impacting the economic, social, and welfare systems of nations. National governments grappled with the daunting task of safeguarding lives and livelihoods while containing infection and mortality rates.

The United Kingdom and Germany presented differing governmental responses and attitudes towards lockdown, which mirror differences in social care models embedded in diverse welfare and regulatory settings. Although both countries faced challenges, Germany, with its generally stronger institutional system, exhibited greater resilience compared to the United Kingdom. In some instances, Germany resorted to familiar regime-specific arrangements to offer support and protection to vulnerable populations, displaying 'institutionally recidivist' tendencies. Conversely, the United Kingdom, with its liberal legacy of flexible labour markets and welfare cutbacks, faced exposure during COVID-19. This prompted significant short-term departures from the conventional liberal approach concerning employment, social protection, health, and residential care (Ellison et al., 2022). However, while our approach aimed to examine how these institutional differences influenced the experiences of care workers, the way workers reconciled their genuine emotions, often suppressed due to COVID-19, did not reveal significant national disparities. This surprising finding suggests that, despite national contexts, the experiences of care workers were relatively similar.

The Selected Countries

The selected countries (i.e. United Kingdom and Germany) conform to the original liberal and social democratic regime types (Esping-Andersen, 1990). Importantly, we use this typology as a theoretical and methodological starting point, rather than a comparative tool, because it raises questions about the resilience of the dissimilarities of outcomes in the light of the existing different institutional arrangements during a period of significant challenges. Despite some evidence of liberalization, social care in Germany largely complies with the welfare ideologies identified by Esping-Andersen (1990). Conversely, social care in the United Kingdom follows an increasingly liberal path, with extensive privatization in residential care settings.

In the United Kingdom, the privatization of care homes began in earnest in the 1980s (Simmonds, 2022) when local authorities, in search of cost savings, outsourced most care for older adults to the private sector (Simmonds, 2022). By mid-2000s, 94% of residential beds for older people were supplied by private providers (Spasova et al., 2018) a process that accelerated the decline in wages associated with such work and increased the use of zero-hours contracts (Rubery & Urwin, 2011; Skills for Care, 2021). Wages overall fell markedly after the financial crisis before climbing to just over 2007 levels by 2019 (Ellison et al., 2022). By contrast, in Germany average wages rose consistently following the downturn of 2007–2008. Moreover, debt levels were consistently more favourable in Germany than those in the United Kingdom between 2015 and 2020 (OECD, 2021). A general snapshot of the pre-COVID state of both residential care systems in Germany and the United Kingdom indicates that funding models and levels of public resourcing differ across the two countries with Germany enjoying higher levels of public funding and slightly increasing bed capacity, while the United Kingdom experiencing real terms funding reductions and declining bed capacity in the lead-up to 2020 (Ellison et al., 2022; Eurostat, 2020).

In summary, Germany's ability to cope with the impact of the virus was bolstered by two primary factors: its robust fiscal standing and the comparative resilience of its social care and health sectors. Notably, while care professionals in Germany benefit from relatively higher wages due to the implementation of the minimum care wage (*Pflegemindestlohn*), our research highlighted a concerning trend: the declining numbers of professional carers in favour of much lower-paid helpers or care assistants. Conversely, the United Kingdom lacks substantial financial incentives for professional carers, resulting in their remuneration being at the same low level as individuals without any formal credentials. This disparity in compensation underscores a significant contrast between the two countries' approaches to remunerating those in the caregiving profession, contributing to divergent trends in the workforce composition which potentially may be expected to impact differently the overall quality of care delivered within these respective healthcare systems.

With these contextual distinctions in mind, we explored how care workers have experienced the disruptions resulting from the COVID-19 pandemic, and how these influenced their motivations for various types of 'emotion management' performances. It was expected that distinctive contexts would be reflected in differences in the workers' emotion management experiences in relation to their genuine or authentic emotions, in an environment where emotions were suppressed due to COVID-19. However, this was not found, thereby suggesting that the nature of the work and the impact of the crisis had the most significant bearing on the emotion management of our respondents.

Data Collection and Analysis

Thirty-nine biographical narrative interviews (Schütze, 2008) were conducted with care workers in residential care homes in United Kingdom (19) and Germany (20) to examine workers' experiences arising from different national contexts (Miles & Huberman, 1994) during the COVID-19 crisis. The data collection took place between May 2020 and January 2022. The interviews were transcribed, in the case of the German sample subsequently translated into English, and later anonymized.

The research sought to examine the experiences of care workers before and during the COVID-19 pandemic, and the ways they related these experiences to their overall life situation. In the first part of the interview respondents were encouraged to tell the story of their life-work experiences. The respondents brought up the topic of COVID-19 independently without the researchers' active intervention. The pandemic thereby represented the last and present stage of their story: an unprecedented crisis that deeply disrupted their everyday lives, exacerbated existing problem constellations, and created new ones.

The COVID-19 pandemic was examined as a collective and 'unintentional' 'crisis experiment'. This is both in analogy with – and in contrast to – Garfinkel's (1967) 'intentional initiation' of extremely disruptive crises in ordinary encounters and situations to detect how members of society establish order in their everyday lives and rely on background expectancies as a matter of course. Scambler (2020) describes COVID-19 as an 'ethnomethodological breaching experiment [.] putting a gigantic spanner in the works' and one that would cast a light on the impact of neoliberal policies in relation to health care. Here, we use primary data to examine how the tumultuous events of the pandemic revealed something of the 'seen but unnoticed' (Garfinkel, 1967, pp. 37–38). COVID-19 created a situation of fracture of practices and relationships for care workers who were suddenly expected to adapt their everyday routines to rapidly changing events and expectations which were unprecedented. For Garfinkel (1967) a fracture enables the basic principles of social interaction which have lain hidden to be unearthed. Thus, we show how care workers have reconciled their personal experiences and emotions within the framework of feeling rules during the COVID-19 pandemic.

The sampling of participants both in the United Kingdom and Germany was purposive. We used our own contacts and the help of trade unions and social media to reach residential care settings of various size (small/large), organizational model (voluntary/private) and care philosophy (person-centred/non-person-centred). Within each care home, we interviewed care workers of different level of experience from care assistants to more senior carers. The great majority of the respondents in our sample are working class women ($N = 36$), only three are men which reflects the overrepresentation of female workers in care jobs in both United Kingdom (Skills for Care, 2021) and Germany (Radtke, 2022), where 81% and

83% of those employed in residential care are women, respectively. Our sample reflects some migration patterns in both countries: nine of our respondents had a migration background, with Turkish and Polish workers in Germany, and Eastern European, Irish, and South African workers in the United Kingdom (Table 4.1). We used the country of origin as a proxy for ethnicity and migration status, regardless of whether the workers have become United Kingdom or German citizens. Our goal was not to avoid essentializing ethnic groups but to get access to a variety of perspectives and work experiences. In Germany, most of our respondents were

Table 4.1. Age, Gender, and Country of Origin of the Respondents.

No.	Name[a]	Age	Gender	Country of Origin
1	Zarima	41	F	Bosnia
2	Julia	42	F	Germany
3	Susanne	52	F	Germany
4	Rashid	29	M	Pakistan
5	Ruby	62	F	Philippines
6	Sinem	39	F	Turkey
7	Marianne	55	F	Germany
8	Nele	53	F	Germany
9	Maggie	62	F	Germany
10	Michaela	60	F	Germany
11	Nadia	56	F	Germany
12	Özlem	45	F	Turkey
13	Eva	53	F	Germany
14	Alina	34	F	Germany
15	Lilly	20	F	Germany
16	Rebekka	55	F	Poland
17	Beate	61	F	Germany
18	Doreen	28	F	Germany
19	Sonja	52	F	Germany
20	Sarah	59	F	Germany
21	Sophia	38	F	United Kingdom
22	Mary	41	F	United Kingdom
23	Diana	33	F	United Kingdom
24	Olivia	25	F	United Kingdom
25	Lynn	33	F	United Kingdom
26	Ciara	19	F	United Kingdom
27	Marc	54	M	United Kingdom
28	Monica	52	F	United Kingdom
29	Joan	54	F	Ireland
30	Matt	53	M	United Kingdom
31	Marika	43	F	Latvia
32	Nelly	58	F	United Kingdom
33	Lina	64	F	Lithuania
34	Marta	34	F	Poland
35	Tina	64	F	United Kingdom
36	Marianne	62	F	South Africa
37	Tara	57	F	United Kingdom
38	Edith	67	F	United Kingdom
39	Marija	37	F	Croatia

Source: Own elaboration.
[a]All names are pseudonyms to protect the interviewees' anonymity.

over the age of 40 and had older children. The average age in the United Kingdom sample was lower and included more respondents with younger children.

Recruiting respondents proved to be difficult, as our fieldwork took place during the pandemic. Therefore, we widened our selection criteria by including social care assistants and activity coordinators in addition to trained care workers who had been our initial focus. These respondents mostly lacked formal credentials but improved their status over time by gaining work experience and tended to work in voluntary care settings or private non-profit elderly care homes; some worked in shared flats or other assisted living facilities, which provide specialized support, for example, for people suffering from dementia. Due to the biographical interview format, we also included a few respondents who were currently engaged in domiciliary care but had previous experiences in residential care work. The interviewees expressed a very caring and positive attitude towards residents, and we acknowledge that this may reflect their reflexivity as they are actors who care about 'how they are seen by others', something literature refers to as impression management (Leary, 1995).

Our interpretation of the transcriptions of the narrative interviews was influenced by the procedures of a sequential socio-linguistically based analysis of social processes, which had primarily been developed in analysing biographical narrative interviews (Schütze, 2008). Several steps were involved in the analysis of the data, starting from the narratives' content, and using inductive reasoning (see also Riemann et al., 2023). First, we read through a subset ($N = 10$) of the 39 narrative interviews to familiarize ourselves with the content. We then proceeded with open coding (Glaser & Strauss, 1967) of all interview transcripts, which was followed by the second step, such as selective coding around the two main themes which had emerged in our analysis namely: the COVID-19 pandemic as a collective 'breaching experiment' and the feeling rules underlying everyday interactions at residential care homes before and during the pandemic.

We treated these two main themes as 'sensitizing concepts' for further analysis (Charmaz, 2003, p. 259). Thus, we used these concepts to interpret the participants' experiences in relation to the feeling rules they created and motivations in the context of restricted facial expression and body movements due to personal protective equipment (PPE) and labour shortage (Schutz & Luckmann, 1973). Four overarching categories emerged through which we studied workers' experiences during COVID-19: (1) Emotion management in pre-pandemic times, (2) COVID-19: smiling through a mask, (3) COVID-19: social distancing and lockdown, and (4) COVID-19: 'Getting through it together'.

EMOTION MANAGEMENT AND PROFESSIONAL FEELING RULES DURING COVID-19

Emotion Management in Pre-pandemic Times

Prior to the pandemic many care homes sought to create an environment as close as possible to a home and community setting. This facilitated trust, familiarity, community, and engagement with the outside world. When speaking about the impact of the COVID-19 crisis on care homes, our informants frequently drew contrastive comparisons to pre-pandemic times, revealing the pride they took in giving residents 'that little extra' or 'a gift' (Bolton, 2005, p. 139):

> Well ... we also did daytrips which aren't taking place anymore, right? We have a ... wish club, where residents can write down their wishes on a card ... someone wrote down: 'I want to fly to the moon'. And my colleague on the other living area had this, in my opinion, great idea and went to the planetarium with them. (Nadia, age 56, Germany)

Nadia commented: 'These are things that we don't think about that much, every day ... because we just do it. You know?', underlining how it took a breach – in this case the pandemic – to realize the central importance of such social activities to foster a sense of inclusion and the value workers attached to their ability to deliver this. Care workers invested considerable energy and effort into reaching residents on a personal level. In order to prevent boredom and routine, care workers report they used to come up with new ideas on a regular basis. Our interviewees described this process as enjoyable, as it also served as source of recognition and authentic self-actualization. Consequently, curtailment of these opportunities was missed:

> We've got two floors in our home, both residents used to mix, we couldn't do any of that during COVID. I used to do some rewarding activities in pre-COVID when I used to bring ingredients and cook for residents. Because I've been to Morocco, I did the Moroccan meal .... I tried to make it like it was a restaurant, cause one resident said to me, 'It's like going out for the night'. But now you can't do anything like that. (Marc, age 54, United Kingdom)

When recalling their approach to planning social activities before COVID-19, care workers expressed pride and sensitivity regarding an 'ethos'. This ethos embodies the fundamental principles guiding their behaviours as 'carers', including acknowledging and celebrating the rich and diverse lives of residents:

> Especially with like, Remembrance Day[2] and everything. We try and do like a two-minute silence and put poppies everywhere. You have to know how to do all this, it requires knowledge, competence and sensitivity which is part of what we do as carers .... Yeah, and we sort of like, try and do lots of reminiscence things as well. So, watching The Crown with them, usually after an episode, we chat with them and ask, 'do you remember that, when that happened?' Or 'Do you remember hearing stories?' It's always good sort of listening to stuff they went through. Because quite a lot of residents have lived through the 2nd world war, and I've spoken to a few of them about it because they were obviously children. And normally, they say to me, that they weren't scared. It was an adventure for them, and they can remember it like it was yesterday. (Sophia, age 38, United Kingdom)

The onset of the COVID-19 pandemic disrupted usual practices and expectations, inadvertently creating a space for care workers to explore their motivations. In particular, and as the following sections will illustrate, the elimination of previously established social activities, coupled with the mandatory use of **PPE** such as masks, gloves, and, in some cases, full-body suits, alongside the enforcement of social distancing and lockdown measures, exposed the genuine enactment of professional feeling rules in emotional management among the care worker respondents during these challenging circumstances. In other words, we show how care workers actively embodied professional feeling rules in their social interactions within the studies residential care homes while also adhering to the established norms within the context of the pandemic.

COVID-19: Smiling Through a Mask

The loss of shared social activities was one of many restrictions and disruptions care workers had to deal with in their everyday work routines and relationships. In an attempt to prevent the virus from spreading, staff were instructed to wear PPE including masks, gloves, aprons, and even entire protective suits. These newly protective measures increased physical demands on workers ('It is an incredible burden. You close the zipper of your suit, and you are already sweating'. Marianne, age 55, Germany), also because they impeded efforts to connect with residents on an emotional level.

Respondents stressed that being able to 'read' the emotional state of residents and being recognized and understood by those they cared for was an essential aspect of their work. The introduction of PPE hampered and disrupted nonverbal communication, as face masks transformed trusted carers into strangers in the eyes of the residents. In order to compensate for the additional barrier, our informants adapted their presentational emotional response:

> [...] a lot of people lip read ... or tell someone's emotions or feelings from their facial expressions. That is a massive thing to people with dementia because that's how you communicate. If you can only see someone's eyes, but it's a big thing because if you go into a room. and this person has seen someone that they have never seen before it can be quite daunting if you put your hands on them ... you have to go in all high pitch and jolly, because they cannot see your face ... because they couldn't see my face and they were quite threatened by it. (Ciara, age 19, United Kingdom)

The usual interaction between elderly individuals and caregivers fell short in the face of the challenges brought on by the pandemic. Mask-wearing mandated care workers to alter their voices and project a positive demeanour as a means of compensating, highlighting the substantial effort required in managing emotions, particularly when they had to suppress their own fears of infection, stress, and excessive workload. Consequently, the demand for emotional support from residents heightened during this crisis, while the ability of care workers to respond adequately was significantly compromised:

> Yeah, again, you've got to put this smile on your face. They can't see that smile .... You know, they're scared. They heard on the news; they're being told it's in the home. They're all being told they must stay in their own rooms. Trying to look after everybody in their own rooms is hard because they're lonely. They're frightened ... in the meantime, you are dealing with these patients that are poorly and with less and less staff because staff are going off [testing positive]. Your family members are ringing you constantly ...'How are you? you've not got it?' (Diana, age 33, United Kingdom)

Ensuring residents receive positive emotional support is a fundamental expectation deeply ingrained in the organizational framework of care homes. Caregivers report to engage in diverse emotional approaches, essential for fostering a comfortable and positive environment – an overarching aim ingrained in the prescribed guidelines within organizational structures. While these actions align with 'professional' codes of behaviour, however, interviews also reveal the genuine nature of the motivation behind them. Respondents highlight that despite perceptions of forced smiles and artificially cheerful tones being viewed as inauthentic, these do not diminish care workers' sincere dedication to those they care for. Instead, these emotional expressions serve as a means to a larger goal, such as to shelter the health and well-being of residents against the challenge of the pandemic. The narratives shared by respondents vividly illustrate how emotional management is pivotal in caregiving, extending far beyond the scope of mere physical tasks. Respondents also emphasized that this facet of their work often goes unnoticed, with the complexity and value of their efforts frequently underestimated:

> I've had people say to me, you know 'Oh, you're just a bum wiper. That's all you are as a job!'. You know, I'm not just somebody, you know, I'm dealing with, I'm someone's last port of call. I'm there with somebody, while they're taking their last breaths. I've been there when they've been in pain. I've been there when they've been frightened. I've been there when they've been happy, I've been there, while they've been joyful. I've seen them, you know, seeing their new great grandchildren being born, you know, I've been ... I've been someone's friend, someone's support worker, you know? (Diana, age 33, United Kingdom)

This quote sheds light on both the breadth of emotion work that is undertaken at elderly care homes and the central importance of the latter for care workers' professional self-identification. It shows that this work involves much more than simply making the elderly smile but also providing comfort and solace at key points in the lives of vulnerable people. Although finding time for social interactions with residents has always been difficult due to severe labour shortages in many care homes, it was deemed crucial, considering it was integral to upholding the dignity and respect the elderly rightfully deserve.

COVID-19: Social Distancing and Lockdown

In addition to the loss of shared activities and the introduction of PPE, social distancing and lockdown measures had a significant impact on residents' well-being. At the height of the pandemic, residential care settings had to close their doors for visitors for extended periods of time. Residents found this difficult to understand, especially those experiencing dementia. Many felt abandoned while others became increasingly alienated from their families:

> It's got worse because they haven't seen their loved ones ... people have kind of forgotten that they have a family ... there was a lady that I spoke with and I was like: 'you know you don't write any letters to your daughter?' And she's like: I have a daughter? I have grandchildren? (Olivia, age 25, United Kingdom)

Throughout the COVID-19 lockdowns, residents experienced prolonged separation from their families, often spanning months. As many of these individuals were approaching the final stages of their lives, the fear of dwindling time with their families became a pressing concern. These conditions often resulted in the rapid deterioration of the well-being of residents within a short period of time. Respondents described how they attempted to re-establish that well-being by compensating residents for the missing emotional support that family relatives provide in 'normal times':

> They are sort of withdrawn in themselves. ... when you go in some of them have just been crying and sobbing, because they can't see their families. And you've got no answer to that because it's not us that stopped it .... And you have to hold it together. (Monica, age 52, United Kingdom)

The commitment to 'holding it together' despite being pushed to one's limits, followed by a release of emotions outside the care home, is a shared experience among other respondents in our study. Respondents employed a form of presentational emotion management to uphold social order within residential care settings. However, this approach was rooted in genuine concern for the well-being of those they cared for. An alternative emotional response, such as openly crying in front of the residents, would likely have escalated the situation, causing increased distress and a potential failure to meet professional standards of maintaining order and providing a sense of security. Respondents frequently empathized with those in residential care, often expressing a shared sentiment of 'if this were me':

> (One resident) said, 'I'm 90, what does it matter if I die of Corona or something else? What matters is I die with my people ... with my child' ... some of them have kids themselves, or a spouse they've been married to for 70 years, right? ... which I understand, personally I wouldn't care either if I can't see my beloved who I've spent 70 years with .... (Sinem, age 39, Germany)

Respondents reported concerns about the disruption of care practices that had importance to them:

> For me it was just horrible ... that I couldn't be there for anyone when they passed away. That was horrible ... I always make sure that I experience this process with the residents .... That is really dear to my heart. Covid is the devil. (Marianne, age 55, Germany)

This simple act of accompanying someone through the process of death was an important part of carers' professional self-identification, which was curtailed during lockdown. Despite extremely challenging circumstances, respondents typically refrained from self-pity and used comparison with the situation of elderly residents to explain and justify their commitment to work. This impacted their thinking both within and outside of the work environment and for many became a continuous point of reflection:

> For me, I can just go out for a walk. I can get in my car and drive to work. That's me getting out of my house. They have to kind of stop ... they can't go outside for fresh air. (Olivia, age 25, United Kingdom)

Ultimately, care workers adapted their emotional management approach to cope with the trauma resulting from disrupted routines and the loss of typical sources of support, for example, the assistance previously provided by visiting relatives. They relied on their genuine empathy for residents and their skilful understanding and experiences of what emotions are appropriate in conjunction with the understandings held by their co-workers during this challenging period.

COVID-19: 'Getting Through it Together'

Prior to the introduction of the COVID-19 vaccines, residential care homes were sites of emotional uncertainty, fear, and stress. It was unclear how long this state of emergency would last. Care work has historically encompassed inherent risks, including stress, accidents, and overwork. However, the contagious and fatal nature of the virus blurred the lines between workers' professional roles and their personal or domestic lives. Respondents felt a sense of guilt that they were the cause of ill health within their own families:

> They tried to get my father to breathe, but we weren't allowed to visit him, we couldn't say goodbye, we couldn't do anything .... Because I was also tested positive first, I told myself: 'It started with me

and I got my entire family sick', and I was scared that others would bring that up to the table, that they would blame me. When I look into their eyes, can I live with that. (Özlem, age 45, Germany)

While this example was unique in its severity, feelings of guilt for putting their family members at risk or forcing them to limit their lives or make compromises, was not uncommon:

My street was full of kids playing out, my boys knew that they couldn't because of the extra risk to them, to my residents and to their own father. My little boys had to sit and watch other children play out of the window .... I didn't just have to worry about my colleagues, I had the worry of my home life. You know, me bringing it home to my husband was the reason that my husband lost his life is an extra fear for me ... there's a lot you could say about Covid-19. But I think the biggest thing I could say is fear is itself. (Diana, age 33, United Kingdom)

The empirical examples vividly depict how care workers had to cope together with an unrelenting fear of infection that consumed their lives around the clock. Despite this pervasive fear, their dedication to their work remained remarkably high. During the peak of the crisis, care workers were offered the choice to relocate to a secure facility due to safety concerns. Considering the immense personal sacrifices this relocation entailed, it is noteworthy that numerous respondents bravely opted for this step. This decision reflects a profound and selfless commitment to their profession and the collective endeavour of safeguarding the residents, signifying an authentic dedication:

There was nine of us, we literally packed a bag and we moved into the home. And just to protect the residents, so we kept them in that bubble .... There was the same staff all the time. We didn't get days off in that ... but it was the same faces. But we were smiling every day, because we knew what we were doing was working, you know, we were hearing of all these homes all around us that were contracting it. And we were still feeling like we were secure in our bubbles ... we were safe. (...) Unfortunately, it (COVID) was going to get in one day. And it was, will that day be today? That was always weighing over your head. ... and eventually today was the day and then you are heartbroken. The vaccine was so close. It was all over the news, it was all, we were getting an email to say it [vaccine] was coming soon. And then we contracted it. And it was like, it just felt like if we could just push that little bit longer, then, you know, it would have been really nice. (Diana, age 33, United Kingdom)

Despite the immense efforts made by respondents to contain the virus, several residential care homes experienced COVID-19 outbreaks. Some individuals perceived these outbreaks as personal failures, attributing them to factors such as 'tracing the virus back to specific workers' (Nele, 53, Germany) or 'persisting while waiting for the vaccine' (Mary, 41, United Kingdom). It was especially during these critical moments that the influence of professional emotional guidelines became evident, as the respondents exhibited an exceptional level of concern for the residents, emphasizing the necessity of maintaining their own emotional balance to effectively carry out their duties. The narratives shared during this time contained distressing accounts of fatal chain reactions, experiences that many respondents were still coping with and trying to comprehend at the time of the interviews:

One after the other got infected and then they stayed in their rooms. Then during that time eleven residents died in a row ... an incredibly hard time for everyone. Yes, so, there was a lot of crying [among staff]. And of course, we were fewer employees. So, you also [did] many, many extra hours ... until you caught it yourself. So yes, this solidarity ... it lasted for a very long time. For the residents, there were many, many conversations as well, and good and then everyone has to deal with their grief and all of us got through that together well. (Marianne, age 55, Germany)

This notion of a 'getting through it together' reveals a deep level of commitment to the emotional management of care work that is driven by an authentic commitment. Faced with significant sacrifice and danger, the responses and actions of the respondents illustrate their reliance on personal insights and experiences as caregivers. This reliance presupposes a foundation built upon principles, values, beliefs, and ethics inherent in their profession. This foundation guided them in discerning which emotions were suitable for expression and which ones needed to be concealed for the well-being of others – be it the residents, their families, or their co-workers. Workers expressed a sense that they were being pushed to their absolute limits under overwhelming pressure. At the same time they also report that they 'keep going':

But you step outside the door, and then you just cry and sob as well. You know, it's just, it's horrible'.... 'Just dreadful. There just seems to be no end. But we keep going and you know, fingers crossed. You have to try to not let the residents see how low we are, this is what we do as carers, this is the 'ethic' of being a career, caring for the others ... it's hard but we know what to do. (Monica, age 52, United Kingdom)

Despite the immense emotional toll and challenges faced in their roles, caregivers maintain a strong ethic centred around shielding residents from their own distress, embodying the essence of selfless care. Their unwavering commitment and resolve reflect the resilience and professionalism integral to their profession. Caregivers collectively worked to navigate the challenge of offering emotional reassurance that often ran counter to their anxiety and personal fears arising from the reality of their day-to-day work. Therefore, they look for safe spaces within which to express together emotions that they felt had to be suppressed in everyday interaction with residents for the sake of maintaining their well-being:

Well, I got to be honest, when we lost two residents, I got really upset about it. That was awful. We all have [.] *most of us had a good cry*. We still do, especially when you start reading about them//I mean the one gentleman I looked him up and it said he was 98. He was in the Navy during the Second World War. He was so brave//The island of Malta he got freedom of Malta and I actually googled his name, and you could find out all the amazing things he did as a young lad and I just thought how sad, you know just die of a disease like that. It's quite upsetting to be honest. (Marc, age 54, United Kingdom)

What helped us was praying together. You know? The contact to God. Yes .... God so, we were so completely empty and completely burnt out .... You just tried to process the grief as much as possible ... and you really talked about it again and everyone could share how they experienced it. So, it was- a part of the processing. Talking, talking, talking ... (...) Each of us fought at work with their own self, with their own grief. You know? There are no more hierarchies then. So, the togetherness was really, really strong during that time. And the sense of being there for each other was strong .... So, there was an incredible need for conversation with one another. Everyone tried to process their grief that way .... Our residents. I mean, there was just the need to talk. We talked a lot and prayed. (Marianne, age 55, Germany)

These real-life examples vividly demonstrate the effects of emotional exhaustion intertwined with an unwavering collective dedication to persist in their professional duties. Marianne's insight highlighted a collective approach to coping that involved containing emotions, evident in workers persevering despite their fears. This collective response extended to the residents, exemplified by finding solace in shared acts such as 'praying together' revealing genuine feelings of grief and powerlessness that each struggled with individually. Despite feeling 'completely burnt out' Marianne and her peers remarkably found the inner strength to provide mutual emotional support, both among themselves and towards the elderly – a display of professionalism that must be considered a genuine expression of care, akin to 'a gift'. The concealment of personal emotions such as fear, anxiety, and grief when caring for others embodies 'the gift' of authenticity and genuine concern. The emergence of collective experiences was significantly influenced by the shared coping mechanisms driven by professional expectations. However, it was the impact of COVID-19 that notably heightened the collective nature of these experiences. The unprecedented challenges brought on by the pandemic compelled workers to unite in their approach, leaning on professional emotional management techniques while preserving their authenticity. This response underscored the pandemic's role in uniting individuals in a shared, cohesive experience, accentuating the need for collective coping strategies guided by professional expectations in navigating the complexities of this unparalleled crisis.

CONCLUSION

This study has explored how emotions motivated by professional feeling rules can retain authenticity particularly where these rules support the worker's emotional expression to care for others.

We utilized Garfinkel's (1967) concept of the 'breaching experiment' to delve into the impact of the COVID-19 crisis, which disrupted normal conditions and placed exceptional pressure on workers. This exploration aimed to understand how the enactment of professional feeling rules was put in practice within residential care in the United Kingdom and Germany. Despite the United Kingdom facing a more challenging situation due to limited institutional capacity and the necessity to implement measures to compensate for shortcomings in the social protection system, respondents in both countries reported similar experiences. These shared experiences were observed across different national contexts, illustrating commonalities in the challenges faced by care workers.

Our findings illustrate the influence of professional feeling rules on care workers, highlighting the expected demonstration of empathetic concern for residents' well-being. It suggests that adhering to professional feeling rules does not compromise authenticity; rather, it emphasizes the symbiotic relationship between adhering to these rules and maintaining genuine care. Within this context professional ethos serves as a motivator for care workers by reinforcing authentic care provision. Thus, the argument is put forward that adhering to professional feeling rules does not undermine genuine care; instead, it bolsters a professional ethos that guides and motivates care workers in managing emotions effectively. In particular, it highlights how care workers, amidst the challenges of the COVID-19 pandemic, enacted professional feeling rules by relying on personal experiences to express appropriate emotions while caring for residents. This showcases the pivotal role of a professional ethos – such as a set of collective principles, values, and beliefs upheld by individuals within a specific professional community – in fostering both altruistic motivations and proficient emotion management practices among care workers during unprecedented times.

Our findings make two important contributions to the literature on emotion management. First, we point to that the adherence of professional feeling rules can be understood as authentic caring, a 'gift', which involves a sincere commitment on the part of workers. Bolton (2005) mainly links authenticity with philanthropic emotion management, contrasting it more often with pecuniary emotion management or commercial feeling rules rather than with prescribed or professional feeling rules. Our study clarifies why authenticity and adherence to professional feeling rules are not mutually exclusive concepts. In particular, it demonstrates that care workers' sincere dedication to being there for residents amidst orchestrated disruptions, significantly affecting emotional management in residential care homes, goes beyond simply putting on a 'professional façade'. It also cannot be solely attributed to philanthropy. Instead, this period represented a collective professional endeavour rooted in authentic and genuine concerns, driven by an understanding of a professional code of conduct. This observation also illuminates the intricate nature of the established conduct among care workers, highlighting that its formation is not solely a product of organizationally driven training or regulatory frameworks dictating emotional expressions. Rather, it signifies a deeply rooted reliance on personal comprehension and familiarity with appropriate emotions, often developed in collaboration with their co-workers. This symbiotic construction of conduct suggests a collective process, where care workers mutually engage in defining and refining the emotional code that governs their interactions and responses within caregiving settings. Moreover, amidst the challenges presented by the COVID-19 pandemic, this collectively constructed code underwent notable shifts and adaptations. The unprecedented circumstances compelled care workers to recalibrate their emotional responses and strategies collaboratively. They drew upon shared experiences, evolving their established conduct to navigate the heightened demands and complexities brought on by the pandemic. This period of intense pressure and shared experiences likely played a pivotal role in further solidifying the collectively constructed emotional code among care workers, emphasizing the dynamic and adaptive nature of their collaborative emotional understanding within the context of their work.

Care work is typically distinguished from traditional professions due to the absence, to different extent in different national contexts, of specific entry requirements, credentials, or qualifications. Additionally, no professional body oversees access to training or regulation of the profession. Similarly, there is little evidence of a professional body that wields political influence to safeguard its importance or define occupational skills. Nevertheless, this study provides compelling evidence that the emotional management of care workers is shaped by the social feeling rules dictated by professional rules of mutual and collective conduct to provide essential work and support for vulnerable people. In response to the challenges posed by COVID-19, respondents consistently emphasized the collective professional nature of their efforts: 'we are in it together', 'we did our best'. Care workers demonstrate a remarkable ability to adapt emotional rules to the unique circumstances presented by the pandemic. Notably, these were rooted in care workers' personal interpretations and experiences of a professional ethos, reflecting the underlying shared moral commitment among care workers.

Thus, and this is the second contribution, which is closely linked to the above, this research illuminates the significance of the professional ethos as a motivating factor for care workers in adhering to the feeling rules of their profession. The term 'profession' is employed here in alignment with how care workers themselves perceive it. They rely on their everyday personal understanding and experiences to decide which emotions to convey. Through the workers' accounts, it became evident that there was a crucial need to create shared spaces where emotions, typically suppressed during daily interactions with residents due to the COVID-19 pandemic, could be openly expressed. This was vital to ensure the well-being of those under their care. It also involved considering the perspectives of their co-workers. Furthermore, care workers narrate their 'professionalism' by recounting how skilfully, carefully, and effectively they have carried out their work under the emotionally intense, complex, and difficult circumstances of the pandemic. They describe relying on their personal experiences to decide which emotions to convey, especially when faced with profound sorrow resulting from the loss of care residents. Caregivers developed collective coping spaces (Korczynski, 2003) where they sustain their continued authentic and professional commitment to their work by 'praying together' during this time of crisis.

Based on these contributions we suggest two ways our study can foster understanding of emotion management in research. We posit that the impetus behind enforcing prescriptive professional emotion management lies in both prioritizing authenticity in caring for others' health and well-being, driven by a professional ethos and genuine altruistic intentions. Care workers consistently went above and beyond expectations outlined in their employment contracts, risking their own health and that of their loved ones, to fulfil the needs of the individuals under their care. This selfless commitment, characterized by actions like 'we literally packed a bag and we moved into the home' to 'live with residents' underscores the profound influence of professional code of conduct, standards, and expectations in fostering philanthropic emotion management. As indicated, it shed light on the significance of professional ethos as a motivating factor for care workers in following the feeling rules of their profession. At the same time, we illuminate the authentic goal and commitment that lie beyond a pure presentational 'façade'. Respondents relied on their personal understanding and experiences to determine which emotions to express to care for the residents during the difficult circumstances of the pandemic. They describe this process as, for example, 'modifying their voice', 'holding together', and 'I experience this process [i.e., dying] with the residents'. This illustrates the essential nature of care work in the realm of emotion management by revealing care workers' expertise and how adeptly and efficiently they engage with work, is both a source of pride and an intrinsic value to them. Professional feeling rules in these circumstances are not predominantly focussed on presenting a distant and aloof demeanour professional caregiver

(Bolton, 2000). These professional rules were applied by our respondents through a compassionate and empathetic regard for the health and well-being of residents. In conclusion, this study serves as a compelling testament to the 'professionalism' exhibited by these caregivers, vividly portraying the demanding and indispensable nature of their contributions within society and labour markets. However, it also underscores a critical discrepancy – the unfortunate undervaluation of these crucial roles despite their profound significance and irreplaceable worth.

Our research has care workers and not residents at its core. How do residents perceive the professional and moral commitment of care workers? How far and how feeling rules and motivations of care workers and residents do bleed into one another? Examining the boundaries, interactions, and mutual impacts of the emotion management, norms, or expectations (feeling rules) set by care workers as well as the motivations, desires, or emotional responses of the residents in a care environment can help delving into the 'authenticity' of feeling rules and motivations by understanding how they might influence, intertwine, or blur between the caregivers and those receiving care.

NOTES

1. Our approach does not make the empirical claim that all work labelled as 'professional work' consistently embodies all of these characteristics to the same degree.
2. The Remembrance Day – also known as 'Armistice Day' – commemorates the end of First World War. Wearing poppies has become a symbol of remembrance and a way to honour military personnel who have died in war.

ACKNOWLEDGEMENTS

This research received funding by the European Research Council (ERC) under the European Union's Horizon 2020 research and innovation programme [grant agreement number 833577] – ResPecTMe AdG project; PI: Valeria Pulignano. We thank the editors, and two anonymous referees for the constructive comments on a previous version of this paper, and Juliane Imbusch for her support during the collection of data.

REFERENCES

Bolton, S. C. (2000). Emotion here, emotion there, emotional organizations everywhere. *Critical Perspectives on Accounting, 11*, 155–171. http://dx.doi.org/10.1006/cpac.1998.0236

Bolton, S. C. (2005). *Emotion management in the workplace*. Palgrave.

Bolton, S. C., & Boyd, C. (2003). Trolley dolly or skilled emotion manager? Moving on from Hochschild's managed heart. *Work, Employment and Society, 17*(2), 289–308. https://doi.org/10.1177/09500170030170020

Charmaz, K. (2003). Grounded theory: Objectivist and constructivist methods. In N. K. Denzin & Y. S. Lincoln (Eds.), *Strategies for qualitative inquiry* (pp. 249–291). Sage.

Duffy, M. (2011). *Making care count: A century of gender, race, and paid care work*. Rutgers University Press.

Ellison, N., Blomqvist, P., & Fleckenstein, T. (2022). Covid (in)equalities: Labor market protection, health, and residential care in Germany, Sweden, and the UK. *Policy & Society, 41*(2), 247–259. https://doi.org/10.1093/polsoc/puac004

Esping-Andersen, G. (1990). *The three worlds of welfare capitalism*. Polity.
Eurostat. (2020). *Long-term care beds in nursing and residential facilities, 2013 and 2018. Health in the European Union* – Facts and figures. Eurostat, Online data code. Retrieved April 20, 2023, from https://hlth_rs_bdsns
Freidson, E. (2001). *Professionalism, the third logic*. Chicago University Press.
Garfinkel, H. (1967). *Studies in ethnomethodology*. Prentice Hall.
Glaser, B., & Strauss, A. (1967). *The discovery of grounded theory: Strategies for qualitative research*. Aldine.
Hatton, E. (2017). Mechanisms of invisibility: Rethinking the concept of invisible work. *Work, Employment & Society, 31*(2), 336–351. https://doi.org/10.1177/0950017017667
Hebson, G., Rubery, J. & Grimshaw, D. (2015). Rethinking job satisfaction in care work: Looking beyond the care debates. *Work, Employment and Society, 29*(2), 314–330. https://doi.org/10.1177/0950017014556412
Hochschild, A. R. (1983). *The managed heart: Commercialization of human feeling*. University of California Press.
James, N. (1989). Emotional labour: Skill and work in the social regulation of feeling. *Sociological Review, 37*(1), 15–42. https://doi.org/10.1111/j.1467-954X.1989.tb00019.x
Korczynski, M. (2003). Communities of coping: Collective emotional labour in service work. *Organization, 10*(1), 55–79. https://doi.org/10.1177/1350508403010001479
Leary, M. R. (1995). *Self-presentation: Impression management and interpersonal behavior*. Brown & Benchmark Publishers.
Lewis, P. (2005). Suppression or expression: An exploration of emotion management in a special care baby unit. *Work, Employment and Society, 19*(3), 565–581. https://doi.org/10.1177/0950017005055673
Miles, M., & Huberman, A. (1994). *Qualitative data analysis: An expanded sourcebook*. Sage.
OECD. (2021). *Sovereign borrowing outlook for OECD countries*. Retrieved April 25, 2023, from https://www.oecd.org/daf/fin/public-debt/Sovereign-Borrowing-Outlook-in-OECD-Countries-2021.pdf
Omdahl, B., & O'Donnell, C. (1999). Emotional contagion, empathic concern and communicative responsiveness as variables affecting nurses' stress and occupational commitment. *Journal of Advanced Nursing, 29*, 1351–1359. https://doi.org/10.1046/j.1365-2648.1999.01021.x
Pugh, M. (2015). *Women and the women's movement in Britain since 1914*. Palgrave.
Radtke, R. (2022). *Distribution of nurses in Germany by type of care and gender 2020*. Retrieved April 27, 2023, from https://de.statista.com/statistik/daten/studie/1029877/umfrage/verteilung-von-pflegekraefte-in-deutschland-nach-pflegeart-und-geschlecht/
Rakovski, C., & Price-Glynn, K. (2010). Caring labour, intersectionality and worker satisfaction. *Sociology of Health and Illness, 32*(3), 400–414. https://doi.org/10.1111/j.1467-9566.2009.01204.x
Riemann, M. L., Mara, C., Domecka, M., & Pulignano, V. (2023). 'If we lower our responsiveness, the algorithm likes us less'. A biographical perspective on (losing) control in the platform economy. *Labour and Industry*. https://doi.org/10.1080/10301763.2023.2252609
Rubery, J. (2005). Reflections on gender mainstreaming: An example of feminist economics in action? *Feminist Economics, 11*(3), 1–26. https://doi.org/10.1080/13545700500300876
Rubery, J., & Urwin, P. (2011). Bringing the employer back in: Why social care needs a standard employment relationship. *Human Resource Management Journal, 21*(2), 122–137. https://doi.org/10.1111/j.1748-8583.2010.00138.x
Scambler, G. (2020). Covid-19 as a 'breaching experiment': Exposing the fractured society. *Health Sociological Review, 29*(2), 140–148. https://doi.org/10.1080/14461242.2020.1784019
Schutz, A., & Luckmann, T. (1973). *The structures of the life-world*. Northwestern University Press.
Schütze, F. (2008). Biography analysis on the empirical base of autobiographical narratives: How to analyse autobiographical narrative interviews. *European Studies on Inequalities and Social Cohesion, 1/2* (Part I), 153–242, and *3/4* (Part II), 5–77.
Sevenhuijsen, S. (2003). The place of care: The relevance of the feminist ethic of care for social policy. *Feminist Theory, 4*(2), 179–197. https://doi.org/10.1177/14647001030042006
Simmonds, B. (2022). *Ageing and the crisis in health and social care: Global and national perspectives*. Policy Press.

Skills for Care. (2021). *The state of the adult social care sector and workforce in England*. Retrieved June 27, 2022, from https://www.skillsforcare.org.uk/adult-social-care-workforce-data/Workforce-intelligence/publications/national-information/The-state-of-the-adult-social-care-sector-and-workforce-in-England.aspx#:~:text=The%20number%20of%20people%20working,%2F20%20and%202020%2F21

Spasova, S., Baeten, R., Coster, S., Ghailani, D., Peña-Casas, R., & Vanhercke, B. (2018). *Challenges in long-term care in Europe. A study of national policies, European Social Policy Network (ESPN)*. European Commission.

Strauss, A., Fagerhaugh, S., Suczek, B., & Wiener, C. (1982). Sentimental work in the technologized hospital. *Sociology of Health and Illness*, *4*(3), 254–278. https://doi.org/10.1111/1467-9566.ep10487954

CHAPTER 5

THE POLITICS OF ESSENTIALITY: PRAISE FOR DIRTY WORK DURING THE COVID-19 PANDEMIC

Nancy Côté[a], Jean-Louis Denis[b], Steven Therrien[a] and Flavia Sofia Ciafre[c]

[a]*Department of Sociology, Université Laval, Quebec, Canada*
[b]*School of Public Health (ESPUM), Université de Montréal, Quebec, Canada*
[c]*Law Faculty, Université de Montréal, Quebec, Canada*

ABSTRACT

This chapter focuses on the COVID-19 pandemic's impact on the recognition through discourses of essentiality, of low-status workers and more specifically of care aides as an occupational group that performs society's 'dirty work'. The pandemic appears as a privileged moment to challenge the normative hegemony of how work is valued within society. However, public recognition through political discourse is a necessary but insufficient element in producing social change. Based on the theory of performativity, this chapter empirically probes conditions and mechanisms that enable a transition from discourse of essentiality to substantive recognition of the work performed by care aides in healthcare organizations. The authors rely on three main sources of data: scientific-scholarly works, documents from government, various associations and unions, and popular media reports published between February 2020 and 1 July 2022. While discourse of essentiality at the highest level of politics is associated with rapid policy response to value the work of care aides, it is embedded in a system structure and culture that restrains the establishment of substantive policy that

Essentiality of Work
Research in the Sociology of Work, Volume 36, 81–108
Copyright © 2024 by Nancy Côté, Jean-Louis Denis, Steven Therrien and Flavia Sofia Ciafre
Published under exclusive licence by Emerald Publishing Limited
ISSN: 0277-2833/doi:10.1108/S0277-283320240000036005

recognizes the nature, complexity, and societal importance of care aide work. The chapter contributes to the literature on performativity by demonstrating the importance of the institutionalization of competing logics in contemporary health and social care systems and how it limits the effectiveness of discourse in promulgating new values and norms and engineering social change.

Keywords: Essentiality; dirty work; care aides; health system; politics; performativity

INTRODUCTION

This chapter examines the impact of the COVID-19 pandemic on recognition of the essentiality of low-status work (Kim et al., 2022; Stevano et al., 2020; Williams et al., 2020), and specifically the work of care aides as an occupational category. The health crisis provides a privileged moment to observe and analyse the impact of a new discourse by political authorities about the essentiality of a low-status occupational category and the conditions that enable or limit the translation of these discourses into tangible improvements in working conditions. Discourses are considered a necessary but insufficient element in producing social change. As suggested by recent works on performativity, discourse must be enacted and embedded in transformative strategies that impact on the structural determinants of differentiation and inequality among social groups (Bowden et al., 2021; Leca & Barin-Cruz, 2021). Discourses of essentiality are considered here as political statements with undetermined effectiveness at producing social change. This is the starting point of our inquiry on essential work in contemporary organizations.

Prior to the pandemic, low status health workers and their poor working conditions were largely invisible to the public and governments in charge of health and social care systems (Hatton, 2017; Rabelo & Mahalingam, 2019). Their marginality and the nature of their work reflected the status of dirty work in society (Hughes, 1951, 1958). During the pandemic, care aides received unusual public recognition in Canada and in many other countries (Bellerose, 2020; Desjardins, 2021; Gosselin, 2020; Hirata, 2021), which contrasted sharply with their actual working conditions and experience of work (Anderson, 2000; Deery et al., 2019). The duality between marginality and the proliferation of discourse praising essential workers offers a unique opportunity to understand the power and limits of discourses in making the labour market more equitable in a time of social disruption.

Recent work on performativity guides our effort to empirically probe the interface between the dirty work of low-status occupational groups and the political discourse of essentiality. A performativity lens sees in discourse a capacity to influence or orient collective action (Bourgoin et al., 2020). Through discourses, social reality takes shape. However, discourse alone is not enough to bring about change and can also be used to maintain inequalities and differentiation among occupational categories. A recent study by Mohammed et al. (2021) documents how the discourse of elected officials during the pandemic promoted a representation of nurses as heroes but had a more conservative than transformative effect, reproducing poor working conditions. Based on Bowden et al. (2021), performativity emphasizes the power of discourse in shaping social reality. Performativity is conceived as a practice of representation in need of anchors in the material world. A performative approach is fundamentally relational and sees discourses gain effectiveness and authority through relations with others (Bourgoin et al., 2020; Bowden et al., 2021). Similarly, Leca and Barin-Cruz (2021) contest the predominant scholasticism of performativity studies and stress the importance of understanding the institutional substrate that makes discourses effective or transformative.

Prior work on performativity situates discourse as embedded within a social system that contributes to either reproducing hierarchy and discrimination or generating opportunities for transformation (Cabantous et al., 2016, 2018). The effect of sudden public recognition in political and public discourse on substantive and lasting change in the valuation of low-status work remains unclear (Hirata, 2021; Rose, 2021; Webb, 2021). In this analysis, we examine the discourse of politicians, unions and care aides in order to identify elements that make the rhetoric of essentiality promoted by political elites more or less effective in valuing the work of care aides. Political elites and low-status occupational groups are not usually found in the same relational space. However, during a major enduring health crisis like the pandemic, political authorities engaged with these groups with the aim of maintaining commitment and mobilization within a system that was facing considerable health human resources challenges even before the pandemic. Our study focuses on these political discourses and the reactions of various groups in society in order to better understand the conditions and mechanisms that may support the translation of discourses into substantive changes of working conditions and recognition of care work.

CONCEPTUAL BACKGROUND
The Social Fabric of Exclusion Within Labour Markets

A significant proportion of the so-called essential work during the pandemic involved low-wage and low-skilled jobs (Anderson et al., 2021; Farris & Bergfeld, 2022; Rose, 2021; Stevano et al., 2020) characterized by significant occupational segregation (Farris & Bergfeld, 2022). Occupational segregation within the labour market is based on differential recognition of the skills necessary to perform a job. Evaluation of skills is not neutral and tends to undervalue invisible and unquantifiable skills that are central to care work (Farris & Bergfeld, 2022; Stevano et al., 2020). Several authors have demonstrated that the work of care is complex, based on a set of technical, relational, and emotional know-how (Guimarães & Hirata, 2021; Molinier, 2010). These 'discrete skills' (Molinier, 2010) are often rendered invisible, considered natural and reduced to feminine qualities (Hirata, 2021).

Effective recognition of care work would challenge the current occupational hierarchy based on gender, social class, and ethnicity (Aubry, 2016; Farris & Bergfeld, 2022). From an intersectional perspective (Crenshaw, 1989), care aides as an occupational group appear doubly marginalized as they both perform dirty work and belong to discriminated groups (Hirata, 2021), with many care aides being racialized women from underprivileged social classes and thereby carrying the weight of multiple systems of oppression (Lightman, 2022; Syed et al., 2016).

Management practices in health and social care organizations often contribute to the invisibility of care aides by excluding them from decisions related to their work (Aubry, 2021; McCaughey et al., 2015). Political and public recognition of the importance of essential workers triggers questioning of their status and working conditions (De Camargo & Whiley, 2020; Farris et al., 2021; Stevano et al., 2020). Many authors consider that the pandemic provides a privileged opportunity to challenge the normative hegemony of what is valued within society (Povinelli, 2011; Slutskaya et al., 2023) and inequities within the labour market (Farris & Bergfeld, 2022; Rose, 2021; Stevano et al., 2020; Webb, 2021). Substantive gains in working conditions appear conditional on being collectively well organized and represented within the public sphere and in institutions where decisions regarding wages and working conditions are made (Stevano et al., 2020). Governments' response to the pandemic, including their attention to health and social care workers and their working conditions, is conditioned by prevalent political regimes and institutions (Greer et al., 2020), not least a neoliberal ideology that seeks to minimize government intervention and emphasizes individual responsibility to improve one's situation on the labour market (McAlevey, 2016). Questions remain around how discourse of essentiality can generate perennial and substantive social transformation to move occupational groups from the periphery to the core of the economy (Bergfeld, 2020; Hirata, 2021).

From Dirty Work to Essentiality in Times of Crisis

The sociologist Everett Hughes coined the term *dirty work* to define occupations where certain tasks are considered degrading or even disgusting (Deery et al., 2019; Hughes, 1951, 1958). The stigma related to tasks is transferred to the workers who perform dirty work (Deery et al., 2019; McMurray & Ward, 2014), distinguished by its physical, social, or moral taint (Blake et al., 1999; Hughes, 1958). For care aides, this taint stems from workers' close contact with bodily fluids and functions (Ostaszkiewicz et al., 2016), with patients who are no longer in control of their emotions and behaviours (Hirata, 2021; Rivera, 2018), and with marginalized populations, resulting in the social stigmatization of workers themselves (Manchha et al., 2022).

Workers performing dirty work are often deemed less socially valuable and visible (Deery et al., 2019; Dick, 2005), and the more efficiently they perform dirty work, the more invisible they become. Ostaszkiewicz et al. (2016) study in long-term care settings shows that care aides develop sophisticated social skills to prevent families and other team members from having to confront the reality of dysfunctional and soiled bodies. They 'keep dirt at a distance' to separate the pure from the impure, as Douglas (1966) states in her work on purity and danger. She argues that dirt is constructed socially to maintain social order, with the impure pushed 'outside' the boundary of usual social life to protect the 'inside' of society

(Douglas, 1966; McMurray & Ward, 2014). Some authors argue that the ability of workers performing dirty work to reposition themselves 'inside' society relies on political alliances with higher status groups (Blake et al., 1999).

The concept of essential workers was mobilized during the COVID-19 pandemic to highlight the crucial work of certain categories of workers who perform dirty work and provide services critical to social and economic well-being during a crisis (Anderson et al., 2021; Farris & Bergfeld, 2022). The central role of care aides in day-to-day care of the most vulnerable members of society means that they were quickly identified as essential workers (Bergfeld, 2020; Parks et al., 2020; Williams et al., 2020). The pandemic revealed the great vulnerability of elderly people living in long-term care facilities, and their heavy dependence on care aides for basic care needed to survive and maintain a certain quality of life. The staggering rates of infection in these settings during the pandemic, combined with the shortage of care aides, created exceptional conditions where the crucial role played by these workers performing dirty work became highly visible. While the discourse of essentiality was associated with increased public recognition of the value of their work, various social processes and forces may operate to sustain the invisibility of their work.

Performativity of Discourse and Social Change

A growing body of work in social sciences, and more specifically in organizational theory, invokes the concept of performativity to understand the role of discourse in the transformation of practices (Garrick & Chan, 2017; Riach et al., 2016) and the production, reproduction, or transformation of social norms and structures (Tyler & Cohen, 2010). Performativity refers to the process of constructing subjects and their identities through discourses and the reiteration of norms (Butler, 1993). Discourse is seen as a social production that reflects symbolic order and the structure of legitimation and domination (Foucault, 1969; Keller, 2007).

Cabantous et al.'s work (2016, 2018) on performativity provides a framework that identifies the mechanisms involved in moving from discourse to substantive political or social change, namely in this case the recognition of the essential work of care aides. These mechanisms rely on both discursive and material resources and practices. The authors propose three areas of focus to analyse how discourse can generate substantive change. First, performativity requires attention to both the content of discourse, such as the essentiality of work, and to the bearers of the discourse, that is, actors and their positions (Cabantous et al., 2016). Through discourse, actors can challenge existing power-knowledge regimes by mobilizing emancipatory normative ideals for care aides and their work (Farris & Bergfeld, 2022; Rose, 2021). Second, performativity involves looking at the capacity of discourse to renew the ontology of organizations, work, and workers, meaning to reveal and reconsider the structural and cultural determinants of occupational hierarchies (Cabantous et al., 2016). Discourse is used to engage in explicit conversations about forms of inequalities and their causes in work settings and society. Scholars have shown the importance of distributed agency to shape situations and orient collective actions (Bourgoin et al., 2020). The participation of actors such as trade unions, the public and the media in promoting emancipatory ideals may contribute to the transformative potential of discourse. Third, performativity calls for consideration of materiality. As Cabantous et al. (2016) point out: 'Performativity happens through the political engineering of sociomaterial agencements that are constituted within and across organizations, institutions and markets' (p. 209). It refers to the ability to materialize emancipatory normative ideals through new alliances and networks of actors or new formal agreements or management systems (measures, incentives, labour agreements) that reflect and align with the new norms.

Our analysis aims to determine whether the discourse produced by political authorities and the discursive practices and reactions of media and unions represent a shift in predominant representations of the work and status of care aides and is potentially conducive to transformative policies within the labour market and organizations.

METHODOLOGY

Research Design

We conducted a case study focusing on discourse of essentiality of care aides during the COVID-19 pandemic (Yin, 2014). Our study focuses on the discourse of a variety of actors (politicians, unions, care aides), on various reactions to this discourse, and on policies introduced to value and recognize the essential work of care aides. More precisely, we aim to (1) describe and assess the response from essential workers, media, unions, and experts to this sudden public recognition and (re-)valuation of care aides' work as well as the reactions of other occupational groups; (2) identify policies introduced to reflect this recognition during the pandemic; and (3) identify challenges and prospects to value essential work and address occupational inequality in a significant way.

Data Sources

We rely on three main sources of data to track discourse of essentiality related to care aides during the pandemic. We extensively review scientific-scholarly works, documents from government and various associations and unions, along with media coverage (daily news and press conferences) from 25 February 2020 to 1 July 2022 (see *Reference list* for media and data sources). This period allows us to assess the valuation of essential workers and recognition of their work through the different phases of the pandemic. Throughout this period, the media played an important role in shaping and circulating discourse surrounding the work of care aides.

The Eureka database of primary media sources enabled us to cover major newspapers in Quebec. We searched for media reports using the (French language equivalent) term 'care aides' in their introduction and title. Of the 4,373 results (the results are not equivalent to the number of original sources, due to the sharing of sources by other media) for the period 25 February, 2020, through 1 July 2022, 150 original sources were retained as relevant. By relevant, we mean that they had care aides as their main subject or described government measures that affect care aides. We therefore excluded sources that included care aides within the broad category of healthcare workers, without referring to them specifically. This choice reflects our objective of studying the specificity of this occupational group, which has only recently been recognized in political and public discourse, in contrast to the more longstanding discourse on other health and social services professionals. Sources include media (newspaper articles and open letters, television and radio, social media) and reports. Online sources were particularly useful. We retrieved information from the Government of Quebec's website to identify policies put in place. We also examined a Facebook group named 'Care aides out of breath' that had 2,400 subscribers as of March 2023 and other social media posts from care aides discussing their working conditions. In addition to the discourse of the workers themselves and political and media actors, we included the discourse of unions that took a stand during the health crisis to defend the rights of care aides. These unions include the Fédération de la santé et des services sociaux (Health and Social Services Federation, over 110,000 members), the Syndicat québécois des employées et employés de service (Québec Union of Service Employees, over 25,000 members), and the Canadian Union of Public Employees (over 125,000 members). The detailed corpus on which our analyses are based includes 1 book on the work of care aides, 98 newspaper articles, 12 government sources including 4 reports and 39 government press briefings. These various sources enabled us to understand the issues of essentiality from the perspective of different actors. Sources were coded according to the three mechanisms of performativity identified by Cabantous et al. (2016, 2018) (see Table 5.2) and a thematic analysis was carried out (Miles et al., 2014).

RESEARCH CONTEXT: STUDY SETTING AND POPULATION

Our empirical analysis is based on the case of care aides in a publicly funded health system in Quebec (Canada). Canada is a federation where legislative competencies are shared between two levels of government (federal and provincial/territorial). The regulation of healthcare systems falls mainly under the responsibility of the provinces and territories, though the federal level can use certain constitutional powers (notably its 'spending power') to influence provincial healthcare systems. Before the pandemic, the Quebec health system could count on a workforce of 41,563 healthcare aides (Aubry & Couturier, 2019; Ministère de la Santé et des Services Sociaux, 2020). Most care aides in Quebec are women (82%) and 30% of the workforce are recent immigrants compared with 16% of the employed population (Cornelissen, 2021; Ministère de la Santé et des Services Sociaux, 2020). The government estimates that there is currently a shortfall of 11,346 care aides in the Quebec healthcare system (Denis, 2023; also see Cabinet du Ministre de la Santé, 2023).

In Quebec, cares aides work in two sectors: private and public. They mostly work in publicly funded long-term care settings called Centres d'hébergement de soins de longue durée (CHSLD) and some work in the private sector. These distinctions are essential, as there are still major differences between the two sectors. For example, while the minimum wage in the public sector, as of September 2023, is $25.81/hour, the minimum wage in the private sector is only $15.31/hour. The average salary for care aides is $30,000, well below the average salary in Quebec which was $40,100 in 2020 (Institut de la Statistique du Québec, 2022), and around the sustainable income in 2023, which ranged from $27,047 to $37,822 depending on the administrative region (Couturier et al., 2023). Table 5.1 compares some of the characteristics of the care aide occupation with other care professions in long-term care settings in Quebec.

With regard to their position in the job market, care aides are not part of a professional association, and they are at the bottom of the hierarchy in care teams, with the shortest training. Their job is to provide basic care to patients, including bodily care, mobility assistance and help with eating. Although they are in direct daily contact with patients, they do not have access to patients' medical records, and in many cases are not invited to clinical discussion meetings (Aubry, 2020). Many care aides experience precarious work, with 33% working part-time (Government of Canada, 2024). Precariousness also manifests in a lack of stability in work teams, as many care aides are moved from one point of service to another to complete their working hours. Working conditions deteriorated in the Quebec health and social services system between 2015–2016 and 2018–2019, with a doubling of overtime hours; the situation is particularly worrisome in the long-term care sector (Commissaire à la Santé et au Bien-être, 2021; Desjardins, 2019). In terms of subjective work experience, data also show a marked increase in psychological distress, accompanied by high levels of physical health problems (Aubry, 2021). Care aides deplore the daily hardships they encounter. In one open letter, entitled 'Feeding someone is as vital as prescribing pills', a former care aide expresses his frustration after the government announced several million dollars in severance bonuses for managers, while 'those who take care of the frail, who wash them, feed them, dress them, change their soiled underwear, make them walk, listen to them, are still considered too expensive for the administration' (*Le Nouvelliste*, 2018).

Overall, labour shortages and the poor working conditions of care aides were well documented before the pandemic but neglected by government. Unions, the media, and workers were particularly vocal in emphasizing the seriousness of the situation and its consequences for patients and care aides (Duchaine et al., 2022). Table 5.2 summarizes our empirical findings on the development of discourse on essentiality and its impact on the working conditions and experience of care aides. It emphasizes mechanisms that enable (or not) the passage from discourses of essentiality to measures that value the work of this occupational group. Our empirical case is structured along three phases of the temporal evolution in discourses of essentiality and incremental adjustments to working conditions that align with the evolution of the pandemic.

Table 5.1. Comparison of Occupations Performing Care Work.

Comparison of Care Professions	Care Aides	Nursing Assistant	Registered Nurse
Training and work regulation	- Fast-track training: 375 hours - Classical training: 870 hours - *Do not belong to a professional association*[a]	- Training: 1,800 hours. - *Belong to a professional association*[b]	- Training: 1,800 hours + 2 years in university OR training: 3–4 years in university (without prior training)[c] - *Belong to a professional association*[d]
Salary	*Public sector:* - Minimum wage: $25.81/hour - Maximum wage: $25.81/hour[e]	*Public sector:* - Minimum wage: $24.21/hour - Maximum wage: $32.32/hour[f]	*Public sector:* - Minimum wage: $27.08/hour - Maximum wage: $47.98/hour[g]
Scope of practice	- Provide basic patient care - No access to patients' medical records	- Help assess people's state of health and implement their care plan - Full access to patient records	- Full access to patient files. - Can administer medication and modify prescriptions - Can assess or diagnose. - Can carry out invasive diagnostic tests, as prescribed
	Cannot administer medication[h]	Can administer medication[i]	Can provide nursing follow-up for people with complex health problems[j]

[a] Gouvernement du Québec. (2023a). *Préposé aux bénéficiaires*, Métiers et professions en santé et services sociaux. https://avenirensante.gouv.qc.ca.
[b] Accès Études Québec. (2023). *Santé, Assistance et soins infirmier*. https://accesetudesquebec.ca/fr/programme-etude/sante-assistance-soins-infirmiers/38/7.
[c] Accès Études Québec (2023).
[d] Ordre des infirmières et infirmiers du Québec. (2023). *Accéder à la profession infirmière au Québec. Exercer au Québec*. https://www.oiiq.org/acceder-profession/exercer-au-quebec.
[e] Comité patronal de négociation du secteur de la santé et des services sociaux. (2023a). *Préposé aux bénéficiaires*, Métiers et professions en santé et services sociaux. (2023a). 3480 – Préposée ou préposé aux bénéficiaires, Titres d'emplois, salaire et primes. https://cpnsss.gouv.qc.ca/titres-demploi-et-salaires/nomenclature-et-mecanisme-de-modification/fiche-demploi/3480-9-0.
[f] Comité patronal de négociation du secteur de la santé et des services sociaux. (2023b). *3455 – Infirmier auxiliaire ou infirmière auxiliaire*, Titres d'emploi, salaire et primes. https://cpnsss.gouv.qc.ca/titres-demploi-et-salaires/nomenclature-et-mecanisme-de-modification/fiche-demploi/3455-14-0.
[g] Comité patronal de négociation du secteur de la santé et des services sociaux. (2023c). *1911 – Infirmier clinicien ou infirmière clinicienne*, Titres d'emploi, salaire et primes. https://cpnsss.gouv.qc.ca/titres-demploi-et-salaires/nomenclature-et-mecanisme-de-modification/fiche-demploi/1911-22-0.
[h] Emploi Préposé. (2023). *Description du métier de Préposés aux bénéficiaires*. https://www.emploisprepose.ca/description-du-metier-de-preposes-aux-beneficiaires.
[i] Placement Premier Soin. (2023). *Quelle différence entre infirmière et infirmière auxiliaire?*. https://www.premiersoin.ca/difference-infirmiere-infirmiere-auxiliaire.
[j] Gouvernement du Québec. (2023b). *Infirmière clinicienne ou infirmier clinicien*, Métiers et professions en santé et services sociaux. https://avenirensante.gouv.qc.ca.

Table 5.2. Dimensions of Performativity During the Three-year Pandemic.

Cabantous and Colleagues' Dimensions of Performativity	Year I February 2020–February 2021 *Start of the* Pandemic	Year II March 2021–February 2022 *Ongoing* Pandemic	Year III March 2022–July 2022 *Beyond the* Pandemic
Content and bearers of discourse	– New discourse by legitimate political actors positions care aides as 'essential' workers – Crisis creates a window of opportunity to renew discourse – Discourse of essentiality is monopolized by government and the political elites	– The rhetoric of 'essential' value of care aides diminishes – A greater plurality of actors produces discourse, sometimes in opposition to the government, and highlights other issues related to recognition of the work of care aides – Union discourse on how to recognize the work of care aides clashes with government discourse	– Wide dissemination of discourses to thank care aides – Some actors highlighted the gap between the rhetoric of recognition of care aide work during the pandemic and the persistence of inadequate working conditions – Some voices in the media seek to render visible the precariousness and risks of the work environment faced by care aides, and the specific issues encounter by immigrants
Capacity of discourse to renew work	– A public inquiry confirms the necessity of reforming working conditions for care aides in long-term care settings – Skills and expertise to perform care work are recognized and made visible by professionals at the top of the hierarchy – Government measures to address the shortage of care aides by mobilizing other professionals are criticized for failing to recognize the complexity of the work of care aides and their specific expertise	– Government discourse remains focussed on managing human resource headcounts and keeps the broader issues of working conditions invisible – Care aides in private and community sectors are not treated the same as those in the public sector, which is seen as a lack of recognition of their important contribution to the well-being of society	– Unions criticize the termination of incentives even as the rhetoric valuing care aides continues – Some media actors highlight the lack of measures to support immigrants within this occupational group – Union demands are oriented towards wages and size of the workforce, remaining rather silent on other issues of recognition – Care aides remain relatively distant from the public arena and participate little in debates on the recognition of their work

The Politics of Essentiality

Consideration of materiality	– Government provides conditional wage premiums as a State of Emergency measure – Temporary fast-track training of new care aides and the mobilization of other types of professionals to perform care work recognizes the sector as a priority	– Other care sectors are starting to recover and care aides have less visibility as essential workers – Unions and care aides point to the lack of significant change in their working conditions – Government keeps focused on short-term measures and does not tackle the structural problems that would enable longer-term transformation in the recognition of the work of care aides	– Gradual reduction of certain salary bonuses in the public and private sectors – Introduction of more flexible management practices to deal with workforce shortages, which is strongly criticized by unions
	Political and public discourse on essentiality	Gradual restoration of the pre-pandemic labour regime	Discrepancies between discourse of essentiality and working conditions

I – YEAR I OF THE PANDEMIC: EMERGENCE OF POLITICAL AND PUBLIC DISCOURSE ON ESSENTIALITY

The first wave of the pandemic began in Québec on 25 February 2020, and ended on 11 July 2020 (Institut National de Santé Publique du Québec, 2022). During this period, Quebec was the province in Canada most affected by the virus, with a total of 59,845 confirmed cases of COVID-19 between March and July 2020, 7,310 hospitalizations and 5,829 deaths (Carazo et al., 2022; Tremblay & Benigeri, 2020). Moreover, 64.3% of COVID-19-related deaths in the province between March and July 2020 were residents of long-term care facilities (Tremblay & Benigeri, 2020). A survey of 5,000 healthcare workers infected during the first wave reveals that 'physicians accounted for 3% of these confirmed cases, while care aides, nursing assistants and nurses accounted for 70%' (Tremblay & Benigeri, 2020). At one point in the crisis, the situation was so dire that politicians requested help from the Canadian army to provide support in long-term care settings. The lack of personal protective equipment and the mobility of staff within and between long-term care homes 'contributed to the spread of the virus' (Summa Stratégie, 2021; see also Le Protecteur du Citoyen, 2021). A public inquiry by the Ombudsman (Le Protecteur du Citoyen, 2021) on the performance of the Quebec health system in the first wave of the pandemic highlighted the systematic neglect of care sectors outside medical and hospital services and the necessity of reforming working conditions for care aides in long-term care settings.

The first wave also saw the Quebec government begin holding televised press briefings up to several times a week. In the month of March 2020, no less than 17 press briefings were held. By the end of the first year, there had been 115 briefings related to COVID-19 (Bourgault-Côté, 2020). These marked a profound change in the way government communicated with the population. In addition, partisan politics were partly set aside, leaving much latitude to the governing party. In this extreme context, discourse was monopolized by government, while the media served as 'transmission belt' for the emergency measures put in place. The content of the discourse focussed on the exceptional qualities of care aides, their dedication, their crucial importance to society and the urgent need to secure enough care aides to provide safe care to the long-term care home population.

The discourse on essentiality was accompanied by concrete recognition measures. The Quebec government announced a first set of measures to enhance the attractiveness of working in the health sector and address labour shortages. Salary bonuses were offered to healthcare employees, including care aides. In the public sector, care aides in long-term care received an 8% bonus and those in the private sector received 4%. In 2019, before the bonus, an entry-level care aide in the public sector earned $20.76 an hour (Comité Patronal de Négociation du Secteur de la Santé et des Services Sociaux, 2023a). The significant increase in wages created concerns around equity with the wages of other professionals (Bellerose, 2020; TVA Nouvelles, 2020):

Quebec's offer is so generous that the 10,000 [new] candidates will benefit from an entry-level salary higher than that of a nurse entering the profession ($24.08 in 2019). A nursing assistant starts at $22.59 per hour. (Bellerose, 2020)

Additional efforts were deployed to attract new personnel and mitigate the effects of a labour shortage exacerbated by the pandemic. Healthcare facilities issued calls for healthcare workers in their region to come and support employees in the most affected care settings, mainly long-term care homes (Gagné, 2020). Furthermore, the Premier of Quebec issued a press release suggesting that individuals whose jobs were compromised because of the pandemic, namely those working in tourism, customer service, and restaurants should consider enrolling to become care aides (Labbé, 2020a). In a press conference, the Premier stressed that 2,000 care aides and nurses were lacking in private and public long-term care homes and called on medical doctors to fill the gap:

I'm asking doctors to come and help in the CHSLDs [long-term care homes]. We're short-handed. We understand that they're overqualified, but we have no one else. We're appealing to the sense of duty and responsibility of the 20,000 doctors in Quebec. Will we be able to find 2,000 of them to come and help us? I don't know how to put it. This is a national emergency. (Premier quoted by Khalkhal, 2020)

In the end, about 2,000 specialized physicians accepted the Premier's 'invitation' (Labbé, 2020b). However, they were 'appalled' by the Premier's insinuation that care aides and nurses could be replaced at any given moment by other healthcare professionals (Labranche, 2020). The language used by the Premier was seen to praise the work of medical specialists while undervaluing the work of care aides, especially considering how much medical specialists would be compensated for their contribution, and how long care aides had been demanding fair wages (Labranche, 2020; Lacoursière, 2020; Lévesque, 2020). As pointed out by a specialist in internal medicine, '[care aides] have their own expertise, experience and professionalism' and thus cannot simply be replaced (Labranche, 2020). She pointed out that specialists are not adequately trained to feed, bathe, and reposition people (Pettersen, 2020). The exchange marked a rare moment when the skills and expertise needed in care work were made publicly visible by professionals at the top of the hierarchy.

In May 2020, the Premier launched a fast-track three-month training programme for future care aides who could then be deployed to work in long-term care settings. Hoping to enrol at least 10,000 trainees, the government offered 21$ per hour throughout the training period and an additional 5$ per hour upon entering the workforce (Crête, 2020; Labbé, 2020a). In mid-September 2020, 7,100 individuals were completing the last modules of their training, and another 3,200 recruits were expected to join the programme that month (Gouvernement du Québec, 2020). Concerns were raised about the capacity to train care aides so quickly due to the complexity of the work.

Overall, year one of the COVID-19 crisis brought health workforce issues to the forefront and specifically highlighted the essentiality of the work of care aides. Politicians at the highest level (Premier, Minister of Health and Social Services) frequently spoke to the population about the dramatic shortage of labour and its consequences for patients and health workers, especially in long-term care facilities. Policy initiatives were taken to increase the supply of care aides, and the government publicly recognized the value of their work and the need to improve their working conditions, mainly through salary increases. Nevertheless, certain core aspects required for an ontological revaluation of the profession seemed to be missing. The measures temporarily subverted the occupational hierarchy, but few changes were made to other working conditions. Among the issues at the forefront were staff-patient ratios, which the unions asked government to review as current practice was responsible for a deterioration in the quality of care and the quality of care aides' working conditions:

> The hecatomb experienced this spring in CHSLDs [long-term care homes] because of COVID-19 must never happen again. The government must accelerate discussions to reduce the work overload, which will make it possible to guarantee the quality and safety of care for the population. (Bédard, 2020 quoted by The Canadian Press, 2020)

Some actors considered that the problems of salary and workforce sufficiency must be accompanied by profound changes to improve working conditions and experience (Lajoie, 2020; The Canadian Press, 2020).

In this first phase, the dominant discourse was led by government. While it focused on both the material and symbolic dimensions of care aides' work, the measures taken aimed to reduce distributive inequalities (e.g. better wages), but failed to tackle other forms of inequality, in particular a fairer recognition of the complexity of the work and the skills required and the critical contribution of this care work for society. Within phase I of our case, discourses of essentiality were limited in their impact on the implementation of new socio-material agencements such as salary increased, bonuses, and training opportunities to increase the size of the workforce in long-term care settings. This is in line with the views of the general public and medical doctors about what needs to be done to better recognize the work of care aids.

II – YEAR II: GRADUAL RESTORATION OF THE PRE-PANDEMIC LABOUR REGIME

In March 2021, the number of COVID-19 infections in Quebec reached their lowest level since the start of the pandemic. This decline continued until December 2021, when the number of cases exploded, accompanied by an increase in hospitalizations and deaths. A significant proportion of deaths still occurred in long-term care facilities and private seniors' residences.

This dramatic rise in cases and deaths, in both public and private sectors, created immense but sporadic pressure on the health system and the workforce during this period (Lacroix, 2022; Larin, 2022; Pilon-Larose, 2022; TVA Nouvelles, 2022). Workforce shortages in the health system persisted due to both surges in demand associated with the pandemic and the need to catch up with procedures that had been postponed during the first year of the pandemic. Despite the persistence of these workforce issues during this period, the government's willingness to maintain improvements to the remuneration of care aides appeared ambivalent, especially for those working in the private and community sector. Private seniors' residences and community organizations saw this as unfair competition with the public sector, especially as they were offering essential services that the public could not provide:

> We don't intend the premiums to be permanent. There are workforce issues in all sectors, not just in the community network. Organizations are autonomous entities and are able to determine the salaries of their employees. (Carmant quoted by Prince, 2021)

This type of discourse was interpreted as a lack of recognition of the contribution made by care aides in these sectors and raised the threat of a certain setback in terms of working conditions, which care aides found very hard to accept after the mobilization efforts deployed during the crisis.

By September 2021, the first wave of care aides to graduate from the accelerated training programme was also expressing themselves. They had been working in long-term care settings for one year, and it seemed that 'many of them are thinking of leaving their jobs' (Nadeau-Lamarche, 2021). Unions 'denounced the working conditions of these new care aides and did not hesitate to speak of broken dreams' (Nadeau-Lamarche, 2021). Moreover, 'after the "year of grace" following their training, during which they had full-time work, the new care aides fell onto recall lists, where some were only offered part-time work' (Duchaine et al., 2022, pp. 202–203). Flexible workforce management, a longstanding practice in Quebec healthcare facilities, was achieved at the expense of job stability and predictable working hours.

Unions and the media strongly criticized the inadequacy of measures put in place by government during this phase of the pandemic. Criticism focused mainly on work overload, exacerbated by the critical shortage of manpower (Archambault, 2021). For many, these conditions also revealed low esteem for the work done by this occupational group (Lévesque, 2021; Nadeau-Lamarche, 2021). Despite criticism calling for improved working conditions, government focused on salaries and measures to increase the care aide workforce.

During the second year of the pandemic, discourse about the work of care aides came from a wider range of actors, namely government, unions, and care aides themselves. While recognition remained at the heart of the discourse, issues surrounding the conditions needed to provide quality care and enable care aides to practice according to their values gained importance:

> I'd like to continue because it's a great job. But it's just volume that we do. Compared to what we were told [i.e., this idea] of taking care of people, it's far from the truth. It's distressing because the first to suffer are the beneficiaries. You give basic care and that's it. (Lévesque, 2021)

However, labour shortages across the health system, partly due to absenteeism related to COVID-19, put this occupational group in competition with others for policy attention. Long-term care, and more broadly care for the most vulnerable, competed with other priorities such as waiting lists for surgery or cancer treatment in the context of a post-COVID recovery leading to a resurgence of competing logics between care and cure. The inability to sustain incentives to care aides was seen by many actors as a gradual re-establishment of the previous occupational hierarchy, which seemed to be accompanied by a decrease in rhetoric around the 'essential' value of care aides in the public and political sphere. By focussing on short-term measures applied now only to the public sector (wage increases, temporary rapid training), the transformative potential of discourse on essentiality appeared limited and is reflected in insufficient, precarious, and time-limited sociomaterial agencements.

III – LIVING WITH THE PANDEMIC: DISCREPANCIES BETWEEN DISCOURSE AND THE SUSTAINABILITY OF IMPROVEMENTS TO WORKING CONDITIONS

March 2022 saw the start of a fifth wave of the pandemic in Quebec; however the number of cases and hospitalizations was lower than in previous months. March 2022 also marked the two-year anniversary of the pandemic, providing an opportunity to again thank the essential workers who 'held the healthcare system together'. Numerous articles in the Quebec press took the opportunity to assess the government's response to the crisis, underline the exceptional contribution of care aides, and question the medical-centric model of care and the place care aides should hold in the occupational hierarchy (Desrosiers, 2022; Max-Gessler, 2022):

> Many point out that the healthcare system revolves too much around doctors, and the pandemic has clearly demonstrated how essential care aides, support staff and nurses are. (Bergeron, 2022)

Despite discourse praising care aides, many still believed that care aides were not sufficiently valued in Quebec society. In April 2022, an opinion letter highlighted recognition issues:

> With COVID-19, protecting seniors was the ubiquitous rhetoric for enforcing health measures. However, while seniors have secured their place in the public debate, the people who actually care for them have not. The occupation of care aides is greatly devalued in today's Quebec society, and they are not given the credit they are due. (Amyot, 2022)

> [...] the inequalities experienced by these individuals were exacerbated during the pandemic: 'There are a lot of people with immigrant backgrounds, some of whom have irregular status, as well as a lot of precariousness. ... These individuals often live together in small apartments. They cannot afford to miss work, even if the conditions under which they must work are dangerous'. (Cossette & Simard quoted by Hébert-Dolbec, 2022)

It was during this third phase that the discourse on recognition issues specific to certain care aide groups, in particular immigrants, became more visible in the public sphere. While some voices sought to shift the debate towards recognition of the precariousness and risks of their work environment, the criticism directed at government, particularly by the unions, remained focused on salary issues and the lack of staff. This debate re-emerged as the government began to phase out the incentives associated with the state of emergency, namely higher wages (Ministère de la Santé et des Services Sociaux, 2022a, 2022b; Théroux, 2022) and lump sums to encourage attendance at work, which could reach $1,000 per four-week period

(Ministère de la Santé et des Services Sociaux, 2022a, 2022b). The government insisted that the temporary status of these measures had been agreed with workers and their unions. On the other hand, unions denounced the abrupt end of the bonuses (Lévesque, 2022), the government's lack of communication and collaboration (Bouchard, 2022 quoted by Lévesque, 2022) and the absence of 'transitional measures' (Lévesque, 2022) which, according to the unions, reflected a lack of real recognition by the government of the care aides' contribution and work.

Therefore, although the valourization of care work achieved during the pandemic seemed to still be supported in the press and in public opinion, the government's determination to keep the value of care aide work on the political agenda seemed to fade during this third phase (Guérin, 2022; Labrecque, 2022; Normandeau, 2022; Radio-Canada, 2022). Its strategies for tackling labour shortages in this sector have involved giving managers greater flexibility in the organization of work such as: (1) 'the possibility of monetizing vacations at the request of employees' (Guérin, 2022; Labrecque, 2022; Normandeau, 2022; Radio-Canada, 2022); (2) 'the possibility of voluntary intra- and inter-establishment employee movement' (Guérin, 2022; Labrecque, 2022; Normandeau, 2022; Radio-Canada, 2022); and (3) promoting the hiring of temporary employees and agency workers. Some unions heavily criticized the maintenance of some of these measures as 'coercive' (Théroux, 2022).

Overall, with partial relief from the pandemic and the end of the state of emergency, a pre-pandemic pattern of valuation and relationship between government and certain occupational groups in the health system seemed to re-emerge. Although care aide unions were present in the media (Guérin, 2022; TVA Nouvelles, 2020), these workers individually and collectively seemed less visible and vocal than nurses and physicians to assert their specific occupational issues in the public arena. In addition, the discourse of government and unions remained around salaries and workforce sufficiency. Treating the issue as one that simply required a wage increase and more workers limited the revalorization of care aide work in time and depth. The structural and cultural issues surrounding recognition of the work of care aides received little public attention and have not translated into sociomaterial agencements capable of sustaining real recognition policies over the long term.

DISCUSSION

Promulgation of Discourse of Essentiality and Signs of Recognition

Our case empirically probes how government in one Canadian province (Québec) relates to and values a specific occupational category that performs dirty work, namely care aides, in the context of the pandemic of COVID-19. Discourse of essentiality promulgated by politicians, the media, and the public during the crisis attests to society's dependence on the work of care aides and attempts to transcend their current marginalization and peripheral status within the labour market. Despite discourse praising the essentiality of the work of care aides, deeper analysis on how discourse is translated into recognition in policies leads us to qualify its transformative capacity. The question this raises is under what conditions and by what mechanisms can discourse be generative of lasting and substantive transformation?

As discussed earlier, the theory of performativity has been criticized for its overestimation of the capacity of discourse to bring about social change and its limited attention to alternate transformative levers such as innovative sectoral policies. Cabantous et al. (2016, 2018) propose three mechanisms to transcend limitations in scholarly work on performativity and better understand how to move from discourse to policies and practices with high impact on labour conditions and the experience of work. Thus, performativity is dependent on both a critique of the structures and cultural matrix in which discourse is deployed as well as on a certain vision of desirable changes and capacities to mobilize resources and effect substantive changes. Our analysis empirically probes the potential of these mechanisms and conditions that favour their emergence.

Government response is shaped by a context where health human resource issues have been neglected for a long time in Québec (Denis et al., 2021). This legacy influences its ability to address deficiencies in health human resources planning and working conditions. Our empirical case illustrates the important role played by the pre-pandemic policy system in shaping government's response to the care aides' situation (Estabrooks et al., 2020). When the pandemic strikes, government recognizes the essentiality of care aides and initiates rapid short-term policy responses to improve their working conditions. The pandemic opens a space in which government and other groups feel legitimate in publicly holding this discourse of essentiality, even at the risk of triggering more substantial demands for change and improvement. However, and in relation to Leca and Barin-Cruiz (2021) study on performativity, the coupling of substantive policy changes that challenge inequalities with reformative discourse is a long temporal process that requires intensive efforts from marginalized groups and other influential actors in the health and social care sectors. Even political elites, with their own institutional conditioning, are not in a position to translate discourses of essentiality into sustainable improvements of working conditions in such a limited timeframe. Changes depend not only on the political determination of elected officials, but they are also constrained by institutional inertia that systematically and historically privileges acute care sectors and specialized medicine through resources allocation (Usher et al., 2021). While the promulgation of discourses of essentiality opens a space for social change, it cannot by itself provide the basis for substantive or transformative change. Discourses of essentiality act both as precursors and enablers of changes but need to be coupled with other transformative strategies to be effective. The state of emergency declared during the pandemic enabled the government to work quickly and on its own, bypassing the performativity work with concerned actors and groups (Leca & Barin-Cruiz, 2021) that is required to tackle issues of care aide recognition.

Discourse, Contestation, and Social Change

Discourse of essentiality not only publicly manifests recognition but also necessarily raises the question of social processes that contribute to the marginalization of care aides and their work – the second transformative mechanism proposed by Cabantous et al. (2016), the capacity of discourse to renew work. This mechanism creates a space where actors (care aides, unions, other professionals) can react to discourses of essentiality by political elites and voice demands to rebalance the labour market and the status of work across occupational groups. However, this deeper questioning of the sources of hierarchy and stratification is rarely raised explicitly by actors and groups in our case. Our research findings show that unions and political elites do not significantly engage in discursive practices to address predominant normative or cultural matrices that define the occupational hierarchy. In the health and social care system, the stratification of professions and occupations is linked to the division between the world of care and the world of cure. The culture of health systems tends to downplay the logic of care and play up the competencies associated with the logic of cure and more broadly value technical virtuosity and proficiency (Glouberman & Mintzberg, 2001). This is a key aspect of the policy legacy that limits the valuation of care aides in a system where cure, technique, and scientific achievement are valued as core elements, and where care is pushed to the periphery (Estabrooks et al., 2020). This reflects a broader social trend within labour markets, namely the valuing of technical skills over interpersonal and relational skills (Farris & Bergfeld, 2022; Stevano et al., 2020). Structural and cultural conditions contribute to the invisibility of workers performing dirty work and act in synergy with formal labour policies to sustain poor valuation and recognition of the work of care aides.

Discourse appears in our case as performative in alerting society to the importance and poor working conditions of care aides but cannot by itself create the cultural and political shift to challenge labour market segmentation and the low status of this occupational group. The importance of generating alternate discourses that counteract predominant logics is not fully recognized and acted upon by unions, the media, or political elites. The low professional status of care aides performing dirty work, and marginalization in work settings that prevent them from voicing their concerns limit the ability to make their situation more visible and to present a vision of desirable changes. Scholarly works on performativity have not yet provided a deep assessment of the role of political mobilization and formal bodies such as unions in creating channels to discuss the cultural and economic marginalization of low-status social or occupational groups. In this process, only certain dimensions of care work, such as salaries and shortages, are made more visible and recognition policies mainly focus on these aspects rather than on the nature and complexity of care work and the specific expertise of care aides. Once the crisis passes, our empirical findings show a risk of being relegated to the invisibility and working conditions that prevailed before the pandemic.

The Challenge of Genuine Valuation of Dirty Work in Society

Our analysis focuses on institutions and labour regimes that create (or not) a favourable space for the objective recognition of dirty work performed by essential workers (Laaser & Karlsson, 2021). We explore how and to what extent politicians' discourse of essentiality in a crisis context creates sufficient momentum to realign the cultural and structural determinants of the value of work (human resources policies at health system level, labour regimes, and the role of unions). This refers to the third mechanism of Canbantous et al.'s (2016) work on performativity, namely the translation of discourse into substantive change via sociomateriel agencements. Real recognition of the value of care workers requires constructing and mobilizing knowledge that considers the real nature of this work and the technical, relational, and emotional demands associated with care. This knowledge has the potential to undermine the dominant knowledge/power regimes and influence the positions of care workers in society and in the hierarchy of professions (Foucault, 1969).

Our case illustrates that it is difficult to sustain political attention (and the attention of the general population) to the working conditions of care aides and the importance of providing decent care to the most vulnerable. Competing logics and demands of various groups, including the general population, for access to acute care after waiting lists dramatically increased during the pandemic are forces that push aside preoccupations for the working conditions of care aides. In addition, in the competition among professional groups for the valuation of their work, the medical profession has historically been effective at securing advantageous working conditions through their unions (Denis et al., 2022), which may impact on the ability to significantly improve the working conditions of care aides. Discourse of essentiality appears relatively weak to counteract these dynamics as can be seen from the discourses present in phase 3 of the pandemic.

Different professional groups may demonstrate high levels of solidarity and recognition for care aides and their work, but within unions (some of which defend the rights of multiple occupational categories) and across major professional unions, there is *de facto* a structural competition where different groups negotiate their working conditions centrally with government (Gagnon, 1998). Our case shows that unions are more active in the early phase of the pandemic in calling attention to the dramatic situation of care aides and demanding immediate corrections. The performativity of discourse is part of this context where different social forces exert pressure to re-establish the dominant order once the crisis subsides. Our findings from phase 3 of the pandemic reveal that once the intensity of the crisis has passed, the interests of the public, other professionals, and political elites push for a return to the invisibility of this occupational group. Institutions, understood in the context of our study as a combination of competing logics (Reay & Hinings, 2009), including a professional and occupational hierarchy embedded in labour regimes, frame the relation between care aides and government, and influence the ability to translate discourse of essentiality into substantive change. Performativity theory has not paid enough attention to the kind of institutionalization of competing logics observed in contemporary health and social care systems and how it constrains the effectiveness of discourse and the promulgation of values and norms in engineering social changes. Essentiality is constitutive of a valuation discourse where worth or value is given to a specific type of work and class of workers (Lamont, 2012). In line with the sociology of dirty work, our case study illustrates how workers seek recognition and affirm the dignity of their work. The issue is how to move from local discourse and practice among workers that creates a positive sense of self, to agentic capacities at a more collective level to intensify institutional mediation (Laaser & Karlsson, 2021). Discourse does not appear sufficient to transcend structural and cultural forces that historically disadvantage care aides. Reports by various groups (journalists, learned societies) that voice the need to move beyond discourse and substantively value care aides and their work do not necessarily increase the political capacity of care aides as an occupational group to voice demands and achieve improvements of their working conditions. Current decisions in government lean more towards returning to the situation that prevailed before the pandemic, albeit with some permanent salary increases.

We note very few propositions from unions or other organized labour groups to install formal mechanisms in the workplace and within labour regimes to ensure that care aides have a stronger voice. That said, Quebec is currently witnessing a historical united movement between unions that together represent 420,000 workers, including health and social care professional and occupational groups, to negotiate better working conditions with the government. It remains to be seen whether this solidarity will take up demands for conditions that give real recognition to care work and care aides.

CONCLUSION

In this chapter, we empirically assess the transformative potential of discourse of essentiality at the highest level of politics, that is, from the Premier and the Minister of Health and Social Services. While this discourse is associated with rapid policy response to value the work of care aides, it is embedded in a system structure and culture that restrains improvements to the working conditions of this occupational group in the short term. Policy legacies within the health system militate in favour of incremental change that improves the situation of care aides in a context where care and cure and a wide range of professional and occupational groups compete for policy attention and resources. Our analysis suggests that the impact of discourse of essentiality depends on three mechanisms as proposed by scholarly works on performativity. Within these mechanisms, what appears crucial is the propensity and ability of actors and groups to identify and reveal structural and cultural determinants of occupational hierarchy and organize politically to translate discourse into substantive policy change. Local work arrangements and organizational policies may help improve the work experience of care aides, but the possibilities of developing high impact and transformative labour policies are largely conditioned by macro dynamics, including subtle social processes, that frame the collective agency of care aides and their ability to rely on favourable institutional mediation. The importance of competing institutional logics and institutional inertia has not been considered empirically by scholarly works on performativity to understand the power and limitations of discourse in societies in bringing about substantive social changes. Research is needed to better understand the mechanisms by which transformative strategies for valuing low-status occupational groups can emerge and be deployed not only within health and social care organizations but within the broader political economy where these competitive interests and occupational status differentials are produced (Denis, 2024). In-depth transformation of care aides recognition policies requires connecting local workforce issues, management practices within organizations, and broader social changes shaping labour conditions and the experience of work (Côté & Denis, 2024).

Three strategies may help move care aides in from the periphery: (1) a closer alliance with the political forces of other professional groups that, during the pandemic, started to publicly recognize the essentiality of the work performed by care aides; (2) the production and dissemination of formal knowledge on the complex work of care aides and more broadly on care work; and (3) more organized and direct reliance on media and unions that from time to time have been effective at creating momentum for change in this sector.

REFERENCES

Accès Études Québec. (2023). *Santé, assistance et soins infirmiers*. Les programmes de formation. https://accesetudesquebec.ca/fr/programme-etude/sante-assistance-soins-infirmiers/38/7

Amyot, L. (2022, April 12). Un métier indispensable, mais sous-estimé. L'Action. https://www.laction.com/article/2022/04/12/un-metier-indispensable-mais-sous-estime

Anderson, B. (2000). *Doing the dirty work? The global politics of domestic labour*. Zed Books.

Anderson, B., Poeschel, F., & Ruhs, M. (2021). Rethinking labour migration: Covid-19, essential work, and systemic resilience. *Comparative Migration Studies*, 9(45), 1–19. https://doi.org/10.1186/s40878-021-00252-2

Archambault, H. (2021, Septembre 19). CHSLD: des ratios inhumains de patients. *Le Journal de Montréal*. https://www.journaldemontreal.com/2021/09/19/des-ratios-inhumains-de-patients

Aubry, F. (2016). Les préposés aux bénéficiaires au Québec: Entre amour du métier et dégoût de la tâche: Comment l'analyse de l'activité permet de comprendre le paradoxe. *Sociologie et Sociétés*, 48(1), 169–189. https://doi.org/10.7202/1036888ar

Aubry, F. (2020). Les préposés aux bénéficiaires en CHSLD face aux prescriptions organisationnelles relatives à la qualité: quand le désengagement individuel prend la place de la résistance collective. *Cahiers de Recherche Sociologique*, 68, 77–99. https://doi.org/10.7202/1086358ar

Aubry, F. (2021). La fragilisation de la santé psychologique au travail des préposés aux bénéficiaires: l'impact d'une forme d'injustice organisationnelle? In S. Moulin (Ed.), *Perceptions de justice et santé au travail* (pp. 141–156). Presses de l'Université Laval.

Aubry, F., & Couturier, Y. (2019). *La fragilisation de la santé au travail des préposés aux bénéficiaires et des auxiliaires en santé et services sociaux du secteur public au Québec*. Interactions. https://centreinteractions.ca/publication/la-fragilisation-de-la-sante-au-travail-des-preposes-aux-beneficiaires-et-des-auxiliaires-en-sante-et-services-sociaux-du-secteur-public-au-quebec/

Bellerose, P. (Director). (2020, May 28). Des préposés aussi bien payés qu'une infirmière. *Journal de Québec*. https://www.journaldequebec.com/2020/05/28/en-directcovid-19-francois-legault-fait-le-point-sur-la-situation-au-quebec

Bergeron, M. (2022, March 5). Les autres leçons de la pandémie. *La Tribune*. https://www.latribune.ca/2022/03/05/les-autres-lecons-de-la-pandemie-c0141f9809d7b421edc836590cb95b5f

Bergfeld, M. (2020, March 5). The insanity of making sick people work. Jacobin. https://jacobin.com/2020/03/coronavirus-workers-rights-health-care-cleaners-gig-economy

Blake, E., Ashforth, B. E., & Kreiner, G. E. (1999). "How can you do it?": Dirty work and the challenge of constructing a positive identity. *The Academy of Management Review*, 24(3), 413–434. https://doi.org/10.2307/259134

Bourgault-Côté, G. (2020, December 22). François Legault, 115 points de presse plus tard. *Le Devoir*. https://www.ledevoir.com/politique/quebec/592154/legault-115-points-de-presse-plus-tard

Bourgeault, I. L., Maier, C. B., Dieleman, M., Ball, J., MacKenzie, A., Nancarrow, S., Nigenda, G., & Sidat, M. (2020). The COVID-19 pandemic presents an opportunity to develop more sustainable health workforces. *Human Resources for Health, 18*(1), 1–8. https://doi.org/10.1186/s12960-020-00529-0

Bowden, V., Gond, J.-P., Nyberg, D., & Wright, C. (2021). Turning back the rising sea: Theory performativity in the shift from climate science to popular authority. *Organization Studies, 42*(12), 1909–1931. https://doi.org/10.1177/01708406211024558

Butler, J. (1993). *Bodies that matter*. Routledge.

Cabantous, L., Gond, J.-P., Harding, N., & Learmonth, M. (2016). Critical essay: Reconsidering critical performativity. *Human Relations, 69*(2), 197–213. https://doi.org/10.1177/0018726715614073

Cabantous, L., Gond, J.-P., & Wright, A. (2018). The performativity of strategy: Taking stock and moving ahead. *Long Range Planning, 51*(3), 407–416.

Cabinet du Ministre de la Santé. (2023, May 16). *Québec veut former plus de préposés aux bénéficiaires*. https://www.quebec.ca/nouvelles/actualites/details/quebec-veut-former-plus-de-preposes-aux-beneficiaires-47862

Carazo, S., Laliberté, D., Villeneuve, J., Martin, R., Deshaies, P., Denis, G., Deshaies, P., Hegg-Deloye, S., & De Serres, G. (2022). Characterization and evolution of infection control practices among severe acute respiratory coronavirus virus 2 (SARS-CoV-2)-infected healthcare workers in acute-care hospitals and long-term care facilities in Québec, Canada, Spring 2020. *Infection Control and Hospital Epidemiology, 43*(4), 481–489. https://doi.org/10.1017/ice.2021.160

Comité Patronal de Négociation du Secteur de la Santé et des Services Sociaux. (2023a). *3480 – Préposé ou préposée aux bénéficiaires*. Titres d'emploi, salaire et primes. https://cpnsss.gouv.qc.ca/titres-demploi-et-salaires/nomenclature-et-mecanisme-de-modification/fiche-demploi/3480-9-0

Comité Patronal de Négociation du Secteur de la Santé et des Services Sociaux. (2023b). *3455 – Infirmier auxiliaire ou infirmière auxiliaire*. Titres d'emploi, salaire et primes. https://cpnsss.gouv.qc.ca/titres-demploi-et-salaires/nomenclature-et-mecanisme-de-modification/fiche-demploi/3455-14-0

Comité Patronal de Négociation du Secteur de la Santé et des Services Sociaux. (2023c). *1911 – Infirmier clinicien ou infirmière clinicienne*. Titres d'emploi, salaire et primes. https://cpnsss.gouv.qc.ca/titres-demploi-et-salaires/nomenclature-et-mecanisme-de-modification/fiche-demploi/1911-22-0

Commissaire à la Santé et au Bien-être. (2021). *Portrait des ressources humaines du système de santé et de services sociaux québécois*. https://www.csbe.gouv.qc.ca/fileadmin/www/2021/Rapportpr%C3%A9liminaire_Mandat/RapportsAssoci%C3%A9s/CSBE_Portrait-Ressources-humaines.pdf

Cornelissen, L. (2021). *Portrait des personnes immigrantes qui exercent une profession infirmière ou d'aide aux soins de santé*. Statistique Canada. https://www150.statcan.gc.ca/n1/pub/75-006-x/2021001/article/00004-fra.pdf

Côté, N., & Denis, J.-L. (2024). Situations of anomie and the health workforce crisis: Policy implications of a socially sensitive and inclusive approach to human resources. *The International Journal of Health Planning and Management, 39*(3), 898–905. https://doi.org/10.1002/hpm.3785

Couturier, E.-L., Nguyen, M., & Labrie, V. (2023). *Le revenu viable 2023: Dans la spirale de l'inflation et des baisses d'impôt*. Institut de recherche et d'informations socioéconomiques. https://iris-recherche.qc.ca/publications/revenu-viable-2023/#Cout_de_la_vie_pour_un_menage_d%E2%80%99une_personne_seule

Crenshaw, K. W. (1989). Demarginalizing the intersection of race and sex: A black feminist critique of antidiscrimination doctrine, feminist theory and antiracist politics. *University of Chicago Legal Forum, 8*, 139–167. https://chicagounbound.uchicago.edu/uclf/vol1989/iss1/8

Crête, M. (2020, June 1). Quel salaire horaire pour les préposés aux bénéficiaires? *Le Devoir*. https://www.ledevoir.com/politique/quebec/579986/quel-salaire-horaire-pour-les-preposes-aux-beneficiaires

De Camargo, C. R., & Whiley, L. A. (2020). The mythologisation of key workers: Occupational prestige gained, sustained… and lost? *International Journal of Sociology and Social Policy, 40*(99), 849–859. https://doi.org/10.1108/IJSSP-07-2020-0310

Deery, S., Kolar, D., & Walsh, J. (2019). Can dirty work be satisfying? A mixed method study of workers doing dirty jobs. *Work, Employment and Society, 33*(4), 631–647. https://doi.org/10.1177/0950017018817307

Denis, J.-L. (2024). Commentary on Part I. Context: A pretext and opportunity for the renovation of human resources policies and practices in health and social care. In A. M. McDermott, P. Hyde, L. FitzGerald, & A. C. Avgar (Eds.), *Research handbook on contemporary human resource management for health care.* (pp. 2–18). Edward Elgar Publishing Limited.

Denis, J. (2023, May 16). *Québec veut former au moins 3000 préposés aux bénéficiaires d'ici la fin de l'année.* Noovo info. https://www.noovo.info/nouvelle/quebec-veut-former-au-moins-3000-preposes-aux-beneficiaires-dici-la-fin-de-lannee.html

Denis, J. L., Côté, N., Fleury, C., Currie, G., & Spyridonidis, D. (2021). Global health and innovation: A panoramic view on health human resources in the COVID-19 pandemic context. *The International Journal of Health Planning and Management, 36*, 58–70. https://doi.org/10.1002/hpm.3129

Denis, J. L., Germain, S., Regis, C., & Veronesi, G. (2022). *Medical doctors in health reforms: A comparative study of England and Canada.* Policy Press.

Desjardins, F. (2019, June 3). Les préposés aux bénéficiaires au bout du rouleau. *Le Devoir.* https://www.ledevoir.com/societe/sante/555842/les-preposes-aux-beneficiaires-sont-a-bout-de-souffle

Desjardins, F. (2021, March 7). *Bourses disponibles pour futurs préposés aux bénéficiaires.* Beauce Média. https://www.beaucemedia.ca/actualites/sante/bourses-disponibles-pour-futurs-preposes-aux-beneficiaires/

Desrosiers, P. K. (2022, March 15). *L'ensemble des travailleurs a fait preuve de solidarité.* Bruno Petrucci. Les 2 Rives (Sorel-Tracy, QC). https://les2rives.com/lensemble-des-travailleurs-a-fait-preuve-de-solidarite-bruno-petrucci/

Dick, P. (2005). Dirty work designations: How police officers account for their use of coercive force. *Human Relations, 58*(11), 1363–1390. https://doi.org/10.1177/0018726705060242

Douglas, M. (1966). *Purity and danger: An analysis of concepts of pollution and taboo.* Routledge and Kegan Paul.

Duchaine, G., Gagnon, K., & Lacoursière, A. (2022). *5060: L'hécatombe de la COVID-19 dans nos CHSLD.* Boréal.

Emploi Préposé. (2023). *Description du métier de Préposés aux bénéficiaires.* https://www.emploiprepose.ca/description-du-metier-de-preposes-aux-beneficiaires

Estabrooks, C. A., Straus, S. E., Flood, C. M., Keefe, J., Armstrong, P., Donner, G. J., Boscart, V., Ducharme, F., Silvius, J. L., & Wolfson, M. C. (2020). Restoring trust: COVID-19 and the future of long-term care in Canada. *FACETS, 5*(1), 651–691. https://doi.org/10.1139/facets-2020-0056

Farris, S. R., & Bergfeld, M. (2022). Low-skill no more! Essential workers, social reproduction and the legitimacy-crisis of the division of labour. *Distinction: Journal of Social Theory, 23*(2–3), 1–17. https://doi.org/10.1080/1600910X.2022.2077400

Farris, S., Yuval-Danis, N., & Rottenberg, C. (2021). The Frontline as performative frame. An analysis of the UK Covid crisis. *State Crime Journal, 10*(2), 284–303. http://resolver.scholarsportal.info/resolve/20466056/v10i0002/284_tfapfaaotucc.xml

Foucault, M. (1969). *L'Archéologie du savoir.* Gallimard.

Gagné, L. (2020, April 12). *Appel de volontaires chez le personnel soignant de la Capitale-Nationale.* Radio-Canada. https://ici.radio-canada.ca/nouvelle/1693400/appel-volontaires-personnel-soignant-cisss-capitale-nationale-reseau-sante-covid-chu-quebec

Gagnon, M.-J. (1998). La « modernisation » du syndicalisme québécois ou la mise à l'épreuve d'une logique représentative. *Sociologie et sociétés, 30*(2), 213–230. https://doi.org/10.7202/001277ar

Garrick, J., & Chan, A. (2017). Knowledge management and professional experience: The uneasy dynamics between tacit knowledge and performativity in organizations. *Journal of Knowledge Management, 21*(4), 872–884. https://doi.org/10.1108/JKM-02-2017-0058

Glouberman, S., & Mintzberg, H. (2001). Managing the care of health and the cure of disease—Part I: Differentiation. *Health Care Management Review, 26*(1), 56–69. https://doi.org/10.1097/00004010-200101000-00006

Gosselin, J. (2020, April 24). On a besoin de vous. *La Presse+.* https://plus.lapresse.ca/screens/0ed848c0-7f54-4dab-becf-97f120bfbb4e%7C_0.html

Government of Canada. (2024). *Guichet-Emplois, Perspectives d'emploi.* Préposé/préposée aux bénéficiaires au Québec. https://nb.guichetemplois.gc.ca/rapportmarche/perspectives-profession/15774/QC

Gouvernement du Québec. (2023a). *Préposé aux bénéficiaires*. Métiers et professions en santé et services sociaux. https://avenirensante.gouv.qc.ca/carrieres/prepose-aux-beneficiaires

Gouvernement du Québec. (2023b). *Infirmière clinicienne ou infirmier clinicien*. Métiers et professions en santé et services sociaux. https://avenirensante.gouv.qc.ca

Gouvernement du Québec. (2020, September 15). *Programme accéléré pour devenir préposé en CHSLD – Les membres de la première cohorte prêts à intégrer le réseau de la santé*. https://www.quebec.ca/nouvelles/actualites/details/programme-accelere-pour-devenir-prepose-en-chsld-les-membresde-la-premiere-cohorte-prets-a-integrer-le-reseau-de-la-sante

Greer, S. L., King, E. J., da Fonseca, E. M., & Peralta-Santos, A. (2020). The comparative politics of COVID-19: The need to understand government responses. *Global Public Health*, 15(9), 1413–1416. https://doi.org/10.1080/17441692.2020.1783340

Guérin, S. (2022, June 15). *Manque de préposés au Bas-Saint-Laurent: Le SCFP a rencontré le cabinet du ministre Dubé*. Radio-Canada. https://ici.radio-canada.ca/nouvelle/1891361/syndicat-prepose-beneficiaire-bas-saint-laurent-christian-dube

Guimarães, N. A., & Hirata, H. (2021). *Care and care workers: A Latin American perspective*. Springer International Publishing.

Hatton, E. (2017). Mechanisms of invisibility: Rethinking the concept of invisible work. *Work, Employment and Society*, 31(2), 336–351. https://doi.org/10.1177/0950017016674894

Hébert-Dolbec, A.-F. (2022, May 16). « Traitements-chocs et tartelettes »: Des experts se prononcent sur la gestion de la pandémie. *Le Devoir*. https://www.ledevoir.com/lire/711627/lire-autopsie-du-discours-pandemique

Hirata, H. (2021). *Le care, théories et pratiques*. La Dispute.

Hughes, E. C. (1951). Studying the nurse's work. *The American Journal of Nursing*, 51(5), 294–295. https://doi.org/10.2307/3459394

Hughes, E. C. (1958). *Men and their work*. Free Press.

Institut de la Statistique du Québec. (2022). *Revenu moyen*. Vitrine statistique sur l'égalité entre les femmes et les hommes. https://statistique.quebec.ca/vitrine/egalite/dimensions-egalite/revenu/revenu-moyen

Institut National de Santé Publique du Québec. (2022). *Données COVID-19 au Québec*. https://www.inspq.qc.ca/covid-19/donnees

Keller, R. (2007). L'analyse de discours comme sociologie de la connaissance. Présentation d'un programme de recherche. *Langage et Société*, 120(2), 55–76. https://doi.org/10.3917/ls.120.0055

Khalkhal, F. (2020). 15 avril: Un appel d'urgence aux médecins. *Le Journal de Chambly*. https://www.journaldechambly.com/15-avril-un-appel-durgence-aux-medecins/

Kim, H. Y., Kim, S., Howell, T. M., Doyle, S. P., Pettit, N. C., & Bizzarro, M. (2022). Are we essential, or sacrificial? The effects of felt public gratitude on essential worker recovery activities during COVID-19. *Social Psychological and Personality Science*, 14(2), 218–227. https://doi.org/10.1177/19485506221077858

Laaser, K., & Karlsson, J. C. (2021). Towards a sociology of meaningful work. *Work, Employment and Society*, 36(5), 798–815. https://doi.org/10.1177/09500170211055998

Labbé, J. (2020a, May 27). *Québec veut recruter 10 000 préposés aux bénéficiaires en offrant des formations payées*. Radio-Canada. https://ici.radio-canada.ca/nouvelle/1706748/coronavirus-bilan-quebec-francois-legault

Labbé, J. (2020b, April 16). *CHSLD: 2000 médecins spécialistes ont répondu à l'appel*. Radio-Canada. https://ici.radio-canada.ca/nouvelle/1694562/coronavirus-covid-legault-gouvernement-quebec-arruda-mccann-bilan

Labranche, M. (2020, April 16). Popos de François Legault: Les médecins spécialistes «attristés», «choqués» et «insultés». *Le Journal de Québec*. https://www.journaldequebec.com/2020/04/16/propos-de-legault-les-medecins-specialistes-attristes-choques-et-insultes

Labrecque, M. (2022, March 31). Plus de 400 emplois disponibles dans le réseau de la santé. *Le Peuple Lotbinière*. https://www.lepeuplelotbiniere.ca/fr/index.aspx?sortcode=1.34.39&id=114249

Lacoursière, A. (2020, April 15). Les médecins spécialistes qui prêteront main-forte recevront 2500 $par jour. *La Presse*. https://www.lapresse.ca/covid-19/2020-04-15/les-medecins-specialistes-qui-preteront-main-forte-recevront-2500-par-jour

Lacroix, S. (2022, January 4). Le réseau de la santé sous haute pression dans la région. *Le Nouvelliste*. https://www.lenouvelliste.ca/2022/01/05/le-reseau-de-la-sante-sous-haute-pression-dans-la-region-fbaf5884bbcdfb4df54cb53c79eb12e6

Lajoie, G. (2020, April 16). Préposés et infirmières en CHSLD: il Faut abaisser les ratios personnel-patients. *Le Journal de Québec*. https://www.journaldequebec.com/2020/04/16/preposes-et-infirmieres-en-chsld-il-faut-abaisser-les-ratios-personnel-patients

Lamont, M. (2012). Toward a comparative sociology of valuation and evaluation. *Annual Review of Sociology, 38,* 201–221. https://doi.org/10.1146/annurev-soc-070308-120022

Larin, V. (2022, January 18). « On est encore dans la tempête »: Trop de pression sur les hôpitaux pour des assouplissements. *Le Journal de Québec*. https://www.journaldequebec.com/2022/01/18/quebec-fait-le-point-sur-la-covid-a-13h-1

Leca, B., & Barin-Cruz, L. (2021). Enabling critical performativity: The role of institutional context and critical performative work. *Organization, 28*(6), 903–929. https://doi.org/10.1177/1350508421995759

Le Nouvelliste. (2018, January 31). *Faire manger quelqu'un est aussi vital que prescrire des pilules.* https://www.lenouvelliste.ca/2018/01/31/faire-manger-quelquun-est-aussi-vital-que-prescrire-des-pilules-13966fb16cbad0b4e04883b3cac6f71f

Lévesque, F. (2021, October 16). « Au bout d'un moment, c'est intenable ». *La Presse+*. https://plus.lapresse.ca/screens/8f328feb-59da-4d23-8c39-2a46168eabcc.html

Lévesque, L. (2020, May 6). La prime des préposés aux bénéficiaires touchée dans le privé, partiellement dans le public. *Le Soleil*. https://www.lesoleil.com/2020/05/06/la-prime-des-preposes-aux-beneficiaires-touchee-dans-le-prive-partiellement-dans-le-public-c2a4d-12f83828a78507cc08959b9cc36

Lévesque, L. (2022, March 1). Fin prochaine de certaines primes COVID, les syndicats auraient aimé une transition. *Le Soleil*. https://www.lesoleil.com/2022/03/11/fin-prochaine-de-certaines-primes-covid-les-syndicats-auraient-aime-une-transition-0f8f91fc0bc2d3e79170559b38858462

Lightman, N. (2022). Caring during the COVID-19 crisis: Intersectional exclusion of immigrant women health care aides in Canadian long-term care. *Health & Social Care in the Community, 30,* 1343–1351. https://doi.org/10.1111/hsc.13541

Manchha, A. V., Way, K. A., Tann, K., & Thai, M. (2022). The social construction of stigma in aged-care work: Implications for health professionals' work intentions. *The Gerontologist, 62*(2), 994–1005. https://doi.org/10.1093/geront/gnac002

McAlevey, J. (2016). *No shortcuts: Organizing for power in the new gilded age*. Oxford University Press.

McCaughey, D., Turner, N., Kim, J., DelliFraine, J., & McGhan, G. E. (2015). Examining workplace hazard perceptions & employee outcomes in the long-term care industry. *Safety Science, 78,* 190–197. https://doi.org/10.1016/j.ssci.2015.04.013

McMurray, R., & Ward, J. (2014). 'Why would you want to do that?': Defining emotional dirty work. *Human Relations, 67*(9), 1123–1143. https://doi.org/10.1177/0018726714525975

Max-Gessler, M. (2022, March 7). Deux ans au front pour le personnel de la santé. *Le Nouvelliste*. https://www.lesoleil.com/2022/03/07/deux-ans-au-front-pour-le-personnel-de-la-sante-77a1f84ad80192a7eefe506dd5a034ba

Miles, M. B., Huberman, A. M., & Saldaña J. (2014). *Qualitative data analysis: A methods sourcebook* (3th ed.). Sage Publications.

Ministère de la Santé et des Services Sociaux. (2020, February 4). *Plan d'action pour l'attraction et la fidélisation des préposés aux bénéficiaires et des auxiliaires aux services de santé et sociaux.* Publications du ministère de la Santé et des Services sociaux. https://publications.msss.gouv.qc.ca/msss/document-002450/

Ministère de la Santé et des Services Sociaux. (2022a, March 31). Loi sur la santé publique », *Arrêté numéro 2022-030 du ministre de la Santé et des Services sociaux en date du 31 mars 2022*. https://cdn-contenu.quebec.ca/cdn-contenu/adm/min/sante-services-sociaux/publications-adm/lois-reglements/AM-2022-030.pdf?1648760032

Ministère de la Santé et des Services Sociaux. (2022b, March 11). *Modifications aux mesures incitatives pour le personnel du réseau de la santé et des services sociaux et des milieux privés.* https://www.msss.gouv.qc.ca/ministere/salle-de-presse/communique-3476/#:~:text=La%20r%C3%A9mun%C3%A9ration%20%C3%A0%20150%20%25%20pour,remboursement%20des%20frais%20de%20stationnement

Mohammed, S., Peter E., Killackey, T., & Maciver, J. (2021). The "nurse as hero" discourse in the COVID-19 pandemic: A poststructural discourse analysis. *International Journal of Nursing Studies, 117*, 1–11. https://doi.org/10.1016/j.ijnurstu.2021.103887

Molinier, P. (2010). Qu'est-ce que le care? Souci des autres, sensibilité. In S. Polinier, S. Laugier, & P. Paperman (Eds.), *Sociétés et jeunesses en difficulté [En ligne], hors-série*. http://journals.openedition.org/sejed/6658

Nadeau-Lamarche, K. (2021, September 14). *Des préposés qui avaient suivi la formation accélérée envisagent de démissionner*. Radio-Canada – ICI Québec. https://ici.radio-canada.ca/nouvelle/1824179/preposee-aux-beneficiaires-chsld-formation-accelere-un-an

Normandeau, A. (2022, April 27). *Côte-Nord: Le réseau de la santé perd des travailleurs*. TVA Nouvelles. https://www.tvanouvelles.ca/2022/04/27/cote-nord-le-reseau-de-la-sante-perd-des-travailleurs

Ordre des infirmières et infirmiers du Québec. (2023). *Accéder à la profession infirmière au Québec. Exercer au Québec*. https://www.oiiq.org/acceder-profession/exercer-au-quebec

Ostaszkiewicz, J., O'Connell, B., & Dunning, T. (2016). "We just do the dirty work": Dealing with incontinence, courtesy stigma and the low occupational status of carework in long-term aged care facilities. *Journal of Clinical Nursing, 25*(17–18), 2528–2541. https://doi.org/10.1111/jocn.13292

Parks, C. A., Nugent, N. B., Fleischhacker, S. E., & Yaroch, A. L. (2020). Food system workers are the unexpected but under protected COVID heroes. *The Journal of Nutrition, 150*(8), 2006–2008. https://doi.org/10.1093/jn/nxaa173

Pettersen, G. (2020, April 15). Médecins spécialistes, descendez de votre piédestal. *Le Journal de Montréal*. https://www.journaldemontreal.com/2020/04/15/medecins-specialistes-descendez-de-votre-piedestal

Pilon-Larose, H. (2022, January 19). Capacités du réseau de la santé: Il faut « explorer toutes les alternatives à l'hôpital ». *La Presse*. https://www.lapresse.ca/actualites/sante/2022-01-19/capacites-du-reseau-de-la-sante/il-faut-explorer-toutes-les-alternatives-a-l-hopital.php

Placement Premier Soin. (2023). *Quelle différence entre infirmière et infirmière auxiliaire?* https://www.premiersoin.ca/difference-infirmiere-et-infirmiere-auxiliaire

Povinelli, E. A. (2011). *Economies of abandonment: Social belonging and endurance in late liberalism*. Duke University Press.

Prince, V. (2021, Octobre, 12). *Crainte d'exodes chez les préposés aux bénéficiaires*. Radio-Canada. https://ici.radio-canada.ca/nouvelle/1830863/organismes-communautaires-exode-preposes-beneficiaires

Le Protecteur du Citoyen. (2021). *La COVID-19 dans les CHSLD durant la première vague de la pandémie – Cibler les causes de la crise, agir, se souvenir*. Rapport spécial du Protecteur du citoyen. https://protecteurducitoyen.qc.ca/sites/default/files/2021-11/rapport-special-chsld-premiere-vague-covid-19.pdf

Rabelo, V., & Mahalingam, R. (2019). "They really don't want to see us": How cleaners experience invisible 'dirty' work. *Journal of Vocational Behavior, 113*, 103–114. https://doi.org/10.1016/j.jvb.2018.10.010

Radio-Canada. (2022, June 10). *Les aides de service du CIUSSS de l'Estrie pourront devenir préposés aux bénéficiaires*. ICI Radio-Canada – Estrie. https://ici.radio-canada.ca/nouvelle/1890032/aide-prepose-penurie-sante

Reay, T., & Hinings, C. R. (2009). Managing the rivalry of competing institutional logics. *Organization Studies, 30*(6), 629–652. https://doi.org/10.1177/0170840609104803

Riach, K., Rumens, N., & Tyler, M. (2016). Towards a Butlerian methodology: Undoing organizational performativity through anti-narrative research. *Human Relations, 69*(11), 2069–2089. https://doi.org/10.1177/0018726716632050

Rivera, K. (2018). Once more, with feeling! Working with emotional taint. In S. B. Thomson & G. Grandy (Eds.), *Stigmas, work and organizations* (pp. 143–164). Palgrave Macmillan. https://doi.org/10.1057/978-1-137-56476-4_8

Rose, J. (2021). Biopolitics, essential labor, and the political-economic crises of COVID-19. *Leisure Sciences, 43*(1–2), 211–217. https://doi.org/10.1080/01490400.2020.1774004

Slutskaya, N., Game, A., Morgan, R., & Newton, T. (2023). When two worlds collide: The role of affect in 'essential' worker responses to shifting evaluative norms. *Sociology, 57*(1), 211–227. https://doi.org/10.1177/00380385221101795

Stevano, S., Ali, R., & Jamieson, M. (2020). Essential for what? A global social reproduction view on the re-organisation of work during the COVID-19 pandemic. *Canadian Journal of Development Studies/Revue Canadienne d'Études du Développement*, *42*(1–2), 178–199. https://doi.org/10.1080/02255189.2020.1834362

Summa Stratégie. (2021). *Rapport cinglant sur les CHSLD à Québec*. https://summastrategies.ca/2021/11/29/rapport-cinglant-sur-les-chsld-a-quebec/

Syed, I., Daly, T., Armstrong, P., Lowndes, R., Chadoin, M., & Naidoo, V. (2016). How do work hierarchies and strict divisions of labour impact care workers' experiences of health and safety? Case studies of long term care in Toronto. *The Journal of Nursing Home Research Sciences*, *2*(1), 41–49. https://www.ncbi.nlm.nih.gov/pmc/articles/PMC5218838/#:~:text=Task%20orientation%20combined%20with%20a,that%20is%20to%20be%20completed

The Canadian Press. (2020, October 21). Les ratios ne sont pas sécuritaires en CHSLD dans plusieurs régions, selon la FIQ. *Le Devoir*. https://www.ledevoir.com/societe/sante/588199/les-ratios-ne-sont-pas-securitaires-en-chsld-dans-plusieurs-regions-selon-la-fiq

Théroux, G. (2022, March 29). *Prolongation des « primes covid » pour au moins quatre semaines*. Noovo-Info. https://www.noovo.info/nouvelle/les-primes-covid-en-sante-continuent-mais.html

Tremblay, É., & Benigeri, M. (2020). *Première vague de la pandémie de COVID-19 au Québec: Regard sur les facteurs associés aux hospitalisations et aux décès – État des pratiques une production de l'Institut national d'excellence en santé et en services sociaux*. Institut National d'Excellence en Santé et en Services Sociaux. https://numerique.banq.qc.ca/patrimoine/details/52327/4198245

TVA Nouvelles. (2020, June 19). *Conditions des futurs préposés: Une injustice pour les autres travailleurs, dénoncent les syndicats*. https://www.tvanouvelles.ca/2020/06/19/conditions-des-futurs-preposes-une-injustice-pour-les-autres-travailleurs-denoncent-les-syndicats

TVA Nouvelles. (2022, January 10). *Les hospitalisations ont quintuplé en seulement 3 semaines au Québec*. https://www.tvanouvelles.ca/2022/01/10/les-hospitalisations-ont-quintuple-en-seulement-3-semaines

Tyler, M., & Cohen, L. (2010). Spaces that matter: Gender performativity and organizational space. *Organization Studies*, *31*(2), 175–198. https://doi.org/10.1177/0170840609357381

Usher, S., Denis, J. L., Préval, J., Baker, R., Chreim, S., Kreindler, S., Breton, M., & Côté-Boileau, É. (2021). Learning from health system reform trajectories in seven Canadian provinces. *Health Economics, Policy and Law*, *14*(4), 383–399. https://doi.org/10.1017/S1744133120000225

Webb, C. (2021). Giving everyone a fish: COVID-19 and the new politics of distribution. *Anthropologica*, *63*(1), 1–16. https://doi.org/10.18357/anthropologica6312021275

Williams, J. C., Anderson, N., Holloway, T., Samford, E., Eugene, J., & Isom, J. (2020). Reopening the United States: Black and Hispanic workers are essential and expendable again. *American Journal of Public Health*, *110*(10), 1506–1508. https://doi.org/10.2105/AJPH.2020.305879

Yin, R. K. (2014). *Case study research design and methods* (5th ed.). Sage Publications.

CHAPTER 6

ESSENTIAL WORKERS IN THE UNITED STATES: AN INTERSECTIONAL PERSPECTIVE

Caroline Hanley[a] and Enobong Hannah Branch[b]

[a]William & Mary, USA
[b]Rutgers University-New Brunswick, USA

ABSTRACT

Public health measures implemented early in the COVID-19 pandemic brought the idea of essential work into the public discourse, as the public reflected upon what types of work are essential for society to function, who performs that work, and how the labour of essential workers is rewarded. This chapter focusses on the rewards associated with essential work. The authors develop an intersectional lens on work that was officially deemed essential in 2020 to highlight longstanding patterns of devaluation among essential workers, including those undergirded by systemic racism in employment and labour law. The authors use quantitative data from the CPS-MORG to examine earnings differences between essential and non-essential workers and investigate whether the essential worker wage gap changed from month to month in 2020. The authors find that patterns of valuation among essential workers cannot be explained by human capital or other standard labour market characteristics. Rather, intersectional wage inequalities in 2020 reflect historical patterns that are highly durable and did not abate in the first year of the global pandemic.

Keywords: Essential work; intersectional; race and ethnicity; gender; wage gap; COVID-19 pandemic

INTRODUCTION

In the first year of the COVID-19 pandemic, the concept of essential work generated popular debate over issues of visibility and valuation. While many Americans sheltered at home in spring 2020 as schools closed and non-essential businesses were shuttered under emergency public health orders, frontline workers employed in fields deemed essential reported to work. Some essential work was performed remotely, and therefore remained less visible, but traditional and social media called new attention to millions of workers whose labour often goes unnoticed: not just the doctors and nurses who staff hospitals, but also the health technicians, cleaners, and cafeteria workers who keep a hospital or nursing home running; not just the cashiers who take our money and bag our purchases in grocery stores but also those who pick, process, and pack our food before it arrives in the stores; and the ranks of transit, warehouse, and postal or other delivery workers who make it possible to purchase almost anything from the comfort of home. In short, in the spring of 2020 and beyond there was a newfound recognition of the interconnectedness of different types of work.

The idea of essential work, which entered public discourse as an administrative concept used to implement state and federal public health emergency measures, quickly took on new resonance and meaning as a concept informing public debate over what types of work are essential for society to function, who performs that work, and how the labour of essential workers is rewarded. In this chapter, we ask *how did essentiality affect wages during the first year of the global pandemic*? To answer this question, we advance an intersectional perspective on the valuation of essential work in the United States that foregrounds the way socially constructed dimensions of difference intersect to shape the social relations that generate and sustain inequalities (Misra et al., 2021). Specifically, we explain how race, ethnicity, and gender have historically been used to assign workers to workplace roles (segregation) and assign value to those roles based on their racial, ethnic, and gender composition (devaluation) such that intersectional inequalities are woven into the fabric of work in the United States (Stainback & Tomaskovic-Devey, 2012). Most jobs officially designated as essential in 2020 have origins in reproductive labour traditionally performed by women and, especially, women of colour (Glenn, 1992; Wooten & Branch, 2013), and as such essential work reflects highly racialized and gendered patterns of devaluation – including those undergirded by the legacy of systemic racism in labour and employment law.

The chapter makes three empirical claims based on quantitative analysis of labour market data from the CPS-MORG in 2020. First, we examine earnings differences between essential and non-essential workers and show that there is a substantial essential work wage gap that cannot be explained by either standard labour market characteristics (including human capital) or workers' race/ethnicity and gender. Rather, the essential worker wage gap in the United States derives from a wider pattern of industrial and occupational wage differences that is highly racialized and gendered. Second, we use the monthly survey design of the CPS-MORG dataset to investigate change in the essential worker wage gap and find no evidence that the effect of essential worker status on wages shifted during the first year of the pandemic, as the sharp rise in unemployment starting in March 2020 that increased earnings in low-wage sectors of the economy (Autor et al., 2023) produced comparable wage gains among essential and non-essential workers. Third, we investigate patterns of valuation among essential workers and find that intersectional wage inequalities reflect historical patterns that are highly durable and did not abate in the first year of the global pandemic. Among essential and non-essential workers, Black and Hispanic/Latinx workers are highly concentrated in the jobs with the lowest pay and weakest employment protections. Gender is an important determinant of pay but the magnitude of the gendered employment advantages that accrue to men and the disadvantages experienced by women vary greatly by race and ethnicity. Intersectional wage gaps are robust to essential worker status and sector, human capital, unionization, detailed industry and occupation, and a range of other controls. Altogether, our empirical findings suggest that essential worker status is less important for understanding the distribution of labour market rewards than is labour market power: long-standing patterns of unequal opportunity and devaluation have served to maintain inequalities among essential workers that mirror the wider labour market. The chapter concludes with a discussion of how essentiality as a cultural frame may be mobilized to advance better pay and working conditions in the future.

WHAT IS ESSENTIAL WORK? WHO ARE ESSENTIAL WORKERS?

In their classic functionalist account of social stratification, sociologists Kingsley Davis and Wilbert E. Moore (1945) argued that essentiality – defined as the necessity of the social function that is fulfilled by a task – is central to explaining both who does what and who gets what in a complex society. According to Davis and Moore, social stability rests on making sure that necessary social roles are filled, and more functionally critical roles must be highly rewarded to encourage people to develop the specialized skills those roles require. Pay therefore aligns with the functional importance of the labour and the scarcity of the skills required to perform the task. In his critique of the Davis and Moore thesis, sociologist Melvin Tumin (1953) observed that socially necessary functions do not always require highly specialized skills; that the process by which individuals aspire to and are matched with particular social roles cannot be reduced to the incentives attached to those roles; and that there is nothing objective or inevitable about the compensation received for performing a particular role in society. Rather, Tumin argued that social inequality rests on social, economic, and political power, including the power to decide what roles are considered functionally important and therefore highly valued in society. In this section, we continue the conversation about essentiality that Davis and Moore started over 70 years ago by examining the concept of essential work from a sociological perspective. We highlight the range of functionally interrelated jobs that were officially considered essential in 2020 and the centrality of race/ethnicity and gender for understanding essential work in the United States.

To advance a sociological perspective on essential work and workers, we build on the concept of reproductive labour. Taking as a starting point Karl Marx's observation that capitalist production relies on the reproduction of workers' labour power with labour to produce the necessities of life, intersectional feminist scholars use the term reproductive labour to more broadly refer to 'the creation and recreation of people as cultural and social, as well as physical, beings' (Glenn, 1992, p.4). According to this conception, reproductive labour includes a wide range of caring and cleaning roles traditionally performed by women in both household and institutional settings: child and elder care, food preparation, healthcare, and cleaning or janitorial work. The commodification of social reproduction deepened the specialization (or task specificity) of such services, such that labour attending to 'emotional support, amusement, and companionship' can also be considered reproductive labour (Glenn, 1992, p. 6). This broad conception of reproductive labour may include recreational and community-based services performed in the private sector or by non-profit and government institutions.

Race, ethnicity, and gender are closely intertwined in reproductive labour, such that it follows a strong racial/ethnic division of labour among women and relies increasingly on the labour of men who are racial and ethnic minorities. Glenn (1992) argues that the commodification of reproductive labour and its attending specialization have divided tasks across a hierarchy in which more visible and 'clean' forms of reproductive labour (including supervisory work) have historically been reserved for white women, while Black, Hispanic or Latinx, and Asian women were traditionally assigned to invisible and 'dirty' work (see also Branch, 2011; Wooten & Branch, 2013). Race and ethnicity also intersect with gender among men in their relationship to reproductive labour. Duffy (2007) shows that from 1900 to 2000, as 'dirty' cleaning and cooking tasks were transformed from relations of household servitude to institutional service work, Black and Hispanic or Latino men became more reliant on this form of work. In the US context, caring and cleaning labour is highly gendered and racialized because its transition to the market progressed from relations of enslavement and servitude – primarily based in white homes and entailing the labour of Black, Mexican American, Asian American, and immigrant women – to a highly specialized and stratified service industry (Branch & Wooten, 2012; Glenn, 1992).

The idea of reproductive labour as rooted in caring and cleaning provides a useful starting point for thinking sociologically about essential work in 2020. Following the World Health Organization's designation of COVID-19 as a pandemic on 11 March, the United States issued a national emergency on 13 March. On 16 March, the federal government announced social distancing guidelines that aimed to 'flatten the curve' of disease transmission by limiting large group gatherings, restricting travel, and urging people to stay at home as much as possible (Gostin et al., 2020; Harris, 2020). On 29 March, the Department of Homeland Security's Cybersecurity and Infrastructure Security Agency (CISA) issued an advisory memo on the identification of 'critical infrastructure' workers to guide state and local responses to the public health emergency (Council of State Governments, n.d.; Krebs, 2020; National Governors Association, 2020). State and local mandates temporarily closed 'non-essential' businesses for varying lengths of time, with some states starting a staged reopening of non-essential businesses as early as April 2020 and the US Department of Labor issuing health and safety guidelines for reopening on 18 June 2020 (McPhillips, 2020; Miller, 2020; U.S. Department of Labor, 2020). The idea of essential work thus emerged as an administrative concept used to guide business closures due to the public health emergency.

The CISA memo's conception of critical infrastructure is broad – ranging from healthcare to commercial custodial and sanitation services; from agriculture and transportation to utilities and finance; and from emergency first responders to government social services. The memo's list of essential jobs also includes retail employees in establishments that sell food and medicine, educators, workers who care for the elderly or the disabled, and childcare workers supporting parents employed in other essential fields (Krebs, 2020). In the days and weeks that followed, state and local governments, activists, and think tanks used the CISA framework to inform regulation and advocacy around essential work.

A close examination of the forms of work included in the CISA report clarifies how the official designation of essentiality aligns with and goes beyond the concept of reproductive labour as rooted in caring and cleaning work. Table 6.1 lists the twelve sectors of work deemed essential in the CISA report, selects detailed occupations included in each of those sectors to illustrate the nature and range of the work included, and each sector's share of all essential work.[1] Based on this definition of essential work, we estimate that about 27% of all jobs performed in the United States were officially designated as essential in 2020. Table 6.1 shows that essential work sectors with close ties to reproductive labour – health care, food and agriculture, and commercial services and sanitation – together account for 57.7% of all essential work. Government and community-based services, which include forms of work that could fall into a broader conception of reproductive labour as discussed above, account for an additional 10.8% of essential work. In addition to work with origins in reproductive labour, transportation, warehouse, and delivery workers account for another 11.1% of all essential work. The CISA report also includes a number of smaller sectors focussed on utilities – communications/information technology (IT) (6.7%), energy (1.1%), and water and wastewater management (0.3%) – along with finance (6.8%), critical manufacturing (3.3%), emergency services (1.7%), and the chemical sector (0.6%) (Krebs, 2020).

Looking at specific occupations included in each essential work sector, we see a wide range of differences in the types of work performed and the social organization of that work. While some sectors include only one occupation, the detailed occupational differences among workers in most sectors speaks to how specialized the labour is in those fields and how interdependent is the labour of differently skilled workers in those sectors. For example, health care work is performed by specialized professional workers (physicians and registered nurses) who work closely with licensed practical nurses, health technicians, and health aides whose training is less specialized but whose role in supporting patient health is no less essential. To keep a hospital or doctor's office running, its workers must be fed and its building must be cleaned; food and other supplies must be delivered and

Table 6.1. Essential Work Sectors with Occupations, 2020.

Essential Sector	Select Occupations	Share of All Essential Jobs (%)
Health care	Registered nurses; nursing and home health aides; occupational therapy assistants and aids; licensed practical and vocational nurses; physicians	23.7
Food and agriculture	Agricultural workers; cooks; food service managers/supervisors (includes all grocery, convenience, and drug store workers)	18.0
Commercial services and sanitation	Construction laborers and carpenters (inc. supervisors); janitors and building cleaners; maids and housekeeping cleaners	16.0
Transportation, warehouse, and delivery	Drivers and truck drivers (inc. public transit); curriers and messengers; postal service mail carriers; labourers and freight/stock/material movers	11.1
Government and community-based services	Lawyers; courts and municipal clerks; public services eligibility interviewers; teachers (pre-K through secondary); childcare; counsellors and social workers	10.8
Financial sector	Financial managers; credit counsellors and loan officers; personal financial advisors; tellers; insurance underwriters	6.8
Communications and IT	Information/records clerks; telecommunications line installers/repairers; reporters; telephone operators; electronic home entertainment installers/repairers	6.7
Critical manufacturing	Welding; machinists; sheet metal workers; electrical/electronics assemblers; machine operators, setters, and tenders (metal and plastic)	3.3
Emergency services	Firefighters; police detectives and criminal investigators; first-line supervisors of police and detectives, correctional officers, and firefighting/prevention workers	1.7
Energy sector	Electrical and electronics engineers; electrical power line installers and repairers; derrick, rotary drill, and service unit operators in oil, gas, and mining; electrical repairs (industrial and utility); electrical and electronics repairs	1.1
Chemical sector	Chemical engineers	0.6
Water and wastewater management	Water and wastewater treatment plant and system operators	0.3

Source: Author calculation of CPS-MORG data; sectors with origins in reproductive labour shaded.

waste removed; stable provision of heating and cooling, water, electricity, and internet/phone service must be maintained; and patients' payments and insurance claims must be processed.

In short, commodified reproductive labour can be found across a wide array of industries and occupations. To maintain essential human and social reproduction, there is a high degree of functional interrelation among essential work sectors and the occupations within those sectors. In the next section, we advance an intersectional perspective on the valuation of essential work that highlights the institutional foundations of its working conditions and articulates expected sources of intersectional pay differences among essential workers. Based on existing studies, we argue that the effect of race, ethnicity, and gender on earnings is not limited to the marginal effects of intersectional status variables on the wages of workers performing the same workplace roles with the same human capital (discrimination). Rather, we explain how race, ethnicity, and gender have historically been used to assign workers to workplace roles (segregation) and assign value to those roles based on their racial, ethnic, and gender composition (devaluation) such that essential work is devalued in the United States.

AN INTERSECTIONAL PERSPECTIVE ON THE VALUATION OF ESSENTIAL WORK

To investigate the valuation of essential work we adopt an intersectional perspective. An intersectional approach to understanding social inequality foregrounds the way socially constructed dimensions of difference intersect to shape experiences and actions (Misra et al., 2021). Intersectional inequality research emphasizes oppression, including the relational operation of power, and it uses comparison to draw attention to the contexts, historical and otherwise, that construct social processes while also illustrating the potential for alternative paths (Misra et al., 2021). In this section, we use existing research to develop analytic tools for investigating the valuation of essential work in the United States through an intersectional lens. In particular, we theorize that low pay and poor working conditions in essential work derive from three interconnected processes: *segregation*, *discrimination*, and *devaluation*. According to this perspective, inequalities in essential work – most of which has its origins in the caring and cleaning work of reproductive labour – do not derive from neutral market-based processes. Rather, racial/ethnic and gender categories are foundational elements of economic life that deeply structure the division of labour (who does what) and patterns of compensation (who gets what). We begin with an overview of the intersectional pay gap literature, and then explain how we use this research to derive expectations for quantitative analysis of the pay gap between essential and non-essential workers, as well as intersectional pay gaps among essential workers.

Historical patterns of employment *segregation* continue to shape the allocation of workers to jobs by race, ethnicity, and gender. Good jobs – jobs that deliver high pay, security, and opportunities for advancement – have traditionally been more accessible to white male workers in the United States than members of other social groups (Bonacich, 1976; Branch, 2011; Branch & Hanley, 2022; Glenn & Tolbert, 1987; Milkman, 2020). Before the Civil Rights Movement and its culminating legislation to ban employment discrimination in 1964, employers routinely used race and gender to match workers with jobs, drawing on conceptions of skill and ideas about the cultural appropriateness of certain workers for certain workplace roles that were firmly rooted in racist and sexist ideologies (Branch, 2011; Glenn, 2004, 2010; Kaufman, 2002; Milkman, 2020; Reskin & Roos, 1990). Restrictions on equal educational opportunity were an additional mechanism that maintained a high degree of employment segregation by race/ethnicity and gender. In the post-Civil Rights Movement period, it is illegal to use race, ethnicity, and gender in hiring decisions but existing statutes are weakly enforced (Stainback & Tomaskovic-Devey, 2012). Despite a burst of progress in reducing racial and gender inequality in occupational outcomes in the 1970s, employer preferences continue to influence the allocation of workers to jobs and the US labour market therefore remains highly stratified (Branch & Hanley, 2022; Browne & Misra, 2003). The degree of racial/ethnic and gender segregation observed in the United States is even greater when employment is measured at the workplace or establishment level (Tomaskovic-Devey et al., 2020). As a result, a racial/ethnic and gender hierarchy in occupational attainment persists despite convergence in educational attainment across racial/ethnic and gender groups (Pettit & Ewert, 2009).

Race/ethnicity and gender continue to shape access to occupational positions and the earnings rewards they carry (Kaufman, 2002). Women in minority racial and ethnic groups sustain smaller gender wage penalties than non-Hispanic white women, relative to men within their own racial and ethnic groups, but the combined effects of race/ethnicity and gender mean that white women are advantaged relative to minority women in pay (Greenman & Xie, 2008). Conversely, men's earnings advantages do not accrue equally across racial and ethnic groups. Racial/ethnic and gender differences in educational and, especially, occupational attainment are important sources of intersectional earnings differences (Dozier, 2010; Greenman & Xie, 2008; Mandel & Semyonov, 2016; Pettit & Ewert, 2009). In addition, union membership is associated with lower racial wage gaps among women (Rosenfeld & Kleykamp, 2012). In a comprehensive analysis spanning the 40-year period of 1970–2010, Mandel and Semyonov (2016) found that racial earnings inequality among men and women narrowed markedly in the 1970s, following a burst of progress in educational and occupational opportunity, declined at a slow rate from 1980 to 2000, and increased in the first decade of the 21st century despite continued improvements in educational attainment. The racial/ethnic and gender wage gap is sustained by high levels of income inequality in the full labour market, the persistence of occupational segregation (including job segregation, see Tomaskovic-Devey et al., 2020), and growth in the unexplained portion of the earnings gap (Mandel & Semyonov, 2016).

An additional source of intersectional wage inequality is *discrimination*, or unequal pay for equal work. Scholars marshal direct and indirect evidence on the persistence of pay discrimination in the US labour market. Unexplained variance in racial/ethnic and gender wage gaps is often attributed to discrimination (e.g. Dozier, 2010; Huffman & Cohen, 2004; Kmec, 2003; Mandel & Semyonov, 2016), and this interpretation is supported by experimental research showing that race/ethnicity and gender bias workplace evaluations of productivity and merit (e.g. Castilla, 2008, 2012, 2015). Discrimination is also understood as an underlying mechanism when members of racial/ethnic minority groups and women derive unequal returns to their educational attainment, ceteris paribus (Moss & Tilly, 2001). For example, Black women receive lower wages than white women, on average, even when they hold the same educational credentials and work in the same occupation and industry groups (Branch & Hanley, 2017; Dozier, 2010).

The persistence of pay discrimination notwithstanding, group differences in earnings across occupations and industries should not be reified as neutral or market-based and, therefore, legitimate. Research on *devaluation* shows that some categories of work are systematically paid less because the people who perform that work are valued less within society (e.g. Cech, 2013; Levanon et al., 2009; Mandel, 2013). The devaluation of work may reflect ongoing dynamics, as when demographic change in an occupational workforce produces a contemporaneous change in its compensation. Alternatively, the historical association of a certain type of work with workers of a lower social status can continue to keep wages low in that field. As a result, the pay differences that accrue to workers across occupational or industrial categories appear to be a result of race- and gender-neutral market processes, when in fact they reflect longstanding patterns of unequal opportunity. Taking a closer look at US labour history clarifies how industrial and occupational differences in compensation reflect a legacy of systemic racial/ethnic and gender inequality.

New Deal legislation defining the terms of the employment relationship in the United States and establishing labour organizing rights was marked by systemic racism. The National Labor Relations Act of 1935, also called the Wagner Act, created a government-adjudicated process for forming a union that does not rely on direct action tactics, along with the right to collective bargaining and protection from retaliation. These organizing rights did not apply to agricultural and domestic workers. The government agency created to enforce the Wagner Act, the National Labor Relations Board (NLRB), holds jurisdiction over a select group of private employers that is defined based on revenue thresholds, meaning that workers employed by smaller establishments – which is common in the retail and hospitality industries – are not covered (National Labor Relations Board, n.d.). The Fair Labor Standards Act (FLSA) of 1938 established wage and hours laws including a federal minimum wage and the right to overtime, based on a legal definition of employers and employees that exempted certain forms of contract and contingent ('nonstandard') employment relations disproportionately performed by women and minorities (Branch & Hanley, 2022). Like the Wagner Act, the FLSA also included industry-based exemptions for agricultural and domestic work, and it formalized the use of tipping and a subminimum wage in the restaurant industry (Jayaraman, 2016). Industry-based exemptions in the Wagner Act and FLSA were not only racially disparate in impact – given the high degree of industrial and occupational segregation in the United States – they were explicitly designed to depress wages and maintain racial/ethnic and gender inequalities in the labour market. Industry-based exemptions were used to build the legislative coalition to pass these measures, which included representatives from Southern and Southwestern states who would not support employment protections that could upset the racial/ethnic and gender division of labour in their districts (Katznelson, 2005; Mettler, 1998; Milkman, 2020; Perea, 2011).

Skill-based occupational pay differences that predate the New Deal similarly reflect highly racialized and gendered processes. Historically, the idea of skilled (vs unskilled) labour was often mobilized on the shop floor to maintain racial/ethnic and gender inequality in access to good jobs and to justify low wages and poor working conditions for Black and Brown workers excluded from such work. The concept of skilled work (expressed in the early 20th-century occupational classification of jobs) developed, in part, to maintain a strict racial-gender division of labour that functioned as a way of maintaining advantages for white and male workers and legitimizing the unequal distribution of workplace rewards across racial and gender lines, including in highly specialized and functionally interdependent divisions of labour (e.g. Branch & Hanley, 2022; Kaufman, 2002; Steinberg, 1990). Over time, occupational roles defined around racialized and gendered ideas about skill have continued to be systematically devalued (Branch, 2011; Kaufman, 2002; Kessler-Harris, 1990; Steinberg, 1990). The rewards associated with skills – observed in occupational classifications or workers' human capital – are therefore rooted in historically unequal social processes that can obscure the interconnectedness of different forms of labour. 'Skill as a productive capacity exists, not in people as isolated individuals, but in relation to the task complexity of jobs as they are linked to other jobs in organizational divisions of labor' (Avent-Holt & Tomaskovic-Devey, 2023, p. 218).

Racialized and gendered conceptions of skill that were mobilized to maintain differences in occupational pay continue to justify low pay for forms of work traditionally performed by women and people of colour, including reproductive labour, even as the explicit racial and gender ideologies that were used to justify occupational pay differences have receded. Weak enforcement of low-wage workers' employment and labour rights, particularly in food-based, janitorial, and other industries highly reliant on immigrant labour, sustain low pay and poor working conditions for workers in those fields today (Milkman, 2020). Workers in small firms that do not meet revenue thresholds for NLRB oversight, which are concentrated in the retail, restaurant, hospitality, and health/childcare industries (Choi & Spletzer, 2012; National Labor Relations Board, n.d.), are particularly vulnerable to low pay and poor working conditions. Forms of work disproportionately performed by women and racial/ethnic minorities are systematically lacking in robust enforcement of employment rights and operate according to workplace norms of low pay that have deep historical roots.

While early research on essential work during the COVID-19 pandemic has confirmed that it is disproportionately performed by women and people of colour, existing studies of essential worker pay and working conditions in the United States have not parsed the intersectional nature of these inequalities by situating them within the context of historically produced inequalities (Tilly, 1998; Tomaskovic-Devey & Avent-Holt, 2019). Contemporary employment conditions – such as the rewards associated with a particular occupation, unionization, or industry norms of consistent enforcement of wage and hours laws – reflect historically rooted patterns of social inequality that are not easily captured in quantitative analysis. This is important for understanding essential work. Most jobs officially designated as essential in 2020 have origins in the caring and cleaning work of reproductive labour that was traditionally performed by women and, especially, women of colour (Glenn, 1992; Wooten & Branch, 2013).

We therefore expect to see lower wages in essential work than in non-essential work, all things equal, owing to the prevalence of devalued reproductive labour in the essential workforce and the way that historical patterns of devaluation have been legitimized by industrial exemptions to labour/employment law and occupational skill classifications. Further, we expect to see intersectional pay gaps among essential workers that mirror the contours of pay inequality in the wider labour market, including those that cannot be explained by observable characteristics of the work or workers. Yet existing research suggests that the effect of race/ethnicity and gender on wages cannot be reduced to the marginal effects of these variables: differences in job quality related to industrial and occupational status reflect the way that race and gender have historically been used to classify different forms of work as more or less valuable based on the social value of the workers. The historical valuation of workers based on racist and sexist ideologies was written into systems of industrial and occupational job classification such that the effect of race/ethnicity and gender on wages cannot be completely disentangled from industry and occupation wage effects. Finally, given the entrenched and durable nature of racial/ethnic and gender inequalities in the US labour market, we expect to find that neither the essential work wage gap nor intersectional wage inequalities among essential workers abated over the first year of the global pandemic, despite the increased visibility of essential work and workers in 2020.

DATA AND METHODS

In this section, we describe the data source and sample, the measurement of key variables, and the analytic strategy that guides the analysis.

Data Source and Sample

To assess the relations between essentiality, the intersection of race/ethnicity and gender, and earnings during the first year of the COVID-19 pandemic, we draw on the Current Population Survey's Merged Outgoing Rotation Group file (CPS-MORG) from 2020, accessed via the National Bureau of Economic Research website. The CPS is a monthly household survey ($n = 50,000–60,000$ households per month) conducted by the US Department of Labor's Bureau of Labor Statistics to measure labour force participation and employment. Each household that enters the nationally representative CPS sample is interviewed each month for four months, ignored for 8 months, then interviewed again for four more months, with hours and earnings questions asked of households in their fourth and eighth month of interviews. The MORG is an extract of CPS data that includes only these 'outgoing' (months 4 and 8) interviews. We limit the analysis to employed household members with valid earnings data, yielding a sample of 126,524 respondents in 2020.

In our description of essential work, we do not limit the sample to only the 'working age' population as is often done in labour market research. Rather, we include all jobholders (public and private sector workers who are not self-employed) including teens and those over retirement age, yielding a jobholding sample that ranges in age from 16 to 84. There are valid reasons to consider excluding these groups of young and old workers when examining earnings, however: assumptions that non-working age populations are weakly attached to the labour market or that their livelihoods do not depend on their earnings could bias certain types of earnings analysis. Yet excluding young and old workers from the sample of employed jobholders could limit our understanding of who performed essential work in the United States during the first year of the global pandemic in substantively meaningful ways. Table AI disaggregates all jobs, all essential jobs, and different sectors of essential work into four age groups: teenagers (16–19), college age (20–23), working age (24–64), and retirement age (65 and older). While teens and retirement age workers comprise 3.2% and 6.6% of all job holders, respectively, the age distribution of some essential sectors varies greatly. For example, 9.1% of food and agricultural workers are teens and 6.1% are 65 years or older. Communications and IT have a high share of teen workers (7.8%), and over 11% of government and community-based service workers are at retirement age. We limit the multivariate analysis of earnings to the working age population, ages 24–64 ($n = 106,609$), to reduce unexplained variance and therefore bolster our interpretation of estimated marginal wage gaps, discussed in more detail below. In analyses in which we utilize the monthly sampling design of the MORG to test whether the effect of essential worker status on earnings changes over time, the sample of working age earners varies from 7,661 (July) to 10,123 (January).

Variable Measurement

The dependent variable in the multivariate analysis is *weekly earnings*. The CPS-MORG reports weekly earnings for all hourly and salaried employees. Self-employed workers are excluded from the analysis due to the difficulty of comparing their compensation with those of employees. We convert the weekly earnings estimate to 2015 dollars using the Consumer Price Index research series (CPI-U-RS $2015). Outliers (i.e. those earning less than $0.50 or more than $100 per hour in 1989 dollars) were trimmed, following the procedures described in Mishel et al. (2009).

We examine the effect of two focal variables on weekly earnings: essential (vs non-essential) worker status; and the intersection of race/ethnicity * gender. We use the terms pay gap and wage gap interchangeably to refer to the marginal effect of a focal variable on weekly wages, relative to the reference category.

We identify essential workers using the Economic Policy Institute's coding scheme, which is based on the US Department of Homeland Security's CISA memo and includes a range of industries and occupations representing both frontline (non-remote) and other critical infrastructure roles (McNicholas & Poydock, 2020). The resulting *essential work* variable includes a non-essential reference category and the following essential sectors (based on both industry and occupation data): food services and agriculture; emergency services; transportation, warehouse, and delivery workers; commercial (building) services and sanitation;

health care; government and community-based services; communications and IT; financial sector; energy sector; water and wastewater management; chemical sector; and critical manufacturing. This inclusive definition of essential work, while rooted in reproductive labour, allows for comparisons across the essential/non-essential divide and across different types of work officially considered essential in 2020, yielding leverage to empirically parse the role of essentiality versus forms of workplace or labour market power in the valuation of work. The analysis does not, however, distinguish between 'frontline' and other essential workers, a distinction based on the ability to work remotely. A pre-pandemic study of telework estimated that only about 8.3% of workers in agriculture and 26% of workers in retail trade or transportation were able to work from home, compared with 69.9% of professional and business services, 65.3% of public administration, and 48.9% of education and health service workers (Dey et al., 2020).

Following an intersectional approach (e.g. Browne & Misra, 2003; Misra et al., 2021), we compare the experiences of men and women across racial and ethnic groups and seek to situate our interpretation of trends in the contextualized social relations of each type of essential employment. We measure *race/ethnicity* with five mutually exclusive categories: non-Hispanic white, non-Hispanic Black; Hispanic or Latino/a, non-Hispanic Asian, and non-Hispanic multiracial. (While interrogating the intersection of race with ethnicity represents an important topic for intersectional labour market research, parsing those dynamics is beyond the scope of this chapter.) We measure *gender* with a dummy variable for female. All descriptive analysis therefore includes 10 separate racial/ethnic and gender groups. Many studies of labour market inequality use separate multivariate models for men and women with a variable for race or ethnicity, making it difficult to foreground comparison of how racial/ethnic earnings effects vary by gender. We choose, instead, to combine women and men in a single model and use interaction terms for *race/ethnicity*gender* to parse intersectional inequalities (reference=non-Hispanic white men).

We include measures of work and worker characteristics to parse the sources of observed wage gaps. We control for *union* membership given the well-documented positive relationship between earnings and unionization, noting the way that labour law designed opportunities to unionize in ways that remain systematically restrictive along racial/ethnic and gender lines. We include a measure of *citizenship* (a dummy variable with US citizens coded 1) to account for the importance of legal status in the application and enforcement of employment rights (e.g. Gleeson, 2016). We control for human capital with measures of educational attainment and *potential experience* (age and age-squared). We measure *educational attainment* with a categorical measure of years of schooling completed: less than high school (less than 12 years education, which is the reference category in multivariate analysis); high school (12 years); some college (1–3 years of postsecondary schooling); college (4 years of postsecondary education); and advanced degree (more than 4 years of postsecondary education). Family structure figures heavily into gendered employment experiences, including hours worked (Tilly, 1996), in ways that vary by race (e.g. Branch & Hanley, 2022). We therefore control for *usual hours worked per week* and *marital status* (never married, which is the reference category; married; and divorced/widowed). Geography shapes exposure to economic opportunity (e.g. Branch & Hanley, 2011). We therefore include a control variable for *region* (Northeast, which is the reference category; Middle Atlantic; South Atlantic; East South Central; West South Central; East North Central; West North Central; Mountain; Pacific) and a dummy variable for *rural* (vs urban) residence.

Beyond these work and worker characteristics, we control for detailed (four-digit) measures of industry and occupation. Enduring patterns of racial/ethnic and gender segregation across industries and, especially, occupations are an important source of earnings gaps. While detailed industry and detailed occupation are not direct measures of segregation, they tap into well-documented patterns of differential access to good job opportunities along racial/ethnic and gender lines, and therefore provide a basis for estimating the contribution of discrimination and/or job (establishment) segregation to observed wage gaps. Within sociological labour market research, *industries* are important for understanding differences in pay and working conditions for two reasons. First, firms that operate within shared product or service markets compete with one another for customers and are therefore responsive to similar competitive pressures that shape managerial practices and labour relations. Second, working conditions and pay within industries reflect an ongoing legacy of historical exemptions from employment and labour law. *Occupations*, by contrast, are important for understanding differences in pay and working conditions because of the central role of skill in earnings determination. The history of skills-based workplace organizing means that occupations reflect not only the shared competencies or skills that workers within those job groupings share, but also the legacy of a process to define those roles as skilled, often in relation to other excluded roles (Avent-Holt & Tomaskovic-Devey, 2023). While this analysis cannot adjudicate competing underlying mechanisms for industrial and occupational effects on earnings, we introduce categorical measures of detailed (4-digit) industry and detailed (4-digit) occupation to evaluate the extent to which they contribute to observed wage gaps (coefficients not shown, available upon request).

Analytic Approach

To investigate the valuation of essential work, including intersectional differences in pay among essential workers, we first describe key characteristics of essential work and workers and then parse the sources of wage gaps associated with two focal variables: (1) essential (vs non-essential) worker status and (2) the intersection of race/ethnicity and gender. We evaluate the impact of essential worker and intersectional status on weekly wages using ordinary least squares (OLS) regression analysis, drawing on different model specifications to highlight the sources of wage gaps. (Statistically significant wage gaps are graphically displayed in the results section; a table with full model results is available in the Appendix.) We report the estimated wage gaps for all essential work (relative to all non-essential work) and then shift our focus to intersectional pay gaps to highlight how the interaction of race/ethnicity and gender shapes earnings among essential and non-essential workers alike. We introduce a categorical measure of *month of survey* (reference = January) to investigate whether essential and intersectional wage gaps vary over time during the first year of the pandemic.

In the baseline model we report a bivariate estimate of the effect of essential status on weekly wages (Model 0). We then strategically introduce the variables discussed above. Model 1 estimates the marginal effect of essential status taking basic labour market controls including human capital into account, Model 2 adds the intersectional status variables discussed above, and Model 3 introduces controls for detailed industry and detailed occupation. Model 4 adds the month of survey variable to test whether essential and intersectional wage gaps moderate over time, and Model 5 asks whether the intersection of month of survey * essential worker status yields a significant effect on wages.

Comparing estimated wage gaps across models shows the extent to which characteristics of the work and workers contribute to the focal wage gaps. We consider the intersectional wage gaps estimated across Models 2–5 to be a range that reflects historically based intersectional processes of valuation. In the interpretation of results, we emphasize that job classifications based on industry and occupation are codifications of historical power inequalities among workers that may also reflect unobserved contemporary dynamics of pay discrimination and/or job (establishment) segregation.

We conclude the analysis with three robustness checks. First, we repeat the analysis described above with a categorical variable specifying wage gaps for different *essential work sectors* (relative to all non-essential work) to check the substantive interpretation of our findings, looking in particular at the wage gaps in sectors with historical origins in reproductive labour and in which the work is disproportionately performed by racial/ethnic minorities and/or women. Attention to wage differences across different sectors of work that were officially deemed essential in 2020 clarifies the role of essentiality versus forms of workplace power in the valuation of work. Second, we repeat our multivariate analysis of the working age population (ages 24–64) for the full jobholding population (age 16–84) to test for disparate results due to the particular employment experiences of teens, college-age workers, and retirement age workers. The findings were substantively similar, so we focus the discussion of results on the working age population (results available upon request). Finally, we also repeated all analyses using the natural log of weekly wages as the dependent variable to test whether wage outliers were driving any of the findings and found no evidence of outlier bias (results available on request).

RESULTS

We begin by describing the characteristics of essential work in 2020, including across essential work sectors, and then document the racial/ethnic and gender division of labour in essential work, before examining essential worker and intersectional status wage gaps. Looking first at the aggregate characteristics of essential work (in bold), Table 6.2 shows that essential workers on average have lower

Table 6.2. Characteristics of Essential Work, 2020.

	Mean Weekly Earnings ($2015)	Share Workers with College Degree Or More (%)	Mean Hours Worked Per Week	Share Workers Part-Time (%)	Share Union Member (%)	Share Workers Women (%)	Share Workers Non-Hispanic White (%)
Health care	917.52	43.6	38.1	18.7	4.8	76.4	65.0
Food and agriculture	634.24	17.4	36.3	26.1	5.2	45.7	56.1
Commercial services and sanitation	813.56	10.7	38.2	11.0	12.0	15.8	55.9
Transportation, warehouse, and delivery	872.47	15.8	40.9	11.4	23.3	24.8	60.5
Government and community-based services	970.86	58.9	37.2	19.6	8.7	73.9	67.2
Financial sector	1,329.97	61.0	40.8	6.0	2.3	58.5	75.6
Communications and IT	700.71	28.0	36.1	21.1	6.7	60.8	64.0
Critical manufacturing	853.47	5.2	41.1	3.5	14.2	10.3	73.7
Emergency services	1,250.15	37.7	48.8	2.9	54.6	14.9	76.4
Energy sector	1,476.12	46.3	43.5	2.2	19.3	5.9	77.7
Chemical sector	1,224.36	50.4	41.8	5.7	10.0	21.0	74.1
Water and wastewater management	969.34	19.4	39.8	2.5	27.3	6.6	85.0
All essential jobs	878.06	31.3	38.4	16.4	9.8	49.7	63.5
All jobs	967.68	40.7	38.1	15.7	10.8	49.0	68.4

Source: Author calculation of CPS-MORG data; sectors with origins in reproductive labour shaded.

weekly earnings than all US workers ($878 per week, compared with $967 per week, respectively) despite the same mean number of hours worked per week (38) and a similar share of work that is part-time (15.7% in the full workforce compared with 16.4% of the essential workforce). Essential workers complete higher education at a lower rate than the full employed population (31.3% with at least a college degree, compared with 40.7%) and have slightly lower rates of union membership (9.8% vs 10.8%). Essential work in the aggregate is comparable to all jobs in its gender composition: about 49% of all workers in 2020 were women, compared with 49.7% of essential workers. Yet essential jobs are disproportionately performed by racial and ethnic minorities, with 68.4% of all jobs but only 63.5% of essential jobs held by non-Hispanic white workers. These aggregate measures of essential work characteristics obscure important variation across essential sectors.

As discussed above, the three largest essential sectors – health care (representing 23.7% of the essential workforce) food and agriculture (18%) and commercial (building) services and sanitation (16%) – are sectors with origins in the caring and cleaning work of reproductive labour. Women are highly overrepresented in health care (76.4%), relative to their share of the total working population, while non-Hispanic white workers are highly under-represented in both food and agriculture and commercial (building) services and sanitation. Rounding out the top five essential worker sectors, transportation, warehouse, and delivery workers account for 11.1% of the essential workforce, and government and community-based service workers comprise 10.8%. Transportation, warehouse, and delivery workers are disproportionately male and non-white, while government and community-based service workers are disproportionately women (73.9%) and non-white. The top essential work sectors vary greatly in terms of their workers' pay, educational attainment, and other characteristics. Low pay among essential workers is not confined to sectors with origins in reproductive labour – communications and IT workers are paid almost as little as workers in food and agriculture – but there is a clear correlation between the racial-ethnic and gender composition of essential work sectors and average compensation. Smaller essential work sectors such as emergency services and the energy and chemical sectors are highly paid, particularly for their workers' levels of educational attainment, and their workforces skew male and white. Rates of union membership are varied across low-pay sectors, ranging from 5.2% in food and agriculture to 12% in commercial (building) services and sanitation.

To what extent is essential work organized around a racial/ethnic and gender division of labour? To answer this question, we use a measure of representation calculated by taking the share of essential work performed by each racial/ethnic and gender group and adjusting it for the overall size of that group in the employed population (Table 6.3). Groups with a measure of representation that is less than 1 are considered under-represented in essential work, whereas values over 1 indicate group over-representation in essential employment. In the aggregate, essential work is highly racialized and gendered. The final row of Table 6.3 (in bold) shows that Hispanic/Latino and Black men are over-represented in essential work, while other groups of men are under-represented relative to

Table 6.3. Racial/Ethnic and Gender Representation in Essential Work Sectors, 2020.[a]

	Men					Women				
	White	Black	Hispanic or Latino	Asian	Multi-racial	White	Black	Hispanic or Latina	Asian	Multi-racial
Health care	0.45	0.68	0.33	0.67	0.67	1.48	2.26	1.46	1.47	1.29
Food and agriculture	0.86	1.17	1.95	1.22	1.17	0.77	0.92	1.68	1.06	1.14
Commercial services and sanitation	1.39	1.29	3.61	0.83	0.83	0.21	0.28	0.98	0.24	0.29
Transportation, warehouse, and delivery	1.31	2.73	1.74	1.14	1.50	0.43	0.92	0.57	0.44	0.57
Government and community-based services	0.56	0.63	0.24	0.42	0.67	1.42	1.98	1.56	1.41	2.00
Financial sector	0.92	0.54	0.46	1.00	0.67	1.30	1.06	0.79	1.15	0.86
Communications and IT	0.74	1.07	0.84	0.61	1.00	1.14	1.74	1.49	0.94	1.29
Critical manufacturing	1.93	1.02	1.84	0.94	1.67	0.18	0.26	0.22	0.38	0.14
Emergency services	1.86	1.78	1.11	0.81	2.33	0.33	0.32	0.19	0.15	0.71
Energy sector	2.09	0.71	1.26	1.92	2.67	0.13	0.08	0.00	0.38	0.00
Chemical sector	1.70	1.51	0.84	1.72	0.83	0.43	0.45	0.08	0.71	2.00
Water and wastewater management	2.26	1.41	0.57	0.92	1.33	0.17	0.00	0.13	0.00	0.00
All essential	**0.92**	**1.12**	**1.31**	**0.86**	**1.00**	**0.94**	**1.30**	**1.21**	**0.97**	**1.00**

Source: Author calculation of CPS-MORG data; sectors with origins in reproductive labour shaded.
[a]Numbers indicate group representation in essential work sector relative to labour market; values over 1 indicate over-representation.

their share of all employment. We see a similar patterning among women, but here it is Black women who are the most over-represented in essential work followed by Hispanic/Latina women. In 2020 essential work was disproportionately performed by Black or Hispanic/Latino/a women and men.

Table 6.3 also provides an intersectional accounting of the way members of different racial-ethnic and gender groups are over- or under-represented in different types of essential employment. We can see that essential sectors reflect a high degree of racial/ethnic and gender differentiation, evidenced by the very different patterns of representation observed across different essential work sectors. Starting with sectors that have clear origins in the caring and cleaning work of reproductive labour, non-Hispanic white, Black, Asian, and multiracial women are highly over-represented in healthcare. Hispanic or Latino/a men and women are highly over-represented in food and agricultural work, as are Black, Asian, and multiracial men. Hispanic or Latino/a men are highly concentrated in commercial services and sanitation, as are Black and non-Hispanic white men. All women (especially Black and multiracial women) are highly concentrated in government or community-based services, which is part of an expanded conception of reproductive labour, while men are highly concentrated in transportation, warehouse, and delivery work (especially Black and Hispanic/Latino men). There is, in short, a strong intersectionality to who performs what type of essential work, whereby race/ethnicity and gender combine to produce disparate patterns of employment. Racial and ethnic minority men and women are, for the most part, over-represented in essential work sectors with origins in the caring and cleaning work of reproductive labour.

In the next subsections we use multivariate analysis to investigate (1) the valuation of essential work and (2) intersectional inequalities among essential workers.

Essential Worker Wage Gaps

Essential work differs from non-essential work in the racial/ethnic and educational composition of its workers, but it has a similar rate of unionization, average working hours, and representation of women workers as the wider workforce (Table 6.2). To what extent can we conclude that, in the aggregate, work that was officially deemed essential in the United States in 2020 is devalued relative to non-essential work?

Fig. 6.1 shows essential worker wage gaps for five model specifications (see Table AII for full model results). The baseline model (Model 0) shows that, on average, essential workers in 2020 were paid $115.32 less per week than non-essential workers. Model 1 shows that more than half of the baseline essential wage gap can be explained by standard labour market controls including human capital (education and potential work experience), usual hours of work, and unionization. Model 2 shows that taking worker characteristics including intersectional and marital status into account yields an essential worker pay gap of only $32.13/per week. However, when we also take detailed industry and detailed occupation into account (Model 3) we estimate a positive essential worker wage gap of $16.29 per week. In other words, if essential and non-essential jobs were

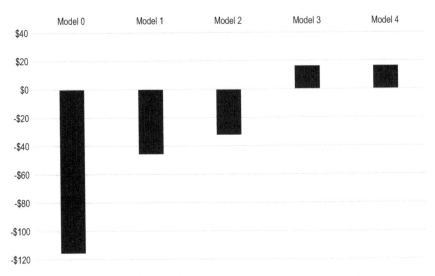

Fig. 6.1. Effect of Essential Worker Status on Weekly Wages, 2020.[a]
[a]Analysis includes working age (24–64) employed earners only. Wage gaps are estimated relative to the reference category of non-essential jobs. Model 0 includes no controls, Model 1 includes a range of basic labour market controls, Model 2 includes intersectional statuses, Model 3 includes detailed occupation and industry, and Model 4 includes month of survey; Model 5, which includes month of survey × essential status, is not shown due to non-significant interaction term (see Table AII for full model results).

in the same industries and with the same occupational positions within those industries, then essential workers would receive a small weekly wage premium. As Model 3 controls for a range of labour market and worker characteristics, this means that low wages among essential workers reflect a combination of the jobs' standard labour market characteristics, the intersectional status of its workers, and the valuation of their industrial and occupational classifications. We elaborate on the interconnections between industry, occupation, and essentiality in the discussion and conclusions section below.

In parsing the independent role of essentiality on weekly wages, one important question for the analysis is whether the emergent public discourse around essential labour had a discernible effect on wages as the first year of the pandemic unfolded. To evaluate change over time in essential worker wage gaps, we introduce a variable for month of survey in Model 4, and an interaction term for month of survey * essential worker status in Model 5. While weekly wages were significantly higher than the reference month of January starting in May 2020, reading a maximum value of $32.80/week in July 2020 (Model 4, Table AII), ceteris paribus, there is no evidence that the pandemic wage premium differed across essential and non-essential worker status: the essential worker wage effect in virtually the same in Models 3 and 4 and non-significant in Model 5. Further, there is no significant interaction between month of survey and essential worker status in 2020. The source of the positive wage effect that emerged starting in July 2020, relative to January 2020, becomes clearer when we consider two pieces of information. First, the observed mean of weekly wages for essential and non-essential workers in 2020 follows an almost identical trend line from month to month (see Fig. A1). Second, monthly unemployment trends for essential and non-essential workers in 2020 are strikingly similar: unemployment spiked in April 2020 and tapered over the summer months before stabilizing at high levels in September 2020 (see Fig. A2, which includes the 2019 unemployment rate as a baseline for distinguishing between seasonal fluctuations and the impact of the pandemic). Altogether the evidence suggests that early pandemic wage gains in the United States, where many non-essential businesses reopened starting in June 2020, likely reflect employers' response to workforce shortages rather than an independent essential work wage bump.

Intersectional Wage Gaps

Fig. 6.2 presents estimated weekly wage gaps by race/ethnicity and gender (see Table AII for full results). All of the estimated wage gaps in the figure represent significant interaction terms, meaning that earnings within each group is significantly different from the reference category of non-Hispanic white men, ceteris

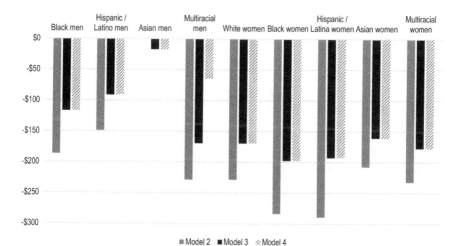

Fig. 6.2. Intersectional Weekly Wage Gaps, 2020.[a]
[a]Analysis includes working age (24–64) employed earners only. Race/ethnicity and gender effects are estimated using interaction terms; wage gaps are estimated relative to the reference category of non-Hispanic white men. Model 2 includes a range of basic labour market controls, Model 3 adds controls for detailed occupation and industry, and Model 4 adds a control for month in sample; Model 5, which adds an interaction term between month of sample and essential worker status, is not shown due to non-significance (see Table AII for full model results).

paribus. Looking first at Model 2, which includes controls for human capital and other basic labour market characteristics, we can see that intersectional status is associated with a significant earnings gap relative to non-Hispanic white men for each group except Asian men. Black and Hispanic/Latino men earn $186 and $148 less than white men, but the wage gaps experienced by women are even great, ranging from $289/week for Hispanic/Latinx women to $207 for Asian women. Even taking detailed industry and occupation into account, Model 3 estimates that Black women are paid $197/week less than non-Hispanic white men, all things equal, compared with $192/week for Hispanic/Latina women, $177/week for multiracial women, $169/week for non-Hispanic white women, and $160/week less for Asian women. Racial/ethnic earnings disadvantages also accrue to men of colour: multiracial men are paid $169 less per week, compared with $116/week for Black men, $90/week for Hispanic/Latino men, and $17/week for Asian men. The magnitude of these intersectional wage gaps is striking, given the range of control variables included in Model 3 including detailed industry and detailed occupation. In short, Black, Hispanic/Latinx, and multiracial men all have significantly lower wages than white men with the same characteristics, but all experience smaller net wage penalties than women across racial/ethnic categories, all things equal.

Introducing controls for month of survey (Model 4) and month of survey * essential worker status (Model 5) yields no change in the estimated intersectional wage gaps. There is no indication that the effect of either essential worker or intersectional status on wages changed over the course of the pandemic's first year.

As a final check on the robustness of our results, we repeated these analyses with a categorical variable for essential worker sector (see Fig. A3). When we use the categorical measure of essentiality instead of the essential worker status dummy variable, we can check to see how different model specifications affect the coefficients for different essential work sectors, effectively providing a test of whether an alternative measure of essentiality would have yielded different results. We see clear evidence of devaluation in the largest essential work sectors, including not only the sectors with origins in reproductive labour (health care, food and agriculture, commercial services, and sanitation), but also in the transportation, warehouse, delivery, and communications and IT sectors. Introducing controls for detailed industry and occupation (Model 3) produces counter-intuitive essential work wage gaps, particularly in relatively advantaged essential work sectors like finance and utilities. This patterning of results supports our larger argument that racialized and gendered devaluation is written into the industrial and occupational structure of the American labour market. Introducing month of survey (Model 4) does not substantively impact the results, and the interaction of month of survey with essential work sector (not shown) produced no significant coefficients. The results suggest that our choice of an essential work measure that includes critical infrastructure and financial services does not bias the direction of our results, though the estimated magnitude of devaluation associated with essential work would be greater with a narrower measure.

Among essential and non-essential workers alike, then, gender is a core axis of earnings inequality with important racial and ethnic differences operating among men and women, even taking detailed industry, detailed occupation, and an array of control variables (including essential worker status and sector) into account.

Fine-grained differences in the types of work performed by members of different racial/ethnic and gender groups contribute to estimated weekly wage gaps but cannot fully explain racial/ethnic and gender gaps observed among either essential or non-essential workers. This analysis suggests that there are multiple sources of low wages among essential workers, including educational attainment, but essentiality itself is less important for understanding labour market rewards than is power, including the historical and intersectional power inequalities that are expressed in the industrial and occupational classification of work. In the next section, we reflect on the broader significance of these results, including implications for ongoing organizing efforts to improve pay and working conditions among essential workers whose labour has long been devalued but who have become more visible since the start of the global pandemic.

CONCLUSIONS

In this chapter we have investigated the valuation of essential work in the United States from an intersectional perspective. Work that was officially classified as essential in the United States in 2020 reflects a wide range of functionally interrelated roles with highly disparate work and worker characteristics, but most essential work has origins in reproductive labour and/or is disproportionately performed by racial-ethnic minorities and women. *We therefore ask how essentiality, race/ethnicity, and gender affected wages during the first year of the global pandemic.*

Our quantitative analysis of weekly wages using data from the CPS-MORG in 2020 supports three main conclusions. First, we find that there is a substantial essential work wage gap that cannot be explained by either standard labour market characteristics, including human capital, or workers' race/ethnicity and gender. Rather, the essential worker wage gap in the United States derives from a wider pattern of industrial and occupational earnings differences that reflect longstanding patterns of segregation and devaluation. Second, based on analysis of monthly data we find no evidence that the effect of essential worker status on wages changed during the first year of the pandemic, as month-to-month earnings trends in 2020 followed a similar pattern for essential and non-essential workers, the essential worker wage gap is robust to controls for month of survey, and an interaction term for essential worker status * month of survey is non-significant. Third, we find that intersectional wage inequalities, in which race/ethnicity and gender intersect to shape earnings, cannot be explained by either standard labour market characteristics or detailed industrial and occupational differences. Gender is the primary axis that shapes earnings, but the effects of gender vary by race and ethnicity to produce a gendered racial/ethnic wage hierarchy in which Black and Brown women experience the highest wage gaps relative to non-Hispanic white men. On the basis of these empirical findings, which we interpret through an intersectional lens, we theorize that essentiality is less important for understanding the distribution of labour market rewards than is labour market power, particularly the way that historical social and political differences along racial/ethnic and gender lines were institutionalized in labour market classifications that continue to shape compensation.

The chapter advances existing scholarship on essentiality and intersectional labour market inequalities by building an analytic bridge between historical (often qualitative) studies of valuation – which emphasize the way that racial, ethnic, and gender inequalities are not deviations from neutral market processes but, rather, foundational elements of the social organization of work in the American context – and contemporary quantitative labour market analysis, which often locates the effects of race, ethnicity, and gender only in their marginal effects. While early research on pandemic-era essential work has shown that it is disproportionately performed by women and people of colour – sometimes but not always publishing statistics that show how race/ethnicity and gender intersect among workers traditionally devalued but newly deemed essential – existing studies have not parsed the intersectional production of these inequalities by situating them within the context of historically produced 'durable' inequalities (Tilly, 1998; Tomaskovic-Devey & Avent-Holt, 2019). In the American context, this means attending to the deep institutional roots of labour market inequalities that were made more visible by the public health emergency, including earnings differences across industries and occupations. Towards this end, we offer an interpretive strategy for quantitative analysis of wages that does not treat workers' industries and occupations as objective market features to account for in service of isolating the independent role of race/ethnicity and gender in earnings determination, but rather as sites of historical classification struggles (Bourdieu & Wacquant, 1992) in which racial, ethnic, and gender inequalities were codified, and which continue to reproduce power differences across different forms of work. While the analysis in this chapter is focussed on the United States, and its conclusions are therefore specific to the American context, the study suggests that research grounded in different national contexts should attend to the way that inequalities around the intersection of race and ethnicity, gender, and other socially defined statuses may be built into the institutional foundations of the employment relationship.

The intersectional inequalities examined in this chapter were relationally produced over decades of unequal educational and occupational access given material consequence by patterns of devaluation that were often codified in industry-based exemptions to labour and employment law. Our findings on the relationship between essentiality and valuation in 2020 therefore reflect the consequences of historical classification struggles; the chapter does not aim to show how the global pandemic has reshaped the contours of work and inequality in the United States, for pandemic-related work disruptions continued beyond December 2020. We confine our analysis to the first year of the pandemic, during which essential worker and intersectional status wage gaps did not abate. Similarly, we are not able in this analysis to parse the way labour force exits, unemployment, and the transition to remote work may have reconfigured essential and non-essential labour, though our findings are consistent with recent research in this area (see Autor et al., 2023). Finally, while our analysis does take detailed industries and occupations into account as a means of tapping into historical devaluation and contemporary discrimination, we do not observe these processes directly or seek to isolate the effect of segregation on wages among essential workers. These are important questions for future analysis.

Nonetheless, we conclude with some observations about how an emergent discourse of essentiality may shape labour market inequality in the future, as policymakers and labour organizers use the concept in ongoing efforts to build institutions that recognize the interconnectedness and dignity of all work. In April 2020, progressive legislators Senator Elizabeth Warren and Representative Ro Khanna proposed an 'Essential Worker Bill of Rights' that sought to use the concept of essentiality to establish universal labour standards including an array of health and safety, compensation, labour organizing, and professionalization measures for all workers (Bhattarai, 2020). In support of the proposed legislation, Representative Khanna observed in April 2020 that, 'Nearly 60 million Americans are still working to keep our internet running, to deliver our groceries, to make sure we have electricity, and to care for the sick' (Warren, 2020). Senator Warren added, 'Essential workers are the backbone of our nation's response to coronavirus. We have a responsibility to make sure essential workers have the protections they need, the rights they are entitled to, and the compensation they deserve' (Warren, 2020). Writing in support of the bill in April 2020, Gene Sperling, national economic advisor to Presidents Bill Clinton and Barack Obama, sought to connect the emergent discourse of essentiality to the unfinished business of the Civil Rights Movement by referencing Dr Martin Luther King, Jr's support for the 1968 Memphis, TN sanitation workers' strike. Quoting Dr King, Sperling wrote,

> One day our society will come to respect the sanitation worker if it is to survive, for the person who picks up our garbage, in the final analysis, is as significant as the physician, for if he doesn't do his job, diseases are rampant. All labor has dignity. (Sperling, 2020)

What would it take to improve access to employment rights and advance the dignity of all work in the United States, including for workers whose labour is systematically devalued? The 'Essential Worker Bill of Rights' did not advance in Congress but union organizing momentum and popular support for organized labour are high (e.g. Hanley, 2022). To the extent that essential worker status, as it was defined in 2020, can be effectively mobilized to organize workers and advance employment rights legislation by countering the racialized and sexist rhetoric of unskilled work and undeserving workers, it may be of consequence for shaping pay and employment conditions in the future. An intersectional perspective on essential work clarifies the stakes of regulations that govern organizing rights and the employment relationship – including statutes that are ostensibly race- and gender-neutral but were crafted with the explicit intent to maintain economic advantages along racial and gender lines – drawing a clear connection between contemporary movements for racial, gender-based, and economic justice.

NOTE

1. Sectors refer to industry groupings, which are defined by shared product or service markets (the output of a particular division of labour), whereas occupations refer to jobs with similar tasks or required skills (labour input). See the 'Methods and Data Section' below for an extended discussion of this measure of essential work, which does not explicitly distinguish between remote and frontline (non-remote) jobs, but that is heavily weighted towards jobs that cannot be performed remotely.

REFERENCES

Autor, D., Dube, A., & McGrew, A. (2023). *The unexpected compression: Competition at work in the low wage labor market* [National Bureau of Economic Research Working Paper 31010]. http://www.nber.org/papers/w31010

Avent-Holt, D., & Tomaskovic-Devey, D. (2023). Skill and power at work: A relational inequality perspective. In M. Tahlin (Ed.), *A research agenda for skills and inequality* (pp. 217–232). Edward Elgar Publishing Limited.

Bhattarai, A. (2020, April 13). Elizabeth Warren urges Congress to enact more protections for 'essential' workers. *The Washington Post*. https://www.washingtonpost.com/business/2020/04/13/elizabeth-warren-workers-protections-coronavirus/

Bonacich, E. (1976, February). Advanced capitalism and Black/White relations in the United States: A split labor market interpretation. *American Sociological Review, 41*(1), 34–51. https://doi.org/10.2307/2094371

Bourdieu, P., & Wacquant, L. J. D. (1992). *An invitation to reflexive sociology*. The University of Chicago Press.

Branch, E. H. (2011). *Opportunity denied: Limiting Black Women to devalued work*. Rutgers University Press.

Branch, E. H., & Hanley, C. (2011). Regional convergence in low-wage work and earnings, 1970–2000. *Sociological Perspectives, 54*(4), 569-592. https://doi.org/10.1525/sop.2011.54.4.569

Branch, E. H., & Hanley, C. (2017). A racial-gender lens on precarious nonstandard employment. In A. L. Kalleberg & S. P. Vallas (Eds.), *Precarious work* (Research in the Sociology of Work, Vol. 31, pp. 183–213). Emerald Publishing. https://doi.org/10.1108/S0277-283320170000031006

Branch, E. H., & Hanley, C. (2022). *Work in Black and White: Striving for the American Dream*. Russell Sage Foundation.

Branch, E. H., & Wooten, M. E. (2012). Suited for service: Racialized rationalizations for the ideal domestic servant from the nineteenth to the early twentieth century. *Social Science History, 36*(2, Summer), 169–189. https://doi.org/10.1017/S0145553200011743

Browne, I., & Misra, J. (2003). The intersection of gender and race in the labor market. *Annual Review of Sociology, 29*, 487–513. https://doi.org/10.1146/annurev.soc.29.010202.100016

Castilla, E. J. (2008). Gender, race, and meritocracy in organizational careers. *American Journal of Sociology, 113*(6), 1479–1526. https://doi.org/10.1086/588738

Castilla, E. J. (2012). Gender, race, and the new (merit-based) employment relationship. *Industrial Relations, 51*(2), 1–35. https://psycnet.apa.org/doi/10.1111/j.1468-232X.2012.00689.x

Castilla, E. J. (2015). Accounting for the gap: A firm study manipulating organizational accountability in pay decisions. *Organization Science, 26*(2), 311–333. https://psycnet.apa.org/doi/10.1287/orsc.2014.0950

Cech, E. (2013, June). Ideological wage inequalities? The technical/social dualism and the gender wage gap in engineering. *Social Forces, 91*(4), 1147–1183. https://doi.org/10.1093/sf/sot024

Choi, E. J., & Spletzer, J. R. (2012, March). The declining average size of establishments: Evidence and explanations. *Monthly Labor Review, March*, 50–65. https://www.bls.gov/opub/mlr/2012/03/art4full.pdf

Council of State Governments. (n.d.). *COVID-19 resources for state leaders, 2020–021 executive orders*. Retrieved March 20, 2022, from https://web.csg.org/covid19/executive-orders/

Davis, K., & Moore, W. E. (1945, April). Some principles of stratification. *American Sociological Review, 10*(2), 242–249. https://doi.org/10.2307/2085643

Dey, M., Frazis, H., & Lowenstein, M. A. (2020, June). Ability to work from home: Evidence from two surveys and implications for the labor market in the COVID-19 pandemic. *Monthly Labor Review*, 1–19. https://doi.org/10.21916/mlr.2020.14

Dozier, R. (2010). The declining relative economic status of Black women workers, 1980–2002. *Social Forces, 88*, 1833–1857. https://www.jstor.org/stable/40645960

Duffy, M. (2007, June). Doing the dirty work: Gender, race, and reproductive labor in historical perspective. *Gender and Society, 21*(3), 313–336. https://doi.org/10.1177/0891243207300764

Gleeson, S. (2016). *Precarious claims: The promise and failure of workplace protections in the United States*. University of California Press.

Glenn, E. N. (1992). From servitude to service work: Historical continuities in the racial division of paid reproductive labor. *Signs, 18*(1 Autumn), 1–43.

Glenn, E. N. (2004). *Unequal freedom: How race and gender shaped American citizenship and labor.* Harvard University Press.

Glenn, E. N. (2010). *Forced to care: Coercion and caregiving in America.* Harvard University Press.

Glenn, E. N., & Tolbert, C. M. II. (1987). Stratification for women of color: Race and gender. In B. D. Wright, M. M. Ferree, G. O. Mellow, L. H. Lewis, M.-L. Daza Sampler, R. Asher, & K. Claspell (Eds.), *Women, work, and technology: Transformations.* University of Michigan Press.

Gostin, L. O., Hodge, J. G., Jr, & Wiley, L. F. (2020). Presidential powers and response to COVID-19. *JAMA, 323*(16), 1547–1548. https://10.1001/jama.2020.4335

Greenman, E., & Xie, Y. (2008, March). Double jeopardy? The intersection of gender and race on earnings in the United States. *Social Forces, 86*(3), 1–28. https://doi.org/10.1353%2Fsof.0.0008

Hanley, C. (2022, August 23). *Despite unions' organizing success, labor law reform is still urgently needed to address inequality.* London School of Economics USAPP Phelan Centre. https://blogs.lse.ac.uk/usappblog/2022/08/23/despite-unions-organizing-successes-labor-law-reform-is-still-urgently-needed-to-address-inequality-in-america/

Harris, R. (2020, March 16). *White House announces new social distancing guidelines around coronavirus.* National Public. Retrieved June 20, 2022, from https://www.npr.org/2020/03/16/816658125/white-house-announces-new-social-distancing-guidelines-around-coronavirus

Huffman, M. L., & Cohen, P. N. (2004). Racial wage inequality: Job segregation and devaluation across U.S. labor markets. *American Journal of Sociology, 109*, 902–936. https://doi.org/10.1086/378928

Jayaraman, S. (2016). *Forked: A new standard for American dining.* Oxford University Press.

Katznelson, I. (2005). *When affirmative action was White: The untold history of racial inequality in twentieth-century America.* W. W. Norton & Company.

Kaufman, R. L. (2002). Assessing alternative perspectives on race and sex employment segregation. *American Sociological Review, 67*(4), 547–572. https://doi.org/10.1177/000312240206700404

Kessler-Harris, A. (1990). *A women's wage: Historical meanings & social consequences.* The University Press of Kentucky.

Kmec, J. (2003). Minority job concentration and wages. *Social Problems, 50*(1), 38–59. https://doi.org/10.1525/sp.2003.50.1.38

Krebs, C. C. (2020, March 28). *Advisory memorandum on identification of essential critical infrastructure workers during COVID-19 response.* U.S. Department of Homeland Security Cybersecurity and Infrastructure Security Agency. Retrieved June 24, 2022, from https://www.federalreserve.gov/supervisionreg/srletters/SR2006a1.pdf

Levanon, A., England, P., & Allison, P. (2009). Occupational feminization and pay: Assessing causal dynamics using 1950–2000 U.S. Census data. *Social Forces, 88*(2), 865–892. https://www.jstor.org/stable/40645826

Mandel, H. (2013). Up the down staircase: Women's upward mobility and the wage penalty for occupational feminization, 1970–2007. *Social Forces, 91*(4), 1183–1207. https://www.jstor.org/stable/43287497

Mandel, H., & Semyonov, M. (2016). Going back in time? Gender differences in trends and sources of the racial pay gap, 1970 to 2010. *American Sociological Review, 81*(5), 1039–1068. https://doi.org/10.1177/0003122416662958

McNicholas, C., & Poydock, M. (2020, May 19). *Who are essential workers? A comprehensive look at their wages, demographics, and unionization rates* [Working Economic Blog]. Economic Policy Institute. https://www.epi.org/blog/who-are-essential-workers-a-comprehensive-look-at-their-wages-demographics-and-unionization-rates/

McPhillips, D. (2020, May 18). *The statistical support for closing non-essential businesses.* U.S. News & World Report. Retrieved June 20, 2022, from https://www.usnews.com/news/articles/2020-05-18/the-statistical-support-for-closing-non-essential-businesses-during-the-coronavirus-pandemic

Mettler, S. (1998). *Dividing citizens: Gender and federalism in new deal public policy.* Cornell University Press.

Miller, H. (2020, April 30). *Reopening America: A state-by-state breakdown of the status of coronavirus shutdowns.* CNBC. Retrieved June 20, 2022, from https://www.cnbc.com/2020/04/30/coronavirus-states-lifting-stay-at-home-orders-reopening-businesses.html

Milkman, R. (2020). *Immigrant labor and the New Precariat*. Polity Press.

Mishel, L., Bernstein, J., & Shierholz, H. (2009). *The state of working America 2008–2009*. Cornell University Press.

Misra, J., Currington, C. V., & Green, V. M. (2021). Methods of intersectional research. *Sociological Spectrum, 41*(1), 9–28. https://doi.org/10.1080/02732173.2020.1791772

Moss, P., & Tilly, C. (2001). *Stories employers tell: Race, skill, and hiring in America*. Russell Sage Foundation.

National Governors Association. (2020, April 13). *Reference chart on state essential business designations*. Retrieved June 20, 2022, from https://www.nga.org/wp-content/uploads/2020/03/Appendix-I-Essential-Business_3.31.20.pdf

National Labor Relations Board. (n.d.). *Jurisdictional standards*. Retrieved March 22, 2023, from https://www.nlrb.gov/about-nlrb/rights-we-protect/the-law/jurisdictional-standards

Perea, J. F. (2011). The echoes of slavery: Recognizing the racist origins of the agricultural and domestic worker exclusion from the National Labor Relations Act. *Ohio State Law Journal, 72*(1), 95–138. https://dx.doi.org/10.2139/ssrn.1646496

Pettit, B., & Ewert, S. (2009). Employment gains and wage declines: The erosion of Black women's relative wages since 1980. *Demography, 46*, 469–492. https://10.1353/dem.0.0061

Reskin, B. F., & Roos, P. A. (1990). *Job queues, gender queues: Explaining women's inroads into male occupations*. Temple University Press.

Rosenfeld, J., & Kleykamp, M. (2012, March). Organized labor and racial wage inequality in the United States. *American Journal of Sociology, 117*(5), 1460–1502. https://doi.org/10.1086%2F663673

Sperling, G. B. (2020, April 24). Martin Luther King Jr. predicted this moment: The coronavirus shows us clearer than ever before that 'All Labor has Dignity'. *New York Times*. https://www.nytimes.com/2020/04/24/opinion/sunday/essential-workers-wages-covid.html?action=click&module=Opinion&pgtype=Homepage

Stainback, K., & Tomaskovic-Devey, D. (2012). *Documenting desegregation: Racial and gender segregation in private-sector employment since the Civil Rights Act*. Russell Sage Foundation.

Steinberg, R. J. (1990). The social construction of skill: Gender, power, and comparable worth. *Work and Occupations, 17*(4), 449–482. https://doi.org/10.1177/0730888490017004004

Tilly, C. (1996). *Half a job: Bad and good part-time jobs in a changing labor market*. Temple University Press.

Tilly, C. (1998). *Durable inequality*. University of California Press.

Tomaskovic-Devey, D., & Avent-Holt, D. (2019). *Relational inequalities: An organizational approach*. Oxford University Press.

Tomaskovic-Devey, D., Rainey, A., Avent-holt, D., Bandelj, N., Boza, I., Cort, D., Godechot, O., Hajdu, G., Hallsten, M., Henriksen, L.F., Hermansen, A.S., Hou, F., Jung, J., Kanjuo-Mrcela, A., King, J., Kodama, N., Kristal, T., Krizkova, A., Lippenyi, Z., Melzer, S.M., Mun, E., Penner, A., Petersen, T., Poje, A., Safi, M., Thaning, M., & Tufail, Z. (2020). Rising between workplace inequalities in high income countries. *Proceedings of the National Academy of Science, 117*, 9277–9283. https://doi.org/10.1073/pnas.1918249117

Tumin, M. M. (1953, August). Some principles of stratification: A critical analysis. *American Sociological Review, 18*(4), 387–394. https://doi.org/10.2307/2087551

U.S. Department of Labor. (2020, June 18). *U.S. Department of Labor issues guidance as non-essential businesses reopen and employees return to work* [News Releases]. U.S. Department of Labor Occupational Safety & Health Administration. Accessed June 20, 2022 https://www.dol.gov/newsroom/releases/osha/osha20200618

Warren, E. (2020, April 13). *Elizabeth Warren and Ro Khanna unveil essential worker bill of rights*. Elizabeth Warren Press Release. https://www.warren.senate.gov/newsroom/press-releases/elizabeth-warren-and-ro-khanna-unveil-essential-workers-bill-of-rights

Wooten, M. E., & Branch, E. H. (2013). Defining appropriate labor: Race, gender, and the idealization of Black women in domestic service. *Race, Gender, & Class, 19*(3–4), 292–308. https://www.jstor.org/stable/43497500

APPENDIX

Table AI. Age Distribution of Essential Workers by Sector, 2020.[a]

	Share Teen (16–19) (%)	Share College Age (20–23) (%)	Share Working Age (24–64) (%)	Share Retirement Age (65+) (%)
Health care	1.6	4.8	85.7	8.0
Food and agriculture	9.1	9.5	75.3	6.1
Commercial services and sanitation	2.5	6.0	85.3	6.2
Transportation, warehouse, delivery	1.5	4.8	85.7	7.9
Government and community-based services	1.9	4.7	81.5	11.8
Financial sector	0.5	3.5	88.5	7.5
Communications and IT	7.8	9.2	77.8	5.2
Critical manufacturing	2.4	7.2	85.4	5.1
Emergency services	0.3	2.1	94.9	2.7
Energy sector	0.2	3.0	91.7	5.1
Chemical sector	0.4	4.0	90.4	5.3
Water and wastewater management	0.8	1.6	92.7	4.8
All essential jobs	**3.4**	**6.0**	**83.3**	**7.3**
All jobs	3.2	6.5	83.7	6.6

Source: Author calculation of CPS-MORG data; sectors with origins in reproductive labour shaded.
[a] Sums to 100% of each job category.

Table AIII. OLS Regression Analysis of Annual Weekly Wages, 2020.[a]

	Model 0	Model 1	Model 2	Model 3	Model 4	Model 5
Essential	−115.32***	−45.62***	−32.13***	16.29*	16.31*	7.57
Race/Ethnicity (ref = White)						
Black			−186.57***	−116.45***	−116.52***	−116.47***
Hispanic or Latino/a			−148.82***	−90.73***	−90.61***	−90.68***
Asian			−1.55	−17.03*	−17.05*	−17.06*
Multi-racial			−84.09***	−64.07***	−64.25***	−64.35***
Female			−228.52***	−169.29***	−169.28***	−169.28***
Race/Ethnicity * Female (ref = White male)						
Black * Female			131.26***	88.11***	88.15***	88.03***
Hispanic or Latino/a * Female			88.20***	67.46***	67.72***	67.70***
Asian * Female			22.75*	25.60*	25.23*	25.12*
Multi-racial * Female			106.67***	96.89***	96.80***	97.14***
Citizen			80.51***	56.25***	56.01***	56.04***
Education (ref = < h.s.)						
High school		73.73***	45.10***	19.01*	19.15**	19.34*
Some college		165.46***	143.01***	53.16***	53.37***	53.55***
College (4 years)		495.91***	465.74***	261.82***	261.86***	261.99***
Advanced degree		715.92***	687.58***	437.75***	437.33***	437.43***
Age		28.27***	26.16***	21.66***	21.69***	21.68***
Age-squared		−0.26***	−0.25***	−0.20***	−0.20***	−0.20***
Union		5.09	1.74	85.21***	85.19***	85.16***
Usual hours of work/wk		25.36***	23.06***	19.54***	19.53***	19.53***
Marital status (ref = single, never married)						
Married			−56.40***	−33.37***	−33.27***	−33.24***
Divorced or widowed			−85.18***	−48.23***	−48.33***	−48.32***

Month (ref=January)				
February			7.74	1.28
March			-1.40	-6.09
April			6.22	1.10
May			23.21***	16.41*
June			23.50***	22.19**
July			32.80***	28.23***
August			31.90***	35.79***
September			23.31***	23.86***
October			24.51***	22.29**
November			18.01**	21.24**
December			25.43***	20.13**
Essential * month (ref=non-essential January)				
Essential*February				23.36
Essential*March				17.31
Essential*April				18.64
Essential*May				24.79
Essential*June				4.56
Essential*July				16.67
Essential*August				-14.81
Essential*September				-2.21
Essential*October				8.01
Essential*November				-11.06
Essential*December				19.38
Constant	1,012.92	-926.82	-658.84	161.47	143.98	146.76
Adj. r^2	0.006	0.406	0.439	0.5244	0.5246	0.5247

[a]Models restricted to working age (24–64) employed earners only. Models 1–5 control for region and rural/urban status. Models 3–5 control for detailed industry and occupation. Full model results available upon request.
*$p \leq 0.05$, **$p \leq 0.01$, and ***$p \leq 0.001$.

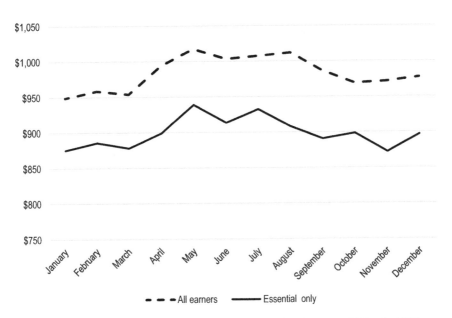

Fig. A1. Mean Weekly Earnings by Essential Worker Status and Month, 2020.

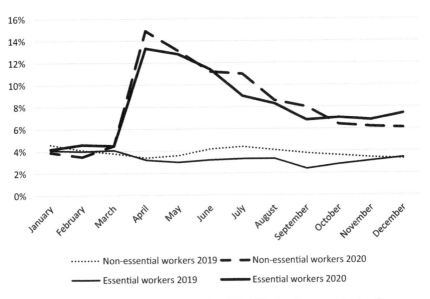

Fig. A2. Unemployment Rate by Essential Worker Status and Month, 2019 and 2020.

Essential Workers Intersectional Perspective 141

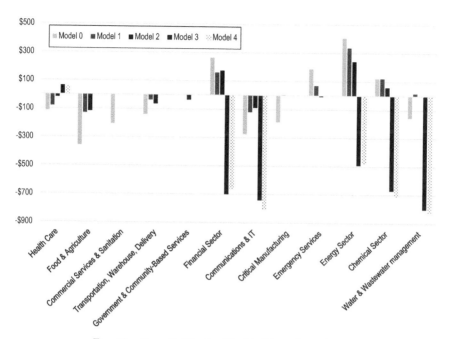

Fig. A3. Essential Sector Weekly Wage Gaps, 2020.*
*Models restricted to working age (24–64) employed earners only. Model 0 introduces control for basic labour market characteristics; model 1 adds intersectional statuses, model 2 adds detailed industry and occupation; model 3 adds month of survey; model 4 adds month of survey * essential sector (not shown). Only significant sector effects shown; full model results available upon request.

A NOTE FROM THE EDITORS: INTRODUCING 'SPOTLIGHT ON ETHNOGRAPHY'

We are excited to introduce our new section: Spotlight on Ethnography. Building on the widespread interest in, and success of, Research in the Sociology of Work *Ethnographies of Work* (Volume 35), we decided to implement this as a regular feature in all upcoming volumes. We do so to encourage ethnographic research on work, seeking to provide an outlet for such research and to showcase creative approaches to ethnographic writing. In other words, we have a permanently open call for submissions dealing with any aspect of ethnographic research. In particular, we encourage empirical submissions which report detailed ethnographic findings about work, including those undertaken as part of doctoral or master's studies. This volume is the first to include this feature section, which consists of three chapters that explore, in unique ways and differing formats, the strength of ethnographic approaches to the study of work.

In the chapter 'Floral Ethics and Aesthetics: Understanding Professional Expertise at Work', Isabelle Zinn brings us into the little-known world of florists. Drawing on 36 months of ethnographic fieldwork in flower shops in Switzerland and Chicago, Zinn contributes to the sociology of work and professions by providing a nuanced understanding of the tensions that can arise between the professional expertise of florists and the aesthetic preferences of customers. The findings on the micro-level reveal that adherence to floral ethics serves as a strategy for protecting and maintaining occupational legitimacy. By uncovering divergent conceptions of what constitutes 'work well done' among florists, the chapter offers a broader argument on the power asymmetry inherent in service relationships.

In the following chapter, Markus Helfen reviews recent exemplars of ethnographic studies of essential work from Germany: Jana Costas' *Dramas of Dignity* and Peter Birke's *Grenzen aus Glas* [literally 'Borders made from Glass']. While Costas is interested in studying how individual cleaners preserve their sense of dignity despite their stigmatizing work roles, Birke is interested in the power resources migrant workers can potentially mobilize to improve their working conditions, despite their multi-dimensional (inter-sectional) precarity. In the context

---

Essentiality of Work
Research in the Sociology of Work, Volume 36, 143–144
Copyright © 2024 by Markus Helfen, Rick Delbridge, Andreas (Andi) Pekarek and Gretchen Purser
Published under exclusive licence by Emerald Publishing Limited
ISSN: 0277-2833/doi:10.1108/S0277-283320240000036012

of German industrial and organizational sociology, both studies represent comparatively rare examples of detailed qualitative and ethnographic work that illuminate the labour process from a workers' perspectives. Although the authors employ different approaches to fieldwork, their studies reveal the precarious nature of being an essential worker in sectors such as meatpacking, warehousing, and cleaning. This general observation gives rise to some concluding speculations about the emancipatory potential of ethnographic work in labour studies and other fields.

In the final chapter, Gretchen Purser revisits Studs Terkel's *Working* on the occasion of the 50th anniversary of its publication. She offers readers a deep dive into the book, which consists of a compilation of interviews carried out with over 130 workers in the United States. While Studs Terkel was widely hailed as a masterful interviewer and oral historian, Purser argues that *Working* serves as an exemplar of ethnographic scholarship on work, capturing the dehumanization and degradation of work as well as workers' unceasing quest for dignity and respect. Furthermore, she spells out the connections between the themes explored in the book and some of the debates that animate the field of sociology of work today, showing that the book remains deeply relevant. *Working*, she argues, remains a 'must read', chock full of ethnographic sensibility and sociological insight.

These three chapters demonstrate our inclusive invitation to ethnographers to submit their research findings, their readings of others' work, and perspectives on an ethnographic approach to studying work. We hope you enjoy this new section and feel suitably encouraged to both undertake such scholarly reflection and empirical studies and submit the subsequent fruits of your own labours to Research on the Sociology of Work!

FURTHER READINGS

Birke, P. (2022). *Grenzen aus Glas. Arbeit, Rassismus und Kämpfe der Migration in Deutschland*. Berlin.
Costas, J. (2022). *Dramas of dignity. Cleaners in the corporate underworld of Berlin*. Cambridge.
Terkel, S. (1972). *Working: People talk about what they do all day and how they feel about what they do*. Pantheon Books.

CHAPTER 7

FLORAL ETHICS AND AESTHETICS: UNDERSTANDING PROFESSIONAL EXPERTISE AT WORK

Isabelle Zinn

Bern University of Applied Sciences and University of Lausanne, Switzerland

ABSTRACT

This chapter presents a study of 'floral ethics', defined as a set of standardized practices for handling flowers shared among members of the florist occupation. Drawing on 36 months of ethnographic fieldwork in flower shops in Switzerland and Chicago, it contributes to the sociology of work and professions by providing a nuanced understanding of the tensions that can arise between the professional expertise of florists and the aesthetic preferences of customers. The findings on the micro-level reveal that adherence to floral ethics serves as a strategy for protecting and maintaining occupational legitimacy. By uncovering divergent conceptions of what constitutes 'work well done' among florists, this chapter offers a broader argument on the power asymmetry inherent in service relationships.

Keywords: Ethnographic fieldwork; expertise; florist; profession; service relationship

INTRODUCTION

The Chicago School's interactionist tradition in the sociology of work and occupations has emphasized the importance of examining how professional work is organized, expertise is developed and controlled, and social boundaries are constructed (Abbott, 1986, 1988; Becker, 1970; Freidson, 1970, 1986; Hughes, 1963, 1971; Liu, 2017). Scholars in this tradition have paid particular attention to how occupational collectives establish jurisdiction over specific tasks and present themselves as professional organizations.

This chapter sheds light on the dynamics of interactions among professionals and customers in the context of the floral industry. While there has been limited research on this topic, the study of standardized practices in the florist occupation provides valuable insights into how expertise and legitimacy are negotiated in the workplace. By examining the perspectives of floral designers in Switzerland and Chicago, the chapter contributes to a more comprehensive understanding of the challenges that arise when the 'floral ethics' clash with customers' aesthetic preferences. The findings highlight the importance of considering the role of expertise in fostering a more balanced relationship between professionals and customers in the floral industry.

The ethnographer's discomfort at observing techniques that did not adhere to standardized practices for handling flowers sparked an inquiry into the specific body of expertise that florists value and prioritize in their work. Through this investigation, I sought to gain a deeper understanding of the practical know-how that florists employ in their craft and the dedication they bring to their profession. Such 'floral ethics', defined as the right practices of handling flowers, are taught during the apprenticeship in Switzerland and tend to establish a common-sense understanding of how to handle flowers. They are based on a set of standardized rules among members of the florist occupation, thus making it possible to distinguish the profession from laypersons such as customers. This idea of 'right' practices corresponds to how I was instructed to handle flowers while working in various florist shops in Switzerland. I use this form of expertise as a sensitizer for both my American and Swiss fieldsites (see also 'Methods, Data, and Setting'). Informants in the field and interviewees often discussed what criteria must be met for florists to be satisfied with their work. Building on these criteria, I will explore the elements that make up a 'good bouquet' and analyse the tensions that arise from the clash between the florists' professional knowledge and the customers' aesthetic preferences.

This research integrates theory from the sociology of work and professions by addressing the asymmetrical relationship in service occupations, both between florists and their customers and, to a lesser extent, between shop owners and their employees. I therefore aim to contribute to a better understanding of the social drama of work (Hughes, 1976). By tackling divergent conceptions of the 'work well done' among florists on the micro-level, the findings will crystallize issues that exceed this situated context of ethnographic research and offer a broader argument on the dramatic asymmetry that characterizes the service relationship, particularly between the people receiving a service and those providing it.

This chapter draws on ethnographic fieldwork carried out in various locations in the florist occupation. The comparative analysis of data from different national contexts has proven to be a valuable heuristic tool for gaining a better understanding of the standardized techniques that were taken for granted or 'seen-but-unnoticed' (Garfinkel, 1967) during the ethnographic fieldwork in a familiar context.

The chapter is structured as follows. First, it will outline the professional ideologies of the florist occupation in Switzerland and Chicago. Next, it will introduce the research methods and data. The subsequent sections will present empirical data that aid in defining floral ethics and work well done. This will be followed by a detailed account of the strategies employed by florists to demonstrate their professional expertise and to avoid an excessively restrictive service relationship. Finally, the discussion and conclusion will summarize the main findings and clarify its contribution to the existing literature, highlighting the social drama of work (Hughes, 1976) in the service industry, and the broader forces that shape the way work is organized and performed.

LICENSING AND EXPERTISE

The trajectories leading to the establishment of the florist profession in Switzerland and the United States are quite different and reflect the broader labour market arrangements in effect in those countries. They are distinct regarding education, training, regulatory framework, and entrepreneurship. Switzerland is known for its vocational education and training system.[1] Under this dual-track apprenticeship system, sometimes defined as the 'Swiss miracle' (Lamamra & Moreau, 2016), apprentices combine on-the-job training with vocational instruction in the classroom, ensuring a recognized qualification upon completion and providing them with direct access to the labour market. More concretely, becoming a florist in Switzerland usually involves a 36-month apprenticeship, leading to a nationally recognized diploma called a 'CFC' (Centre Suisse de Services Formation Professionnelle, Orientation Professionnelle, Universitaire et de Carrière, 2012). This is acquired either through an apprenticeship in an established floral business such as an independent floral shop or garden centre, during which the would-be florists have class once a week.[2] Alternatively, students can obtain this diploma through a dedicated course at a vocational school, during which the students do more limited internships in floral shops. Although it is legally possible to set up a floral business or work as a florist without a certified diploma, more than 80% of Swiss florists are qualified in this way (Office Fédérale de la Statistique, 2011).

The education system in Switzerland echoes the rhetoric that E. C. Hughes (1963) has qualified as 'professional ideology': occupational groups seek to delimit the boundaries of their territory and develop a distinctive body of expertise over their core tasks through boundary work (Abbott, 1986; Gieryn, 1983; Hughes, 1994; Liu, 2017; Murphy & Kreiner, 2020). Such distinct expertise distinguishes professionals from laypersons. Boundary work has the 'aim to gain advantage for their collective entity in the turf battles over jurisdiction' (Liu, 2017, p. 48). Professionals profile themselves as professionals in order to be recognized as such and to assert their monopoly (Abbott, 1986, 1988) and independent judgement (Gormon & Vallas, 2020). Professions therefore set up training courses and entrance examinations to exclude the unqualified, create professional associations, issue codes of good conduct in order to standardize rules and practices (Evetts, 2013; Nicklich et al., 2020), and seek conventional or legal protections (Abbott, 1986). Then, each profession tends to control the tasks performed in their jurisdiction (Abbott, 1988; Bechky, 2003) and asks to be trusted in their expertise and skills (Hughes, 1963). Hughes (1984) even sees in the demonstration of professional competencies 'the essence of the idea of profession and the pretensions it implies' (p. 108).

The legal situation in the United States is different: there is no standardized or mandatory educational path for florists. The floral design programmes and courses in place are not as structured as the Swiss apprenticeship system: the diploma for 'Certified Floral Designers (CFD)' delivered by the 'American Institute for Floral Designers'[3] and 'programs in floral design and caring techniques for flowers' are available through private floral schools, vocational schools, and community colleges.[4] However, according to the US Bureau of Labor Statistics, most of the florists:

> typically get hands-on experience working with an experienced floral designer. They may start by preparing simple flower arrangements and practicing the basics of tying bows and ribbons, cutting stems to appropriate lengths, and learning about the proper handling and care of flowers (...). Most floral designers have a high school diploma or the equivalent and learn their skills on the job over the course of a few months.[5]

This indicates that there is no such thing as 'interns' or formal apprentices and that the boundaries between being a florist and not being a florist hence are much thinner in the United States than in Switzerland where only trained and licenced florists can possibly claim this label.

While in Switzerland the formalized standards for the florist occupation led to a nationally recognized label that distinguishes florists from non-professionally licenced and therefore lay workers, the distinct labour market and educational arrangements mean that floral designers in the United States acquire their knowledge more often through hands-on experience. Moreover, the US labour market more easily encourages entrepreneurship,[6] which potentially translates into a wide range of business models and career paths within the florist profession. Florists in the United States therefore less often share a common and standardized professional knowledge. Many sociologists have argued that expertise is acquired through both academic knowledge and practical work experience (Abbott, 1986; Bechky, 2003; Freidson, 1986; Liu, 2017). I do not want to imply that the formalized apprenticeship in Switzerland necessarily creates a cohesive set of values shared by all its members, nor do I intend to suggest that American florists lack any form of professional knowledge. However, the official florist diploma in Switzerland provides workers with recognition and an understanding of appropriate conduct within their occupation (Hughes, 1984), complementing

Floral Ethics and Aesthetics 149

their practical work experience. In this sense, it might be more challenging for floral designers in the United States to assert such moral authority and a distinct form of expertise. According to the interactionist concept of 'license',[7] formalized by Hughes (1963), professional ideologies tend to create certain values among the members of the group and professionals might be able to claim more easily '(…) the exclusive right to practice, as a vocation, the arts which they profess to know, and to give the kind of advice derived from their special lines of knowledge' (p. 656).

METHODS, DATA, AND SETTING[8]

The data used to build the arguments in this chapter are derived from field notes and interviews gathered between 2012 and 2016 across various occupational settings, such as vocational training schools, flower markets, and florist shops. Additional data were collected during a three-month unpaid internship at a florist in Chicago during spring 2014. The data consist of semi-structured interviews – tape-recorded and transcribed – with florists and teachers, informal discussions with workers in the workplace and participant observation. Twelve formal interviews with female (7) and male (5) florists in Switzerland were conducted. Half of the participants were shop-owners, one a florist teacher and the others were salaried florists and apprentices. The observations spanned over several months, starting with a full week on-site, followed by shorter periods once a month. My role in the field can be described as both an ethnographic researcher and florist trainee as I became an intern to do 'observant participation' (Seim, 2021): I acted with hands-on involvement in the daily activities of the shop – that is, consistent participation in the tasks, following the florists around, and doing the small tasks that I was asked to do. As I spent over three years doing fieldwork, I became an experienced florist trainee to the point where some florists thought they needed no longer to explain certain tasks to me, because I was already familiar with them. The following vignette features such a situation.

'An experienced trainee' (Field notes, 8 September 2014, Switzerland)

I arrive at the garden center around 8:30 a.m. for my first day of internship. I head directly to the flower section. Marielle, with whom I had arranged this internship, told me she did not work on Mondays but that she would inform her colleagues of my arrival. I greet the two florists and introduce myself as the intern for the week. Lisa shows me the locker where I can leave my belongings. As we return, she says to me, 'Could you please arrange the vases? Marielle mentioned that you have already done many internships …'.

Lisa clearly assigned me the role of an intern with enough experience not to require explanations on 'arranging the vases', assuming that I could handle it on my own. When she gave me other tasks during the morning, she would often say, 'You know how to do this, right?' In doing so, she immediately assigned me a certain role that implied a specific level of engagement on my side. The fact that one is no longer considered a novice but has acquired both a certain level of experience and specific knowledge is an important element for the further development of my argument.

Most of the tasks assigned to me were clearly more those for an unskilled worker – like preparing and processing flowers, cleaning, carrying equipment, and delivering flowers. But I was regularly empowered to do florists' tasks as well, such as designing various arrangements and bouquets that were sold in the shop. My work generally followed the standard processes of integrating trainees into the occupation in Switzerland, where becoming a floral designer involves a formal apprenticeship (see above). Each teenager who wants to train as a floral designer is obliged to do an internship prior to the apprenticeship. Given the importance of apprenticeships and hands-on training, my presence did not appear incongruous.

The American and the Swiss contexts are clearly distinct regarding education and apprenticeship and therefore might be hardly comparable. However, the main purpose of grounding this research upon fieldwork carried out in both Switzerland and the United States is not a direct comparison (comparing A to B) but instead draws on what Dodier et al. (1997) have labelled 'combinatory ethnography' where the ethnographer circulates across different fieldsites as she attempts to follow the phenomenon or activity she is interested in. Multiplying locations and contexts enables us to tease out how the phenomenon articulates according to the situation under study. In other words, starting a new fieldsite has helped recognize new patterns emerging. More specifically, thanks to the confrontation with a new fieldsite in Chicago, I was able to better understand what meaning the florists in Switzerland attach to their work and what they define as 'work well done'. While I first tried to avoid looking through preformed research glasses and simply observe what was going on in the flower shop in Chicago, I decided to not only accept this vantage point but also to use it to better understand the field in Switzerland. In this sense, the data collected on the American fieldsite were used as a sensitizer for certain processes that take place in the field in Switzerland and to focus this new lens on the data.

In order to understand the meaning of 'work well done', the starting point has been a strong discomfort felt when – on the third day of the fieldwork in Chicago – I realized that some of the 'best practices' learned would not be valid in this new fieldsite. The analysis of my own 'emotional behaviour' regarding situations in which the floral ethics were not effective has helped me to look more deeply into the conception of work well done. It is possible for the ethnographer herself to draw 'upon her own reactions to identify issues of possible importance to people in the setting (...)' (Emerson et al., 1995, p. 29). In this sense, the emotions are an analytical category as they reveal something significant about the field, that is, divergent conceptions of work well done.

FLORAL ETHICS AND AESTHETICS

In order to characterize a bouquet, the florists I met during fieldwork in Switzerland make a clear-cut distinction between a client's taste, which they label as personal and 'immediate', the 'floral style', and the formal rules and techniques, that is, the ethics of their occupation. In other words, there is no general consensus of what is considered a 'beautiful' bouquet, yet there are some rules that have to be respected in floral design. If florists do certainly have their personal tastes, my observations clearly indicate that their occupational aesthetic (Fine, 1992; Karlsson, 2012) does not play an important role on the job as the florists do not impose their tastes on the customers. However, specific floral styles do play a role: when florists describe their approaches to designing arrangements or evaluating bouquets created by others, there is a relatively consensual categorization of 'styles'. Three main styles can be identified, which are also taught during apprenticeship: 'traditional or decorative', 'modern or linear', and 'natural or vegetative'. Most stores adopt a particular style, and this is how stores themselves become labelled as, for example, 'modern' or 'traditional'. This does not exclude the preparation and sale of bouquets belonging to other styles. In fact, a store usually offers arrangements of various styles while having a preferred one, often embodied by the floral style of the shop owner. Here is what Marielle says about the different floral styles and the importance she attributes to mastering several of them:

> I spent three years in an apprenticeship at an extremely traditional store, where I could still enjoy doing some unusual things when the owners were not there because I was often alone in the afternoon. And then I arrived at [store name], which was very, very modern. So, what's good now here where we do everything, I can do just as well to make a traditional round basket or something hyper-classic as a modern thing, you see? So, it's good, honestly, I've seen a bit of different settings.

If different 'floral styles' exist, certain formalized techniques taught during the apprenticeship in Switzerland tend to establish a common understanding of how to handle flowers, regardless of the florists' individual style. Although these rules possibly include some aesthetic elements, such as the positioning of the flowers, dimension, and relation between different accessories, and complementary colours, they refer more to ethical questions of how to treat flowers so that they last. Floral ethics thus refer to the right practices of handling flowers defined by a set of shared rules among members of the florist occupation. Each profession has a certain 'professional moral' (Becker, 2006 [1962]), rules that define 'what matters' (Bidet et al., 2011; Sayer, 2011), and to what a positive value is attached. In this sense, floral ethics refers to a practical know-how that highlights what the florists value, what they are dedicated to, and what they are concerned about (Dewey, 1939). Furthermore, these rules and values make it possible to claim what distinguishes professionals in the field from others, including laypersons such as customers.

Andrew Sayer (2011) argues that actions are ethical not only because they align with our understanding of social norms but also because they consider (the well-being of) those involved. Therefore, the term floral ethics I choose to coin pertains to both the flowers and their dignity (*lasting longer in their beauty*), the florists' work ethics (*doing work well done*), and the customers (*achieving loyalty*).

The general 'floral culture' – workplace procedures, customer service, type of flowers, and orders are very similar in my Chicagoan and Swiss fieldsites. Basic elements therefore tend to establish a certain common sense for florists *here* and *there*. However, two vignettes that indicate differences in formalized techniques will be presented. The first vignette highlights a strong discomfort felt when I was confronted with techniques found to be inconsistent with standardized practices from previous fieldsites in Switzerland.

> 'Roses & Tulips' (Field notes, 3 May 2014, Chicago)
>
> Pat, one of the part-time florists, is in the middle of designing an arrangement when I get to the back of the shop. I'm more than surprised when I see that she combines tulips with roses in the same arrangement. This is something florists in Switzerland generally would not do as these two types of flowers need different treatment: roses need a lot of water, while tulips need only very little, otherwise they continue to grow very quickly, lose their form, and fade. A bouquet that combines both types of flowers necessarily ensures either too much water for the tulips or not enough for the roses. I watch Pat for a moment. I do not say anything but feel very uncomfortable in knowing that this bouquet will not keep very long.

It is not about the style of a bouquet or whether I personally find it beautiful to combine roses and tulips. It is, therefore, neither about aesthetics nor about the researcher's personal taste, but about ethical standards: I felt responsible for the quality of the product so that the flowers would last as long as possible. Speaking of ethics means imagining and evaluating the consequences of our actions (Dewey, 1939). This strong discomfort was felt because I considered it unethical to combine roses and tulips, which is akin to selling a product that lacks value to the customers.

A closer look at the above vignette with Pat reveals that the emotional behaviour involves an evaluative dimension of what Pat is doing: I consider the way she assembles the bouquet to be inadequate and make a normative judgment, thinking that her way of doing does not respect the ethical codes. While making normative judgments about the behaviour or work of our respondents is not what I strive to do as an ethnographer, it is intriguing to analyse the reasons when it does occur. Throughout my fieldwork, I gained insight into what is generally considered 'work well done' by the florists in Switzerland and have developed a similar appreciation for it. I have adopted their *valuation* (Dewey, 1939) and begun to attach great importance to floral ethics. Thus, my emotional response, which can be regarded as evaluative emotion (Sayer, 2011), reflects the significance of what matters to my Swiss informants. My evaluation of her bouquet relates to verifiable qualities of the bouquet, namely the presence of two types of flowers in the same bouquet that have incompatible needs in water. The reaction is thus mediated by the occupational rules that govern the fieldsites I have been working in for more than two years. Sandra, a florist employee from Switzerland, had told me about the kind of request she would decline because it contradicts her 'floral ethics', namely when a customer asks for a bouquet with tulips and roses:

> Some customers want to have tulips and roses because it looks beautiful. I then explain that these two types of flowers cannot be put together because of the amount of water they both need. Tulips need very little and roses a lot of water. Otherwise, they don't do well. For me, this is clearly a no-go because I want to sell good products that last, this is my job!

Katz's (1999) stance that discrepancies between existing schemes would create emotion seems to be very accurate in understanding why my reaction is so strong.

The emotional behaviour not only has a goal but also a tendency to action (Elster, 1995): I would like to prevent Pat from combining the two types of flowers by explaining that this is something a professional floral designer would not do. I do not dare to do it, as the vignette suggests, as I do not feel empowered to tell Pat how she is supposed to do her job. The role in the field, an intern and ethnographer, does not cover that way to react (*correcting her*) to what she, a floral designer, does. Here is a second vignette that accounts for a similar situation:

'Cutting them wrongly' (Field notes, 3 May 2014, Chicago)

Scott takes the bucket with the white roses from the cooling room and starts preparing them. He says they should stay fresh at least until Monday because they want to use them for various arrangements, they have to design next week. He cuts them with scissors instead of a knife as I've learned it, and the florists always insisted upon – and if he cuts a bias it was, according to my experience, not clearly enough angled (the cut resembles much more a straight cut). We chat and I watch him cutting the roses. I hesitate a lot to make any comment, or at least gently ask how he cuts the roses ... or anything that would stop him doing it. If he wants them to keep as long as possible, I think to myself, I should definitely say something. I remain silent.

Scott's use of scissors makes me uncomfortable because I have learned that it would be better to cut the stems without crushing the internal tubules. This is why, according to the formalized rules, it is more appropriate to use a well-sharpened knife and to cut in a certain angle. In other words, it takes the 'right' technique to respect the floral ethics.

Here is a third ethnographic vignette from one of the fieldsites in Switzerland that underlines the importance a florist attaches to floral ethics.

'Rose Petals' (Field notes, 24 September 2013, Switzerland)

A female customer enters the shop and walks towards one of the buckets filled with roses; Marielle approaches her. The customer wants to buy three roses and insists on choosing them herself. Marielle tries to show her which are the most attractive ones, but the customer does not follow her advice and states: 'I don't like all these petals beneath the flower. I think it's ugly. Can you take them away?' Marielle then explains that this specific type of rose naturally features these tiny petals to protect the main petals that form the flower and gently adds:

'There are other roses that have fewer of these petals. As a florist, I personally think it's a pity to take them away because they are part of the flower itself', to which the customer replies: 'Gha, but I'm not a florist, and I don't like them!' Marielle finally agrees to cut off every single 'superfluous' petal, but I can read in her face that she is really unhappy about it.

It can be difficult for floral designers to find a balance between 'service' and 'servitude' since some customers impose their opinions in a very determined way. The client's reaction is particularly hard to bear for Marielle because it is difficult to give up to what she attributes a positive value (Joas, 2008). This customer questions her expert knowledge by not trusting her advice, and by not wanting to let her do her job the way she intends to do it.

Let's have a closer look at how Marielle tries to convince the customer to keep the petals – she brings forward various arguments which can be associated with work ethics. First of all, she does not contradict the client by replying that the petals *are* pretty. Then, by saying that the type of roses naturally features these petals, she refers to a certain dignity of the product that should afford the ability to retain these petals. Finally, the customer's reply, 'I am not a florist and I do not like it' indicates that the customer contradicts the ethical know-how of the florist by claiming her own personal taste. The result is that the customer gets her own way and requires that Marielle remove the 'superfluous' petals.

To avoid an overly restrictive service relationship, florists often put in place a number of elements that allow them to deal with possible subordination (Jeantet, 2003). However, in this case, putting forward an ethical argument has not had the desired effect: Marielle has to face a relationship of servitude and ends up with simply executing what is being asked from her.

In this sense, to avoid subordination, Marielle probably should have more clearly expressed her expertise as a specialist of flowers and then opposed resistance by claiming the 'floral ethics': removing these petals from the rose will make the flower fade much more quickly. During a more formalized interview with Marielle, I wanted to know why Marielle did not insist by explaining to the customer that the roses will fade more quickly without those little petals that protect the actual flower. Marielle said she was about to insist, but the client really just interrupted her, and so she decided to give up on her, not invest more energy into the relationship, and let her pay the consequences.

AVOIDING SUBORDINATION: THE IMPORTANCE OF 'FACE-SAVING-STRATEGIES'

While the adherence to floral ethics remains crucial for floral designers, they must also navigate commercial imperatives, effectively combining ethical considerations with customer service. Florists are not just individuals with imaginative inclinations; they should also possess the social skills necessary to earn recognition for this from their clients through sales and customer loyalty. A good florist must therefore also excel as a salesperson (Zinn, 2019). The following vignette features a situation witnessed in a flower shop when a customer asked to bring her own flowers for assembly into a floral arrangement.

'Certainly, no chrysanthemum' (Field notes, 20 October 2014, Switzerland)

At around 11 a.m. a customer enters the shop and would like to speak to Sophie, the shop owner. I am processing fresh flowers just behind the counter and can follow the conversation. The customer wants to order a graveside flower arrangement for her father, either a funeral basket or a sheaf. Sophie explains that for a basket one must count at least a hundred Swiss francs and for a sheaf 120 francs. While she shows the customer various pictures of different flower arrangements in a book, she explains what she might create and how much it would cost. The customer does not seem pleased and says she does not like any of these arrangements, stating: 'I want something very natural, not so compact and stiff, but airy!' Sophie shows some more pictures of arrangements that feature flowers like dahlias, asters, roses, and chrysanthemums. 'Oh no, certainly no chrysanthemum, and no roses, really something natural and pastoral! Like this for instance' (she points to an arrangement on the table that Sophie has just created). Sophie explains that this arrangement is for a doctor's office and that a funeral basket would not look like this. The client does not want to hear this and instead insists, 'Maybe I can bring my own flowers so that you can assemble them into a sheaf or basket?' Sophie remains very polite and suggests quite quickly that she will prepare the base for the sheaf, the greenery in particular, and that the customer should come back two days later to see whether or not she likes it and decide on the flowers she would like to add. The customer agrees on that offer and leaves the store. Sophie joins us and I can hear her sigh. 'She wants to bring her own flowers!? I guess this is the type of customer you do not necessarily like very much, right?', I ask. 'Well, it's not really a question of whether I like it or not, we try to adapt, so it's more of a challenge to find an agreement and to satisfy everyone's wish'.

It was a surprise to see that Sophie had offered such a deal and in fact considered using the customer's own flowers, instead of creating, as usual, an arrangement from beginning to end. It actually contradicted the floral ethics witnessed in other flower shops. Customers who question expert knowledge and do not let the florists do their work are generally considered highly undesirable. Most of the florists would grumble about them and consider them 'bad customers'.

Through my observations and informal discussions, I have come to understand that the 'ideal customer' is someone who recognizes and values the professional expertise of florists and, as a result, places trust in them. Florists indeed expect customers to acknowledge their professional expertise in the form of recognition. This recognition is an important source for attributing meaning to their work (Gernet & Dejours, 2009). As one of my informants in Chicago pointed it out: 'I would be happy if only customers let us do our job'. Gold (1964) identified a similar element when doing research among janitors in Chicago: tenants who do not follow the building rules and do not cooperate are particularly disliked by the janitors.

The notion of trust is indeed crucial in service relationships (Jeantet, 2003). As these ethnographic vignettes have shown, as soon as a customer challenges the florists' expertise, their professionalism comes into question. Florists therefore adopt certain strategies to distance the aesthetic sensibility of laypersons. Floral ethics can be used as 'face-saving strategies'[9] (Le Feuvre & Zinn, 2013): demonstrating professional competence and convincing customers through know-how that such laypersons do not have. In this sense, selling valuable products – an element they are generally able to master by themselves – becomes their 'work well done' and enables them in the meantime to cast themselves as professionals and to stand out from non-experts, their customers. Although the florists are willing to serve their clients and accept the objective of 'customer service', they usually reject any relationship that could be identified as close to 'servitude' (Jeantet, 2003). In other words, although the florists display deference to certain customers, they clearly maintain their professional dignity through these face-saving strategies. As pointed out with the previous ethnographic vignettes, these strategies are displayed towards the customers – by directly or indirectly questioning the saying: 'the customer is always right'. A good bouquet is not a priori the one that is easily saleable, but a confection that complies with formalized and standardized rules. Indeed, the professional prestige of florists crystallizes among the 'floral ethics' and florists do not hesitate to educate their customers to restore a balance in the service relationship (Mennerick, 1974). The floral ethics therefore serves as both a sales strategy and to 'educate' their customers, not unlike the janitors (Gold, 1964, p. 20) who were actively trying to change 'the "bad" tenants into "good," and (...) to keep the "good" ones "good"'. This is why it is even more surprising that Sophie did not oppose the customers' request of bringing her own flowers.

By accepting such a deal, Sophie seems to condone an uneven relationship with her customer. Her expertise is mistrusted.

However, if the ethics are a crucial element, they do not necessarily guarantee commercial success. To 'hold on financially', as Marielle insisted upon, floral designers have to create bouquets 'that please' or, for instance, like Marielle, to remove petals that do not please or even accept that customers bring their own flowers. If for Marielle to sell the rose without these 'superfluous' petals is equivalent to selling a product in poor condition – contradicting her conception of work well done – she has at least been able to sell a few roses. The same holds true for Sophie. In adapting to her customer, she was able to sell the base of the basket instead of nothing at all. Here is an excerpt from one of the interviews with Marielle that shows how 'floral ethics' and commercial imperatives are directly linked:

> After all I am trying to respect a minimum of rules, there are flowers that you cannot put together in a bouquet. Some florists would do it anyway, like roses with tulips. A tulip needs very little water, and a rose needs a lot of water, you cannot put them together. Some florists will do it because they want the customer to be happy. But the bouquet will not last, so in the end it's bad customer service (...). We are here to advise customers, we have the know-how and should use it. Exotic flowers go into warm water, you cannot put them with roses who really need cold water, right!? ... I don't think it's fair to let the customer do as they wish, it's bad advice ... and after all they will come back and complain about the bouquet that didn't last.

To solely respond to requests from customers, even if they demand a practice that contradicts the 'floral ethics' may ultimately fail to satisfy them and thus prove to be bad service. The bad service rendered is of course likely to have a negative impact on the commercial relationship: customers whose bouquet has faded very quickly are not inclined to return to the store for future purchases. While professionalism in service relationships focusses on instant customer satisfaction (Barber, 2016), this does not mean that florists will just back down. It is about finding the right balance between floral ethics and customer service to avoid a relationship of servitude with their customers and to provide 'work well done'. Balancing floral ethics and customer requests is only one aspect of the potential tensions in service work that the florists are confronted with. There are at least three key actors in the service industry: workers, bosses, and customers. Let's examine the asymmetrical relationship between owners and their employees to get a clearer picture of the social drama of work.

'A question of style' (Field notes 23 December 2013, Switzerland)

> Tension is rising, everyone is stressed. As soon as Peter is in the store in the front, Marielle complains about him: 'he decides everything, controls everything, and doesn't let me work the way I want. He makes us work too much, he's always right, and he's not open to anything else!' She manages to somewhat hide her discontent, and the atmosphere remains bearable, but every time Peter says something, she looks at me and rolls her eyes, while responding to him with kindness. One situation pushed her over the edge: she welcomes a customer for whom she had prepared an arrangement in advance. When she goes to fetch the order, set aside, to give it to him, she sees that Peter had added a large quantity of Christmas decorations. Kitsch, everything she hates. Furthermore, the customer had specified, and she had indicated as customary on the order form, that it should not look 'too Christmassy'. Since she only noticed these additions at the moment of serving the customer, she is no longer able to remove the decorations and is forced to sell the arrangement as it is.

This vignette illustrates how the asymmetrical – and hierarchical – relationship between the shop owner and one of the florists who disagrees with him imposing his 'Christmassy style' on one of her arrangements creates tensions among them. From Marielle's perspective, Peter altered her creation by adding Christmas decorations without asking for her opinion or even informing her. She rebels, explaining to me that the arrangement sold did not match what the customer had requested. Doing 'work well done' also means responding positively, to the extent possible and without contradicting floral ethics, to the expressed wishes of the customers. The way Peter behaved goes against this conception.

DISCUSSION

Starting a new fieldsite was useful for recognizing new patterns emerging. The data collected in the American fieldsite served as a sensitizer for my fieldwork in Switzerland and made it possible to better understand what florists attach great importance to. In order to be able to profess and to do their job satisfactorily, the florists studied adopt certain strategies that distance the aesthetic sensibility of their lay customers. Their purpose is to establish a monopoly over expertise in order to avoid subordination and create symmetry in the service relationship. According to Hughes (1963): 'Professionals profess. They profess to know better than others the nature of certain matters, and to know better than their clients what ails them or their affairs (...)' (p. 656).

The data presented, particularly the 'superfluous petals' vignette, accurately reflects the confrontation between aesthetic and ethical elements and the tensions that result from this dilemma: the customer wants an aesthetic rose (without the petals) and the florist wants the product she sells to conform with the formalized rules. This vignette gives us an idea as to why the floral designers attach so much importance to their expertise: aesthetic sensibility seems to be lost ground as each customer has their own tastes and thus will not necessarily take advice from a florist or may even oppose their expertise. To demonstrate their professional skills, the floral designers have to take a different approach to convince customers and that is by demonstrating professional knowledge. These findings echo Howard Becker's (1963) research on jazz musicians. Becker underscored a similar dilemma for the musicians he studied. Their professional prestige was based on how much they adapted to the audience from the one extreme of 'playing what you feel' (Becker, 1963, p. 108) to 'do anything for a dollar' (Becker, 1963, p. 108). Buscatto (2003) identified very similar mechanisms for the musicians she studied in the French jazz world. Many of them had to constantly balance professional imperatives with vocation and need for creative self-expression. With florists, a similar question arises: how does one please the customers and maintain one's artistic ideal within floristry? Just as Becker's (1963) musicians find a way out of the dilemma by paying more attention to playing 'correctly' (p. 112) (i.e. properly reading and playing music) and no longer concerning themselves with the style of music they play, the florists adopt a similar strategy. Marielle says that if the clients very clearly specify their wishes, she will be ready to follow their request even when it does not match with her floral style. However, she would not willingly offer to sell the same arrangement in her own shop. The principle she always sticks to is the quality of the products she is selling: 'Although I tend to adapt to my customers' requests, I would never sell mouldy flowers to any client!' What the 'correctness' (Becker, 1963) of a song is for the musicians is here the freshness of flowers for the florists. I have coined it as floral ethics, which means demonstrating professional competence and expertise and convincing others through know-how that non-florist customers do not have. Floral ethics, then, become part of such strategies to demonstrate professional excellence, to control their body of expertise and to construct an occupational mandate (Fayard et al., 2017) in support of their jurisdiction. In this sense, the floral ethics as a form of an occupational rhetoric (Fine, 1996) can become a strategy that helps the florist navigate between commercial imperatives and craftsmanship. This brings in the question of who retains the legitimate know-how and expertise (Sherman, 2010; Stokes, 2021). The tensions between floral ethics and customers' aesthetics can be well understood with what is analysed as the 'occupation-profession' dilemma in the sociology of work: in the 1950s, there was a growing critique of the functionalist paradigm, centred around Talcott Parsons (1939), within the sociology of professions. The latter adopted a restricted conception of what could be considered a profession and therefore of what was worthy of investigation: it was mostly the prestigious or 'proud' (Hughes, 1963) occupations, largely autonomous, and self-regulating institutions, such as lawyers and physicians (Freidson, 1970). This growing critique has been taken up by interactionist scholars, including Everett C. Hughes and a group of students at the University of Chicago – who by now can be defined as being part of the second Chicago School (Fine, 1995) – who stated that any occupation, no matter its status, structure, or recognition – was a potential profession and that the interesting point to investigate is precisely how an occupational group would acquire distinct expertise. More current debates still question any apparent difference between so-called professions and ordinary occupations suggesting moving away from the long-standing sociological approach influenced by Talcott Parsons, considering 'professions' as occupations with very distinct characteristics (Crompton, 1990). This stance has led to broadening the field of investigation within the discipline ever since.

Meanwhile, drawing from my field experience, clients often maintain a specific perception of what defines a professional. If they were to view florists as fully fledged professionals, they would be less likely to challenge their expertise. Ideally, professionals hope for complete trust from their customers regarding their skills. In reality, and as the various vignettes highlighted indicate, customers do not always trust the professionals, but judge the practices of florists and question their expertise: 'Wherever you find people at work, there is some basic difference in the situation of the people receiving the service and the situation of the person giving it. That is an essential part of what I mean by the work drama or social drama' (Hughes, 1976, p. 3). Each occupation tries to present itself as a profession and to achieve its typical characteristics, such as autonomy (Becker, 2006 [1962]). Some professions have more or less room for manoeuvre and enjoy increasing autonomy (Valli et al., 2002). This is not the case with florists who try to become 'good' florists by insisting on floral ethics. By cultivating service relationships (Bigus, 1972) through face-saving strategies they try to make the relationship more symmetrical.

CONCLUSION

This chapter sheds light on the ways in which professional expertise is shaped and enacted, and how it can be at odds with the practices and preferences of customers. The ethnographer's emotional response, characterized by a strong discomfort with non-conforming practices that contradicted floral ethics, provided an entry point for understanding the significance that florists place on particular aspects of their work and their desire to assert themselves as professionals. Conducting fieldwork in different locations allowed me to recognize new patterns and examine taken-for-granted categories more deeply. By examining divergent conceptions of 'work well done' I gained closer insight into familiar data and deepened the understanding of various processes, as well as my position as an ethnographer in the field. The experience of discomfort also revealed the extent to which I had developed member skills and a similar system of evaluation as the respondents in the Swiss fieldsite. Such emotions are not instinctive but an expression of a set of standardized norms. According to Hochschild (1979, p. 15), feeling rules are reflective of social membership, and the emotional response to non-conforming practices can be considered 'luminous data' (Katz, 2001) that sheds light on standardized norms of a social group, in this case, the florists with whom I worked in Switzerland.

Florists face a challenge in meeting their clients' demands while also trying to maintain a sense of professional autonomy. To balance this tension and establish their legitimacy as professionals, they develop and uphold a set of standardized practices defined as 'floral ethics' which guide their work and infuse it with a sense of moral responsibility. By doing so, florists establish their expertise and lay claim to a distinct body of knowledge that sets them apart from others. This helps them maintain a sense of control over their work and to carve out a mandate for constructing occupational expertise. This contribution shows that floral ethics are not merely part of an occupational rhetoric (Fine, 1996) for navigating commercial pressures, but rather a central component of the florist's professional identity. Such boundary work (Gieryn, 1983; Liu, 2017) serves as a strategy for legitimizing their work, protecting, and maintaining occupational legitimacy and establishing monopoly over their expertise.

The observations made at the micro-level regarding the conceptions of 'work well done' extend far beyond the immediate context of ethnographic research. These findings provide a vivid illustration of the 'social drama of work' (Hughes, 1976) and reveal the profound asymmetry that characterizes the service industry, particularly the relationship between those who provide a service and those receiving it. Professionalism, expertise at work, and customer service are guided not only by social norms but also by how our actions affect us and others. These actions can sometimes be ethically flawed such as when a florist trims off unsightly petals to please a customer. In essence, these findings highlight the broader social, economic, and political forces that shape the way work is organized and performed, and how they impact the interactions between workers and their bosses, and customers.

NOTES

1. https://www.eda.admin.ch/aboutswitzerland/en/home/bildung-wissenschaft/bildung/berufsbildung-lehre.html
2. Eighty per cent of the young people who choose to take on an apprenticeship in Switzerland will follow this 'dual system' and will alternate between theoretical training at school and practical training in a floral business (Lamamra & Moreau, 2016; Zinn, 2016).
3. http://aifd.org/membership/become-cfd-and-aifd/, accessed on 15 June 2021.
4. http://www.bls.gov/ooh/arts-and-design/floral-designers.htm, accessed on 15 June 2021.
5. https://www.bls.gov/ooh/arts-and-design/floral-designers.htm#tab-4, accessed on 15 June 2021.
6. https://www.bls.gov/bdm/entrepreneurship/entrepreneurship.htm, accessed on 29 September 2023.
7. As Hughes (1963, p. 656) argues, 'Both in the narrow sense of legal permission and in the broader sense that the public allows those in a profession a certain leeway in their practice and perhaps in their very way of living and thinking'.
8. See also Zinn (2019) for a similar description of methods and data.
9. Such strategies can also be displayed towards other florists, for instance, when florists want to create boundaries towards their colleagues and demarcate themselves from their floral techniques.

ACKNOWLEDGEMENT

I extend my gratitude to the reviewers and editors for their insightful and constructive comments on a previous version of my chapter. I gratefully thank the participants in the Ethnography Workshop at Northwestern University and the group of sociologists from the Social Theory and Evidence Workshop at the University of Chicago for their insightful comments on a previous version of this paper that I presented in 2018. I also want to thank my fellow students from the seminar "Ethnographic Methods" (2014) at the University of Chicago.

REFERENCES

Abbott, A. (1986). Jurisdictional conflicts: A new approach to the development of the legal professions. *American Bar Foundation Research Journal, 11*(2), 187–224.

Abbott, A. (1988). *The system of professions*. The University of Chicago Press.

Barber, K. (2016). "Men wanted": Heterosexual aesthetic labor in the masculinization of the hair salon. *Gender & Society, 30*(4), 618–642.

Bechky, B. A. (2003). Object lessons: Workplace artifacts as representations of occupational jurisdiction. *American Journal of Sociology, 109*(3), 720–752.

Becker, H. S. (1963). *Outsiders: Studies in the sociology of deviance*. The Free Press.

Becker, H. S. (1970). *Sociological work*. Aldine Publishing Co.

Becker, H. S. (2006). La nature d'une profession. In H. S. Becker (Ed.), *Le travail sociologique. méthode et substance* (pp. 131–152). Academic Press.

Bidet, A., Quéré, L., & Truc, G. (2011). Ce à quoi nous tenons. Dewey et la formation des valeurs. Introduction à John Dewey. In A. Bidet, L. Quéré, & G. Truc (Eds.), *La formation des Valeurs* (pp. 5–64). La Découverte.

Bigus, O. E. (1972). The milkman and his customer: A cultivated relationship. *Journal of Contemporary Ethnography*, *1*(2), 131–165. https://doi.org/10.1177/089124167200100201

Buscatto, M. (2003). Chanteuse de Jazz n'est Point Métier D'homme. *Revue française de Sociologie*, *44*(1), 35–62.

Centre Suisse de Services Formation Professionnelle, Orientation Professionnelle, Universitaire et de Carrière. (2012). *CFC sans apprentissage (article 32)*. Centre Suisse de services. Formation professionnelle, orientation professionnelle, universitaire et de carrière (Csfo). http://www.berufsberatung.ch/dyn/10641.aspx

Crompton, R. (1990). Professions in the current context. *Work, Employment and Society*, *4*(5), 147–166. https://doi.org/10.1177/0950017090004005008

Dewey, J. (1939). Theory of valuation. *International Encyclopedia of Unified Science*, *2*(4), vii + 67.

Dodier, N., & Baszanger, I. (1997). Totalisation et Altérité dans L'enquête Ethnographique. *Revue Française de Sociologie*, *38*(1), 37–66.

Elster, J. (1995). Rationalité émotions et normes sociales. In P. Articleman & R. Ogien (Eds.), *La Couleur des pensées. Sentiments, émotions, intentions* (pp. 33–64). Éditions de l'École des Hautes Études en Sciences Sociales.

Emerson, R. M., Fretz, R. I., & Shaw, L. L. (1995). *Writing ethnographic fieldnotes*. University of Chicago Press.

Evetts, J. (2013). Professionalism: Value and ideology. *Current Sociology*, *61*(5–6), 778–796. https://doi.org/10.1177/0011392113479316

Fayard, A. L., Stigliani, I., & Bechky, B. A. (2017). How nascent occupations construct a mandate: The case of service designers' ethos. *Administrative Science Quarterly*, *62*(2), 270–303. https://doi.org/10.1177/0001839216665805

Fine, G. A. (1992). The culture of production: Aesthetic choices and constraints in culinary work. *American Journal of Sociology*, *97*(5), 1268–1294.

Fine, G. A. (1995). *A Second Chicago School: The development of a postwar American sociology*. University of Chicago Press.

Fine, G. A. (1996). Justifying work: Occupational rhetorics as resources in restaurant kitchens. *Administrative Science Quarterly*, *41*(1), 90–116.

Freidson, E. (1970). *Profession of medicine. A study of the sociology of applied knowledge*. The University of Chicago Press.

Freidson, E. (1986). *Professional powers: A study of the institutionalization of formal knowledge*. University of Chicago Press.

Garfinkel, H. (1967). *Studies in ethnomethodology*. Prentice-Hall.

Gernet, I., & Dejours, C. (2009). Évaluation du travail et reconnaissance. *Nouvelle Revue de Psychosociologie*, *2*(8), 27–36.

Gieryn, T. F. (1983). Boundary-work and the demarcation of science from non-science: Strains and interests in professional ideologies of scientists. *American Sociological Review*, *48*(6), 781–795. https://doi.org/10.2307/2095325

Gold, R. (1964). In the basement: The apartment-building janitor. In P. L. Berger (Ed.), *The human shape of work: Studies in the sociology of occupations* (pp. 1–49). Macmillan.

Gormon, E., & Vallas, S. (2020). Introduction: Expertise and the changing structure of professional work. In E. H. Gorman & S. P. Vallas (Eds.), *Professional work: Knowledge, power and social inequalities* (Research in the Sociology of Work, Vol. 34, pp. 1–8). Emerald.

Hochschild, A. R. (1979). Emotion work, feeling rules, and social structure. *American Journal of Sociology*, *85*(3), 551–575.

Hughes, E. C. (1963). Professions. *Daedalus*, *92*(4), 655–668.

Hughes, E. C. (1971). *The sociological eye: Selected papers*. Transactions.

Hughes, E. C. (1976). The social drama of work. *Mid-American Review of Sociology*, *1*(1), 1–7.

Hughes, E. C. (1984). *The sociological eye. Selected articles*. Transaction Books.

Hughes, E. C. (1994). *On work, race, and the sociological imagination*. University of Chicago Press.

Jeantet, A. (2003). 'A Votre service.' La Relation de Service Comme Rapport Social. *Sociologie du Travail*, *45*, 191–209.

Joas, H. (2008). The cultural values of Europe. An introduction. In H. Joas & K. Wiegandt (Eds.), *The cultural values of Europe* (pp. 1–21). Liverpool University Press.

Karlsson, J. C. (2012). Looking good and sounding right: Aesthetic labour. *Economic and Industrial Democracy*, *33*(1), 51–64.

Katz, J. (1999). *How emotions work*. The University of Chicago Press.

Katz, J. (2001). From how to why I. *Ethnography*, *2*(4), 443–473.

Lamamra, N., & Moreau, G. (2016). Introduction: Les Faux-semblants de L'apprentissage en Suisse. *Formation Emploi*, *1*(133), 7–16. http://www.cairn.info/revue-formation-emploi-2016-1-page-7.htm

Le Feuvre, N., & Zinn, I. (2013). Ambivalent gender accountability: Male florists in the Swiss context. *Recherches Sociologiques et Anthropologiques*, *44*(2), 21–45. https://rsa.revues.org/1027

Liu, S. (2017). Boundaries and professions: Toward a processual theory of action. *Journal of Professions and Organization*, *5*(1), 45–57. https://doi.org/10.1093/jpo/jox012

Mennerick, L. A. (1974). Client typologies: A method of coping with conflict in the service worker–client relationship. *Work and Occupations*, *1*(4), 396–418.

Murphy, C., & Kreiner, G. E. (2020). Occupational boundary play: Crafting a sense of identity legitimacy in an emerging occupation. *Journal Organizational Behavior*, *41*, 871–894. https://doi.org/10.1002/job.2473

Nicklich, M., Braun, T., & Fortwengel, J. (2020). Forever a profession in the making? The intermediate status of project managers in Germany. *Journal of Professions and Organization*, *7*(3), 374–394. https://doi.org/10.1093/jpo/joaa020

Office Fédérale de la Statistique. (2011). *Erwerbstätige nach Geschlecht sowie beruflicher Tätigkeit und höchster abgeschlossener Ausbildung (aggregiert) sowie Fünfjahresaltersklassen, 1970–2000*, Neuchâtel.

Parsons, T. (1939). The professions and social structure. *Social Forces*, *17*(4), 457–467. https://doi.org/10.2307/2570695

Sayer, A. (2011). *Why things matter to people: Social science, values and ethical life*. Cambridge University Press. https://doi.org/10.1017/CBO9780511734779

Seim, J. (2021). Participant observation, observant participation, and hybrid ethnography. *Sociological Methods & Research*, *53*(1), 0049124120986209. https://doi.org/10.1177/0049124120986209

Sherman, R. (2010). "Time is our commodity": Gender and the struggle for occupational legitimacy among personal concierges. *Work and Occupations*, *37*(1), 81–114. https://doi.org/10.1177/0730888409354270

Stokes, A. (2021). Masters of none? How cultural workers use reframing to achieve legitimacy in portfolio careers. *Work, Employment and Society*, *35*(2), 350–368. https://doi.org/10.1177/0950017020977324

Valli, M., Martin, H., & Hertz, E. (2002). Le "Feeling" des Agents de L'Etat Providence. Analyse des Logiques Sous-jacentes aux Régimes de L'assurance Chômage et de L'aide Sociale. *Ethnologie Française*, *37*, 221–231.

Zinn, I. (2016). La formation professionnelle au service de la division sexuelle du travail. L'exemple du métier de la viande en Suisse. *Formation Emploi*, *133*, 199–214. http://formationemploi.revues.org/4689

Zinn, I. (2019). The "truly creative" floral designers. When creativity becomes a gendered privilege. *Journal of Contemporary Ethnography*, *48*(3), 429–447. https://journals.sagepub.com/doi/10.1177/0891241618792074

CHAPTER 8

ETHNOGRAPHIC STUDIES OF ESSENTIAL WORK: JANA COSTAS' 'DRAMAS OF DIGNITY' AND PETER BIRKE'S 'GRENZEN AUS GLAS' AS TWO GERMAN EXEMPLARS

Markus Helfen

Hertie School Berlin, Germany

ABSTRACT

This comparative book review is concerned with two recent studies of essential workers in Germany: Jana Costas' Dramas of Dignity and Peter Birke's Grenzen aus Glas [literally 'borders made from glass']. While Costas is interested in studying how individual cleaners preserve their sense of dignity despite their widely believed stigmatizing work roles, Birke is interested in the power resources migrant workers can potentially mobilize for improving their working conditions despite the multi-dimensional (inter-sectional) precarity they confront in their life situation. In the context of German industrial and organizational sociology, both studies represent comparatively rare exemplars of detailed qualitative and ethnographic work that illuminate the labour process from taking a workers' perspective. Using different approaches to fieldwork, both studies reveal the precarious nature of being an essential worker in areas such as meat packing, warehouse work, and cleaning. This general observation gives rise to some concluding speculations about the emancipatory potential of ethnographic research, in labour studies and beyond.

Keywords: Essential work; ethnographic studies; precarity; service work; labour studies; emancipation; Germany

INTRODUCTION

The twin challenges of ethnography as a social research strategy are the identification of the general aspects in a special case, on the one hand, while excavating the peculiar quality of a general phenomenon, on the other. Ethnographers engage with these challenges by choosing the 'particular' as their starting point: They collect data on human practice in context, that is, by going there to look, hear, smell, and touch and talk, and then to compare what they experience and they observe (e.g. Zilber, 2020). But, as indicated in Goethe's quote above, how is it possible, then, to identify the general from observing a single or small number of unique cases in their specific social contexts? And what exactly indicates to us in a specific context which aspect of a single case illuminates the special, yet unnoticed, quality of a development or process of general interest?

This 'polarity of universalism and particularity' (Streeck, 2023, p. 18) can be interpreted in light of the varieties of the 'structure-agency' dilemma (Reed, 1997) influencing not only the choice of research approaches and methodologies but also shaping the real-world dynamics of human action in a variety of contexts from the politics of the workplace to the varieties of institutional change in societies. Applying more widely, this polarity is also encountered in ethnographies and qualitative studies of the labour process in general (e.g. Delbridge et al., 2023), and those studies aim at understanding the realities of essential work, in particular; 'essential work' here understood as the work that is assigned the status of ultimate necessity of being performed for societies to function, but also work which is generally marked by a high risk of precarious working conditions and occupational status (ILO – International Labour Organization, 2023).

If conducted thoroughly, ethnographic studies can contribute to the unearthing and explanation of the general meaning of essential work within and across societal contexts, exactly because they provide exploratory insights into less well-researched phenomena or provides new explanatory insights into the social mechanisms, dynamics, and processes unobserved by other methods. However, while it is a strength of ethnographic and qualitative work in locating and interpreting the specific observations within a meaningful context that offers novel explanation, there is also a caveat to drawing too widespread generalizations about a phenomenon from a single case. In other words, if one looks too closely at the practices around essential work as a specific category of work within a single context, one may overlook relevant aspects of the bigger picture shaping that very observation. As a result, comparison across cases becomes key for reducing the limitations of the single case by putting it in contrast with other cases across contexts such as time, field, industry, geography, or organization.

Ethnographic Studies of Essential Work 165

A good example to illustrate the value of comparison in the context of studying essential work is the recent qualitative research around Amazon warehouses. In these studies, using different qualitative methodologies and observing diverse work sites of the same organization, the simultaneous occurrence of a variety in workplace control strategies is excavated and made subject to contextual explanations by institutions or changes in labour market conditions (Butollo & Koepp, 2020; Delfanti, 2021; Vallas et al., 2022; Zanoni & Miszczyński, 2023). Revealing those peculiarities of this essential work setting that otherwise remain unnoticed by applying the more coarse-grained radar of quantifying methodologies, the comparative conclusion to be drawn from these studies is that 'conflicted collaboration' (Delbridge, 2007) is as relevant as are despotic varieties of Taylorist work organization. And, these academic studies taken together illuminate diversity, while they also correct media reports either highlighting rather uncritically the 'jobs miracle' around that peculiar company or scandalizing single examples of rock bottom working conditions in it.

CONTEXTUALIZING AND INTRODUCING THE STUDIES

Against this background, let us now turn to the two books under consideration here: Jana Costas' *Dramas of Dignity*, and Peter Birke's *Grenzen aus Glas*. In these books, a close look into how cleaners, meatpackers, and warehouse workers experience their daily work practice within organizational and societal contexts – as seen from the point of view of the workers – is given. For situating the books in the broader discourse, a contrasting with other genres reporting qualitatively about work is helpful, also because ethnographic practices – as opposed to neighbouring qualitative methods such as case studies or discourse analysis – have not been widely used in German academic studies of work.

One contrasting genre is the comparatively rich and vital genre of workers' literature in Germany, beginning in the early 20th century with realist novels (for an archetypical exemplar see Traven, 1928/1983, *Das Totenschiff*) or reportages (for an archetypical exemplar, see Kisch, 1928/2019, *Bei Ford in Detroit*), and continued by political journalism in the 1970s and 1980s (for an archetypical exemplar, see Wallraff, 1985, *Ganz unten*). One recent example, dealing with care workers' experiences during the Covid pandemic, sits at the borderline between reportage and documentation: Frederic Valin's (2022) collection of the individual stories of care workers. Having been a care worker himself, Valin curates a bundle of work-related personal accounts of care workers. These workers' accounts are compiled as stand-alone reports with minimal annotation, editing, and contextualization by the respective author, not unlike the curated selection of oral accounts documented by Studs Terkel (see Purser, this volume, Chapter 9).

In these novels, reportages, and accounts, however, one usually does not find a sophisticated apparatus for interpreting the empirical materials for the purpose of finding novel theorizations according to the standards of academic discourse. For example, the workers' literature regularly lacks a proper theory and method section or academic referencing and rarely clarifies the methodological requirements of ethnographic studies proper. Nevertheless, these accounts carry weight and value as a documentation of oral history in which the 'data' talk explicitly about the often-dire realities of work, especially when the working conditions on the frontline of essential work are documented. Thereby, and from a more mainstream research perspective, the authors of the literary genres deliver illuminating descriptions of those aspects of work that usually escape the radar of official reporting systems and inform struggles for emancipation by conveying the workers' view on their working life; a theory of practice of a different, practical sort.

In contrast with that literature, the two books discussed here clearly belong to the academic genre as they carry a lot of baggage in explaining their theories, methods, and findings. Taking a wide perspective on what is ethnographic work, both books report about a self-confident practice of ethnographic and qualitative methods observable also in other domains of social research (e.g. in management and organizational sociology, see Zilber, 2020). Whereas Jana Costas' *Dramas of Dignity* is a unique case of ethnographic work in German management studies, Peter Birke's *Grenzen aus Glas* follows in large parts the established traditions of German qualitative labour sociology.

The books' major commonality is that both place their focus on those work settings which have received sudden attention during the pandemic as 'essential work'. The methods and samples used are obviously different, but the data have been collected during a similar recent period and within the same country context: Germany. In Germany, what has become known as 'essential' work in Anglo-Saxon countries has been called 'system relevant' work, prioritizing a system's stability as the central yardstick for necessity. Of course, it is debatable whether this difference in terminology carries enough weight for capturing the diverging work cultures of the two countries – and for that matter how essential work is evaluated differently within these cultures – however, system relevance implicitly speaks to a generalized collective and public value of the work in question, whereas 'essential' carries a connotation for what necessary work is, leaving open for whom and what end.

Both authors accomplish their goal of giving a thick description of the social situations around essential work they observe and, thereby, examine, sort, and map the details of a complex reality in areas of work otherwise remaining invisible below the radar. There are a couple of pronounced differences between the two books, however, especially in how the authors participate in the lifeworld of essential work.

While Costas chose a participant observation in becoming a cleaner herself – not unlike Burawoy's (1982) classic study on metal workers in a small-piece producing unit – Birke reports an in-depth qualitative field study of workers in meat-processing plants and warehouses including workers' life worlds beyond the workplace. The Birke study combines various forms of narratively interviewing workers, managers, and experts, going also beyond the factory in participating in collective activities outside of the workplace. Engaging in such a variant of action research, that is, going into the private off-work spaces of workers' lifeworld, and participating in meetings with activist students, unionists, or public service officials – the researchers tap into the lifeworld of their interviewees in much more depth than a workplace-related style of data collection would have allowed. Also, both works give their study a different focus: While Costas is interested in studying how individual cleaners preserve their sense of dignity despite their widely believed stigmatizing work roles, Birke is interested in the power resources migrant workers can potentially mobilize for improving their working conditions despite the multi-dimensional (inter-sectional) precarity they experience in their life situation.

In what follows, I summarize the respective texts and identify some of their commonalities as well as their differences. For this, I focus on how these studies have been performed. Of course, in the peculiar context of work ethnography, such a discussion can't do without also reflecting upon the substantive findings of the studies. In the contexts chosen, I will do so by briefly touching upon the issue of workers' emancipation.

DRAMAS OF DIGNITY BY JANA COSTAS

In *Dramas of Dignity*, Jana Costas provides an in-depth ethnography of cleaners' work in what the author calls the 'corporate underworld' of Potsdamer Platz, one of the icons of post-unification Berlin. Producing a lot of insight into what it means to be an essential service worker, this ethnographic approach is very rare within contemporary German business and management studies. 'Underworld' here means the separated areas of the 'lower space' in multi-storey buildings, that is, the 'minus area' (as on elevators' control panels) in which the cleaners prepare for their work before they go out and clean toilets, office floors and desks, or the recreational areas in shopping malls. For cleaners, being in the Underworld brings along a feeling of 'invisibility' about their work and themselves as persons. Not unlike other essential workers such as careworkers or transport workers, cleaners are often doing their job in places and at day times separated from the regular flow of public activity. 'Invisibility' also entails a disconnection from personal interaction with the persons benefitting from their work. Although their presence is taken for granted, cleaners as persons tend to be overlooked by clients due to a lack of attention to their work and direct experience of them working. Costas captures this contradictory situation of the cleaners by calling them the 'absent–present' ones. For cleaners, this often means that their presence is felt by others only when they are absent, that is, not functionally present in physical space: the uncleaned space consisting of dirty and odious places with rubbish all over.

Jana Costas began her journey into the world of cleaners long before the actual study that has been written up in her book. Working a late shift as a business consultant, she noticed a cleaning woman around her age in one of the offices. For Costas, this brief encounter triggered a sudden learning about status differences and social inequality, a realization that although people are the same there are differences in class and status. Whatever such a realization means and how it is interpreted and enacted upon by the individual, it is fair to say that having such a realization of social distinction as a 'late' experience indicates the author's privileged position. Those at the other side of the societal demarcation, the ones 'in darkness' in Brecht's song text, grow up with this reality from the start of their life (Tilly, 1998).

Years later, Costas' participant observation begins with her first shift as a cleaner. She communicates her role as a researcher transparently from the start, so her experiences might have been somewhat different under more obscured investigative circumstances. However, through what is reported in the following pages of the book, this formal positioning seems to have resided into the background during the fieldwork. As for the workers, this positioning triggers different reactions ranging from being afraid of the researcher as a management mole to reactions like this one from Michaela, a 62-year-old cleaner: 'Finally, somebody is coming here to pay attention instead of taking us for granted all the time' (p. 4).

The study is put into the context of a variety of critical management studies, in that it aims to understand what 'dirty work' means for the workers at the point of service production. In the case of cleaning, the 'dirty' part comes from dealing with matter that human beings 'prefer not to see, smell or touch' (p. 4). Rather than being cherished and compensated for carrying this burden for the rest of us, those working in these 'dirty jobs' are relegated regularly to the lower bounds of the occupational and organizational hierarchy as well as pay scales, stigmatized even socially, and enjoying 'little, if any, prestige or respect' (p. 4). In that context, Costas raises the important question about these workers' dignity, and how the workers may or may not overcome their invisibility by reinstating their presence as the equal human beings they are. That question is what gives the book its title, *Dramas of Dignity*, indicating that Costas aims at illuminating, 'how and whether [workers'] sense of worth is undermined or maintained when they interact with others' (p. 9); the others being managers, corporate clients, customers, colleagues, unions, and society more generally.

The findings are presented in an order that follows the analysis of cleaning as service work: (1) the work sites, that is, as physical place(s) and as social space(s), (2) the work process, that is, the combination of a variety of single tasks and activities as well as the instruments necessary for completing these tasks that define cleaning as a human activity for others, (3) the work group, that is, the mapping of the interactions of co-workers and line managers, (4) the interaction with clients, that is, how the client/customer is involved as third factor in the work process, and (5) the multi-faceted control relationships in cleaning, that is, the manifold ways in which the invisible are controlled ranging from personal control by supervisors and clients to electronic and video surveillance in the buildings. In all this, Costas concentrates on illuminating how the workers perceive, make sense, discuss, and relate to their workspace, their work tasks, their colleagues, the clients, and the management and themselves as persons struggling for dignity and self-worth in the cleaning setting. Therefore, she introduces explicitly four individual characters, as she calls it, right after describing the Potsdamer Platz scenery and worksite, before moving on to an in-depth analysis of the labour process. The book provides a rich description of cleaners and their work experience from which a realistic idea can be derived about what it means to work as a cleaner.

The rich detail can't be reproduced here, but a couple of summarizing observations are in order: The individuals working as cleaners come from various social backgrounds that are not directly related to cleaning, rarely there is anyone who started out wanting to make a career as a cleaner. Rather, often biographies show a sign of crisis, disruption, or disadvantage that bring people into cleaning. Nevertheless, cleaners seem to experience their work as a steppingstone into society and draw self-respect from their work. The work of cleaning is organized to be invisible through various additional mechanisms beyond being prepared for in a physical building's underworld: (1) work schedules are set by management so that cleaning takes place early or late in the day when buildings aren't populated, (2) direct contact with clients is organizationally blocked through the subcontracting of the cleaning activities, (3) in direct encounters during work time communication is reduced to narrow task-related aspects, and (4) the sense of being proud of one's work isn't communicable with outsiders before and after work. If cleaners occasionally seize opportunities for stepping over the boundaries of cleaning, a wide array of control mechanisms keeps them in check: buildings' electronic and video surveillance, the critical look (subordinating gaze) of white-collar workers and other customers, the security guards' controlling the building, and the team managers. One aspect of this boundary making is group control in which cleaners remind each other of the boundaries, but also through how they organize themselves as a group. In that context, Costas observes that cleaners discriminate against each other on gender and race when building a 'pecking order' in the group. As Costas shows, these group struggles do hurt the individual cleaners, but not in a way that matches up with the injuries the cleaners experience from the lack of societal, institutional, organizational, and individual support they should receive. In fact, cleaners – in Costas' case at least – cannot form a community of solidarity based on an identity as cleaners alone; a strong sign that becoming a cleaner is first and foremost a matter of instrumentality to earn a living under the force of disadvantageous circumstances, not a matter of unfettered individual choice.

In sum, Costas manages to provide an excellent piece of ethnographic research by getting as close as possible to the work situation of cleaners while being aware of various immediate contexts, which are the physical space, the social relations, and the cultural framings around cleaning work. During her fieldwork, Costas sticks with participant observation which entails the role-taking of being a cleaner – even while remaining in the role of an observer and taking field notes for data collection. She is also very clear and transparent about her own societal positioning towards the cleaners, identifying herself as a relatively privileged university professor with a non-working-class background and professional experience as a business consultant. She also made her positioning as a researcher clear to the workers she studied. Regardless of this positioning, she wants to give a voice to the cleaners by observing them in their work context and writing about them. There is a question, however, of whether Costas' approach is restricting her. In augmenting the evidence gathered from observations and from the informal talks with the cleaners, it is not clear why she opted not to undertake structured interviews with the cleaners. In such interaction, cleaners would have got a chance to challenge her interpretations, give their own views themselves, and explain their interpretations of specific observations. There is no doubt that Costas respects the cleaners as the human beings they are. But if one doesn't want to reaffirm society's status assignment to work roles such as those of the cleaners through one's own ethnographic research (p. 10), giving workers a direct voice seems to be key. Furthermore, the book appears to be somewhat silent on the management's intentions and motives to allow Costas to do her study. For example, one wants to learn more about management's ambitions to reframe cleaning work despite society's dominant ascriptions (pp. 43–45): Are these actions informed by benevolent convictions about improving cleaners' working conditions or do they follow a profit motive in that relabelling cleaners' work successfully may increase the exchange value of their service work or both? One can imagine that there is a very material conflict lurking behind all the talk about dignity, one that concerns how cleaners can increase their share in the benefits of their hard work in hard currency. Cleaners' low unionization levels also points to another open question that is directly concerned with the issue of emancipation but remains unasked: If one doesn't want to see cleaners as passively enduring their fate, but as human beings with agency struggling for dignity, reflections on how it may be possible to instil the sense of collective action needed to alter their conditions in practice would have been an advisable extension to Costas' insightful study.

GRENZEN AUS GLAS BY PETER BIRKE

In Peter Birke's *Grenzen aus Glas* [literally 'borders made from glass'] considerations about action research and collective empowerment are made much more prominent than in Jana Costas' study. Birke's book reports on a selection of single research projects within a larger research project on migrant work in Germany (2017–2021). The reported studies concern two areas of essential work, the meat-packing industry and warehouses, in which a majority of line workers have a precarious status due to their migration background. As in Costas' book, the precarity of the work is intertwined with multiple forms of precarity in the life world of the migrant workers, including their status and dignity as workers and as members of society. In Birke's account, however, the migration dimension of labour market segmentation and fragmentation is of much more explicit concern and made the central focus of the research. The boundaries made from glass in Birke's book consist of the social preconfiguration of the labour market that emerges from a construction of inferior legal and social entitlements for migrant workers and leads to a segregation of migrant workers into lower quality jobs. As a result, blatant forms of direct discrimination are rarely observed in workplace settings, because the segmentation into certain jobs appears to be 'natural', and hence the discriminatory boundary is invisible as if it was made from glass.

In the preface and in the concluding section, Peter Birke makes clear that his research interest is also motivated in his subjective lifeworld in being a parent to a child of mixed-ethnic origin. Many of his reflections in interpreting this life situation inform the interest in studying how discrimination of migrant workers is produced and reproduced in the workplace and beyond. Beyond this personal access to the study's subject, the reported findings are embedded in a larger, publicly funded, and regularly institutionalized research project aimed at understanding how refugees enter the German labour market ('refugees@work', SOFI Goettingen). Hence, the context of Birke's study is also an academic one although the author explains in detail how the research connects with unions' and civil society organizations' activities to ameliorate the situation of the migrant workforces in meat-packaging and warehouses. Building from and extending socio-economic considerations of a Marxian tradition, the ambition is to excavate the processes and practices that explain the connection between value production and valourization in a labour process that rests on the segmentation of workers into migrant and German workers. From there, the peculiar power resources of migrant workers are to be identified, as they – however disadvantaged they may be or appear – retain their capacity for agency (see Thompson et al., 2013).

The findings are reported in a straightforward manner that follows the standards in German industrial sociology in studying workplaces. Methodologically, in this study the problem-centred interview – in a variety allowing for open and narrative styles of talking – is the dominant form of data collection (134 interviews in total) which is accompanied by various forms of direct observation in workplaces. What is especially important is that the project contains data from 51 interviews directly held with line workers. Of these, most interviews were conducted in workers' life contexts beyond the workplace. For both industries, the Birke book delivers a detailed account of the labour process, illuminating the sequence of work tasks and activities in warehouses and meat-packing facilities as well as the working and housing conditions of the migrant workforces.

These findings are embedded in a detailed description of the industry context as well the respective organizational contexts of the five facilities studied (three meat-packing sites and two warehouses). Given the focus on migration, Birke invests also considerable care in delineating the details of the German migration regime by discussing the current state of the law as well as the historical origins of institutions governing migrant workers' lives. In addition to that core, the research team also managed to prolong its activities into the period of the Covid pandemic, that is, the years 2020 and 2021. For this period, the researchers could follow the developments in both industries while there was a public debate about how the 'essential' workers had been treated in the workplace and beyond. Eventually, this debate led to regulatory changes for the meat-processing industry in which the use of subcontracting was legally curtailed.

Like in Costas' book, the overall account of the work reality is rich in detail. A few summarizing observations may be reported here: First, the precarious status of migrant work has to be seen within the context of state regulation which entails the definition of various forms of being a migrant, spelling out a hierarchy of individual rights and entitlements as well as a varying degree of 'punishments' that threaten migrants with informalization. For those forms that carry the lowest entitlements, migrant status forces workers into an inferior labour market position. This can be justifiably regarded as a form of coercion to accept jobs that are generally low in status and working conditions and carry precarious employment conditions. In addition, the migrant workers are subject to what Birke calls 'multiple precariousness' in that the inferior conditions at work are mirrored in the precarity of their lifeworld, for example, their housing situation or their participation in communal life. As for the workplace, rather than being the result of genuine market processes, the outcome of this regulatory migration regime is ascriptions of status and worth that segregate workers based on their migration status into certain work roles despite the proclaimed inclusiveness of employers. This is expressed in a straightforward manner in one quotation taken from the fieldwork: 'On the line you don't find Germans, (...), they are foremen or managers only'. (p. 110)

Birke argues that companies explicitly use these demarcations of the workforce for their own benefit, although in somewhat different forms: Whereas in the meat-processing plants the entire work regime has been built on bringing in temporarily posted groups of EU migrants, in the warehouses, a broader array of migrant biographies can be observed as recruitment is directed towards local communities with a high percentage of immigrant workers of heterogeneous origins. As in Costas' account, the workers working in the warehouse or in meat processing do these jobs not because they have chosen them voluntarily as a career but because their social contexts force them into accepting these jobs to earn a living under extremely constrained circumstances. Birke labels the work regimes observed either as a more traditional variety of Taylorism (meat processing) or as a subjectified form of Taylorism (warehousing). As for the latter, Birke explains why the idea of complete digital control is not observed in the warehouses, although the public image often depicts them as technologically integrated, well-calculated automatons running smoothly through sophisticated software, robots, and hand-helds. On the contrary, many mechanisms of cultural control are used by management with the intention to make workforces fit into the workplace regime (from make-out competitions between floors to displaying ratings on screens). In Birke's interpretation, these attempts at cultural manipulation are important because they indicate an absence of total technological control.

At the same time, in both industries, line worker management is done by what Birke calls a 'management by labor turnover' (p. 362), negatively influencing workers' capacity to form social ties. However, lack of total technological control and scarcity effects in local labour supply occasionally turn into a power resource for migrant workers. At times, workers can credibly threaten to leave the workplace which makes local site managers think about how to ensure the work capacity they need for a smooth and continuous operation of the respective site. This also points towards migrant workers' independent capacities for collective action (not unlike in earlier accounts in a US context, see e.g. Milkman, 2006). This is a surprising observation for those following the dominant view which holds migrant workers' power resources as extremely limited in structural, institutional, and organizational terms. Instead, Birke reports occasional wildcat strikes and other forms of non-unionized resistance that point towards a potential pathway for migrant workers to organize, if adequately supported in that endeavour.

Peter Birke's book makes for an insightful reading for various reasons, of which here the focus is on the potential of ethnographic studies to deliver an innovative and fresh insight into workplace realities in areas of essential work otherwise rarely studied. At the same time, Birke's book nicely illuminates the potential for researchers to involve themselves beyond academia by informing the initiatives struggling to improve working conditions. Here, it would have been interesting to have learnt more about the meetings the research group held with activist students, interested unionists, or public service officials. This would have been illuminating beyond the reflection about the researchers own positioning regarding how to give migrant workers a direct voice through interviewing them.

While the author reflects extensively about his own interpretations of interviewees' responses (pp. 199–126), these considerations lack – as compared to Costas – a clear and explicit self-description of where the author believes himself to be positioned in the struggles of the migrant workers. This makes it difficult for readers to see or interpret how much filtering the author brought to bear on the direct voices of the migrant workers interviewed in the studies. Hence, as a reader one struggles to understand how the author developed his own narrative of the migrant workers' situation. In that context, for example, it appears at least to this reader as an irritating move to place interviews with managers into the category of a 'perspective from the outside' (p. 130). This move leaves open questions about who constitutes the workplace – and the point of production – in the first place.

Regardless of that shortcoming, notably, Birke's careful reflections on how the workers themselves can be empowered to improve their working conditions are instructive. In a double meaning, Birke argues that these workers need not wait for a 'white knight' as a saviour, at least if they could be empowered to take care of themselves. Moreover, Birke suggests a widening of German unions' perspective towards migrants' civic empowerment as it could also assist in tackling the fragmented realities of 'fissured workplaces' (Weil, 2019) to the benefit of all workers. Here, some doubts are justified about whether the study places too much weight on excavating the power resources and collective action opportunities of migrant workers to empower themselves as political actors on their own. In a different reading, the study runs the risk of neglecting the migrant workers' manifold disempowerments resulting from the variety of social, organizational, and individual disadvantages, dependencies, and weaknesses they may have experienced not only in their current life situation but also throughout their biographies.

Of course, Birke is aware that there are constraints that relegate the empowerment of migrant workers to something more often pleaded for than achieved in practice. Especially in his closing remarks, Birke highlights several current developments that may even point in the opposite direction, that is, increasing conflicts over who carries the burden of the climate crisis, rising inequalities along global supply chains, or xenophobia in various forms, which provide obstacles to achieving empowerment. For example, it would already help migrant workers a great deal if those state regulations that relegate them to inferior working positions (in several cases, regardless of their true occupational achievements) were relaxed. Such a move would effectively support the upholding of the working conditions of workers doing similarly strenuous work, regardless of where they are coming from. Exactly such a relaxation appears to be difficult to achieve against extant migration laws crafted to sort people into those welcome and those deemed illegitimate.

These considerations about the state intervening in migrants' labour market position also points to another interesting aspect, methodologically as well as substantively: In both ethnographies, the state's labour inspection isn't mentioned as a prominent aspect of the workers' experience. There seems to be a gap here, especially where the conditions in meat-packing facilities and warehouses are concerned. In fact, in Birke's book, labour inspection is mentioned briefly within the context of discussing the newly introduced legislation – the 'Arbeitsschutzkontrollgesetz' (literally translated 'work protection control law'). However, in what follows the state as having a decisive role in overseeing workplace realities through labour inspection is not discussed in both books in any detail. Admittedly, from standing outside of the fieldwork, it is difficult to assess whether labour inspection does have an influence here in practice or not. However, the neglect of labour inspection points to the challenges of a 'close look' ethnography in that it is also important to reflect upon what is missing in a given social situation; an interpretative skill that needs to be carefully trained in order to enlarge the insights from ground-level ethnographic work.

CONCLUSION

Given what has been written so far, it should not come as a big surprise that doing work ethnographies for studying essential work is often related to emancipatory projects, that is, aimed explicitly – as in Birke's book – or implicitly – as in Costas' – at bettering the situation of those studied. More generally, one could even argue that the ultimate proof of theorizations, not only of those derived from qualitative work and ethnographic studies, is whether the understandings developed can be fruitfully applied to solving a social problem and improving people's life in social reality.

Properly executed, qualitative research in general, and ethnographic work in particular, is well-suited to supporting that sort of pragmatic problem-solving capacity in three ways: (1) by studying the problem in context, ethnographic work helps to identify where and how exactly wider structures impinge on the agency of the persons involved, (2) by moving close to a given social situation, it assists in identifying those practices that can be changed directly, and (3) by placing the spotlight on extreme forms of injustice in depth and with colour, it can provide a strong mobilizing force for action. However, building emancipatory potential from academic study regularly meets resistance through extant structures, enshrined institutions, and powerful incumbents and beneficiaries of the status quo, in academia and beyond (e.g. DeCoster & Zanoni, 2023; Delbridge et al., 2024; Schiller-Merkens, 2022).

Excavating the varieties of dominating structuration in work settings and moving towards a practice that also empowers the practitioners to act individually or collectively to improve their situation also brings along profound additional responsibilities for researchers. One of these responsibilities is being transparent about the researchers' ambitions and positionings to explicate to others how the researchers use the research for what end. As Adler (2002) explained, acknowledging domination as a social fact also entails not hiding abstractly behind labels such as 'critical' but also being explicit by giving an answer to the questions of 'for whom' and 'for what' a study is undertaken. This sort of transparency goes beyond the 'comfort zone' of the standard requirements for communicating all research processes, that is, making theoretical views, methodological decisions, and empirical findings intersubjectively understandable (Scherer & Steinmann, 1999). Nevertheless, transparency is vital for the researcher and equally valuable to the public for at least three reasons: (1) for allowing a critique of one's own conclusions and actions against stated ambitions; (2) for making transparent where a study crosses the boundaries between academic discourse and public and political debate; and (3) for avoiding the pitfalls of technocratic illusions about social science and how its results are informing societal practice. As for the latter, and especially when studying work in business contexts, this reflexivity also includes an awareness about the relative social positioning of the researchers, not least for protecting those in the work situation studied. Essentially, the least an ethnographic approach to the study of essential work can do for supporting such ambitions for emancipation is to bring to light those areas of darkness made invisible, forgotten, or neglected.

REFERENCES

Adler, P. (2002). Critical in the name of whom and what? *Organization*, *9*(3), 387–395. https://doi.org/10.1177/135050840293003

Birke, P. (2022). *Grenzen aus Glas. Arbeit, Rassismus und Kämpfe der Migration in Deutschland*. Mandelbaum.

Burawoy, M. (1982). *Manufacturing consent. Changes in the labor process under monopoly capitalism*. University of Chicago Press. (original work published in 1979).

Butollo, F., & Koepp, R. (2020). Die doppelte Einbettung der Logistikarbeit und die Grenzen prekärer Beschäftigung. *WSI Mitteilungen*, *73*(3), 174–181. https://doi.org/10.5771/0342-300X-2020-3-174

Costas, J. (2022). *Dramas of dignity. Cleaners in the corporate underworld of Berlin*. Cambridge University Press.

DeCoster, M., & Zanoni, P. (2023). More than prefigurative politics? Redefining institutional frames to reduce precarity under neoliberal capitalism. *Organization Studies*, *44*(6), 939–960. https://doi.org/10.1177/01708406221113110

Delbridge, R. (2007). Explaining conflicted collaboration: A critical realist approach to hegemony. *Organization Studies*, *28*(9), 1347–1357. https://doi.org/10.1177/0170840607080744

Delbridge, R., Helfen, M., Pekarek, A., & Purser, G. (2023). Why ethnographies of work? An introduction. In R. Delbridge, M. Helfen, A. Pekarek, & G. Purser (Eds.), *Ethnographies of work* (Research in the Sociology of Work, Vol. 35, pp. 1–8). Emerald. https://doi.org/10.1108/S0277-283320230000035001

Delbridge, R., Helfen, M., Pekarek, A., Schüßler, E., & Zietsma, C. (2024). Organizing sustainably: Introduction to the special issue. *Organization Studies*, *45*(1), 1–23. https://doi.org/10.1177/01708406231217143

Delfanti, A. (2021). *The warehouse. Workers and robots at Amazon*. Pluto Press.

ILO – International Labour Organization. (2023). *World Employment and Social Outlook 2023: The value of essential work*. ILO.

Kisch, E. O. (2019). *Paradies Amerika*. Null Papier. (Original work published 1928)

Milkman, R. (2006). *L.A. Story: Immigrant workers and the future of the U.S. labor movement*. Russell Sage Foundation.

Purser, G. (2024). 'More than a slight ache': on the ethnographic sensibility and enduring relevance of Studs Terkel's working. In M. Helfen, R. Delbridge, A. Pekarek, & G. Purser (Eds.), *Ethnographies of work* (Research in the Sociology of Work, Vol. 36, 177–188). Emerald.

Reed, M. (1997). In praise of duality and dualism: Rethinking agency and structure in organizational analysis. *Organization Studies*, *18*(1), 21–42. https://doi.org/10.1177/017084069701800103

Scherer, A. G., & Steinmann, H. (1999). Some remarks on the problem of incommensurability in organization studies. *Organization Studies*, *20*(3), 519–544. https://doi.org/10.1177/0170840699203006

Schiller-Merkens, S. (2022). Prefiguring an alternative economy. Understanding prefigurative organizing and its struggles. *Organization*, *31*(3), 458–476. https://doi.org/10.1177/13505084221124189

Streeck, W. (2023). Reflections on the particular and the universal: Unity and diversity in social life and social theory. *Society Register*, *7*(2), 7–20. https://doi.org/10.14746/sr.2023.7.2.01

Thompson, P., Newsome, K., & Commander, J. (2013). 'Good when they want to be': Migrant workers in the supermarket supply chain. *Human Resources Management Journal*, *23*(2), 129–143. https://doi.org/10.1111/j.1748-8583.2011.00186.x

Tilly, C. (1998). *Durable inequality*. University of California Press.

Traven, B. (1983). *Das Totenschiff*. Diogenes. (Original work published 1928)

Valin, F. (2022). *Pflege Protokolle*. Verbrecher.

Vallas, S. P., Johnston, H., & Mommadova, Y. (2022). Prime suspect: Mechanisms of labor control at Amazon's warehouses. *Work and Occupations*, *49*(4), 421–456. https://doi.org/10.1177/07308884221106922

Wallraff, G. (1985). *Ganz unten*. Kiepenheuer & Witsch.

Weil, D. (2019). Understanding the present and future of work in the fissured workplace context. *Russell Sage Foundation Journal of the Social Sciences*, *5*(5), 147–165. https://doi.org/10.7758/RSF.2019.5.5.08

Zanoni, P., & Miszczyński, M. (2023). Post-diversity, precarious work for all: Unmaking borders to govern labour in the Amazon warehouse. *Organization Studies*, 1–22. https://doi.org/10.1177/01708406231191336

Zilber, T. B. (2020). The methodology/theory interface: Ethnography and the microfoundations of institutions. *Organization Theory*, *1*, 1–27. https://doi.org/10.1177/2631787720919439

CHAPTER 9

'MORE THAN A SLIGHT ACHE': ON THE ETHNOGRAPHIC SENSIBILITY AND ENDURING RELEVANCE OF STUDS TERKEL'S *WORKING**

Gretchen Purser

Syracuse University, USA

ABSTRACT

It has been 50 years since the publication of Studs Terkel's groundbreaking book, Working, *which consists of a compilation of interviews carried out with over 130 workers in the United States. In this chapter, the author revisits this masterpiece, which offers a penetrating analysis of the dehumanization and degradation of work. The author argues that* Working *is an ode to, and guide for, ethnographic scholarship on work and that it remains as powerful and relevant today as when it was originally published a half of a century ago.*

Keywords: Studs Terkel; working; ethnography; interviews; oral history; alienation

---

*Excerpts from *Working: People Talk About What They Do All Day and How They Feel About What They Do* – Copyright © 2004 by Studs Terkel. Reprinted by permission of The New Press. www.thenewpress.com.

A half of a century has passed since the release of Studs Terkel's iconic *Working*, a compendium of interviews carried out with over 130 workers including steelworkers, lawyers, clerks, teachers, metre readers, waitresses, janitors, cab drivers, receptionists, and more. Arguably no book has done a better job of capturing how workers think and feel about their jobs than *Working*. A national best-seller, the book has been turned into a Broadway musical. It has spawned several copycat sequels (Alvarez, 2022; Bowe et al., 2000). And, most recently, it served as the inspiration for a new docuseries on Netflix, hosted – rather curiously, given Studs' stalwart commitment to ordinary people and to history 'from the bottom up' – by former US President Barack Obama. The book is a work of biting social criticism, documenting in penetrating detail widespread worker alienation. It is also a kind of ode to, and guide for, ethnographic research on work.

Let me begin with a personal note. I first encountered Studs' work as a high school student living in our shared hometown of Chicago. From an early age, I sought to understand the striking inequities that characterize the social geography of the city. I grew up in walking distance to both the city's Gold Coast and the infamous public housing project – since torn down – Cabrini Green. As a kid, my yellow school bus regularly crossed Division Street into the Cabrini Green housing development. 'Windows up, heads down!' the bus driver would yell. We obediently crouched down below the sightline, lest a stray bullet fly by, while our schoolmates boarded the bus for a trip of less than two miles westward. Given such early childhood experiences, it should come as little surprise that my first encounter with Studs' work was via his first book of oral histories, *Division Street*, which explored urban inequality in Chicago.

Yet, no book has had a more lasting influence on me and my work than *Working*. When I set off for graduate school at the University of California at Berkeley, I was armed with little more than a voice recorder – the tool of the trade – and a deep curiosity about peoples' experiences at work. Much of the appeal of *Working*, as some have observed, 'is the very wealth of coverage, the chance to peer into worlds rarely subject to outside observation, let alone analysis' (Fink, 2010, p. 386). For a quite similar reason, for my dissertation I embarked on a study of day labour staffing agencies (or 'slave marts', as one of the interviewees in *Working* refers to them, p. 538), a study which gave me access to all kinds of workplaces: construction sites, car auctions, kitchens, factories, warehouses, stadiums, and eviction crews (e.g. Purser, 2012, 2019).

I have been so inspired and influenced by Studs Terkel that, even today, I have a signed and framed portrait of him hanging on a wall of my home.

ETHNOGRAPHIC ENCOUNTERS

Studs Terkel, born in 1912 to Russian Jewish immigrants, lived and worked up until the ripe old age of 96. He was a prize-winning author and a prominent radio host with an unusually expansive range of interests and talents. Perhaps this is best encapsulated in his admission: 'I was out to swallow the world' (Terkel, 1997, p. 222). Studs is routinely lauded as one of the greatest interviewers, social critics, documentarians, and oral historians of all time. But he was also, as scholars

Hirsch and Cornfield (2010) have pointed out, a sociologist and 'peerless participant observer' (p. 40).

Studs eschewed formulaic question-and-answer style interviews. 'The question-and-answer technique', he writes,

> may be of some value in determining favored detergents, toothpaste, and deodorants, but not in the discovery of men and women. There were questions, of course. But they were casual in nature – in the beginning: the kind you would ask while having a drink with someone; the kind he would ask you. The talk was idiomatic rather than academic. In short, it was conversation. In time, the sluice gates of damned up hurts and dreams were opened. (pp. xx–xxi)

Studs recognized that to understand the human experience, one had to go beyond the interview. To learn something about the 'scars, psychic and physical' experienced by workers, one had to immerse themselves in their world and closely attend to their thoughts and feelings (p. xi). The extended conversations that make up *Working* represent what Studs referred to via the more ethnographic language of 'encounters'.

Studs talks about his method as a form of prospecting, of searching for something even if one doesn't know at first what one is searching for. All fieldwork is a kind of quest, requiring an embrace of uncertainty and serendipity. 'I may have, on more occasions than I had imagined, struck gold', he writes. 'I was constantly astonished by the extraordinary dreams of ordinary people' (p. xxiv). But this analogy between ethnography and mining is doubly significant. By characterizing his method as a form of prospecting for gold, Studs acknowledges, and grapples with, the inherently extractive nature of ethnographic research. 'I was no more than a wayfaring stranger, taking much and giving little', he reflects.

> True, there were dinners, lunches, drinks, breakfasts, in posh as well as short order places ... [but] I was the beneficiary of others' generosity. My tape recorder, as ubiquitous as the carpenter's tool chest or the doctor's black satchel, carried away valuables beyond price. (p. xviii)

What were these valuables? 'It was the daily experience of others, their private hurts, real and fancied' (p. xviii). Studs recognized that being asked to reflect upon one's experiences and aspirations could elicit considerable pain. Yet he also knew that these conversations often led to self-clarification and mutual recognition. 'On one occasion, during a play-back, my companion murmured in wonder, "I never realized I felt that way". And I was filled with wonder, too' (p. xix). These encounters could be transformative, even liberating, offering people the opportunity to express themselves to an attentive and empathic listener.

> My experiences tell me that people with buried grievances and dreams unexpressed do want to let go. Let things out. Lance the boil, they say; there is too much pus. The hurts, though private, are, I trust, felt by others too. (p. xix)

ON THE JOB

And therein lies the power and, hence, popularity of the book. The hurts and grievances crisscrossing these pages, while experienced as deeply personal, are felt and shared by others. Take, for instance, the conversation with Bob Sanders, a strip miner living in Indiana near the border with Kentucky. Bob worries about the harm he's done to the earth. 'There's a lot of things I don't like about my work', he says. 'I've never really appreciated seeing ground tore up. Especially if that ground could be made into something. I think about it all the time' (p. 21). Or take the conversation with Brett Hauser, a 17-year-old box boy at a supermarket, who has learned at a young age about the indignities of service work. 'You have to be terribly subservient to people' (p. 279). Or consider the conversation with Barbara Herrick, a script supervisor and producer at a large advertising agency who, at 30, is anxious about growing older in a workplace that places a premium on youth. 'I have a fear of hanging on past my usefulness', she admits. 'The danger of aging, beyond touch, out of reach with the younger market' (pp. 70–71). Who among us hasn't felt – like Bob, Brett and Barbara – a similar kind of regret, shame, and/or anxiety about our work?

Readers of all backgrounds recognize themselves within the accounts of these strangers, who – on the basis of that shared recognition – become far less strange. Terkel lets each individual come alive on the page, giving us a clear glimpse into the way they think about their situation. But he also generalizes from these encounters, telling us something broader about the nature of work and offering a deep sociological analysis of labour under capitalism. 'This book', writes Studs,

> being about work, is, by its very nature, about violence – —to the spirit as well as to the body. It is about ulcers as well as accidents, about shouting matches as well as fistfights, about nervous breakdowns as well as kicking the dog around. It is, above all (or beneath all), about daily humiliations.

Terkel continues,

> It is about a search, too, for daily meaning as well as daily bread, for recognition as well as cash, for astonishment rather than torpor; in short, for a sort of life rather than a Monday through Friday sort of dying. (p. xi)

No interview more clearly demonstrates this search for daily meaning as well as daily bread than that with Nora Watson, a 28-year-old staff writer. 'Jobs are not big enough for people', Nora opines.

> A job like mine, if you really put your spirit into it, you would sabotage immediately. You don't dare. So you absent your spirit from it … You want it to be a million things that it's not and you want to give it a million parts of yourself that nobody else wants there … It's so demeaning to be there and not be challenged. It's humiliation, because I feel I'm being forced into doing something I would never do of my own free will – which is simply waste itself … I know I'm vegetating and being paid to do exactly that … Somebody has bought the right to you for eight hours a day. The manner in which they use you is completely at their discretion. You know what I mean? (p. 521)

Nora, reflecting on her father's vocation as a preacher, later adds, 'there's nothing I would enjoy more than a job that was so meaningful to me that I brought it home'. Trapped in what we would characterize as a 'bullshit job' (Graeber, 2018), Nora recognizes the allure of following one's passion (Cech, 2021). Nevertheless, she does not fully embrace the 'do what you love' mantra. Instead, Nora finds herself 'coming to a less moralistic attitude toward work' altogether (p. 524). 'I don't think I have a calling – at this moment – except to be me'.

Other workers featured in the book find that the job 'possesses' them even after quitting time, becoming – wittingly or unwittingly – a kind of 'singular preoccupation' (p. xv). Take, for example, Pat Zimmerman, the 'headmaster' and administrator of an alternative school in the gritty Chicago neighbourhood of Uptown, working with kids from the ages of 6 to 17. He embraces the job as his singular preoccupation. 'My work is everything to me', Pat admits.

> I find myself trying to get an hour or two of personal life now and then – in vain. I'd rather die for my work life than for my personal life. I guess you can't really separate them. The school's not an institution. We have a building, that's where the school exists. But it also exists when we leave (p. 491).

For others, the preoccupation stems from the ways in which the job lingers upon, or breaks down, the body. Take Lincoln James, for instance, who works in a rendering and glue factory, cooking animal fat and bones down into grease. Despite wearing rubber gloves, 'there'd still be an odor to your hand'. Lincoln explains, 'The odor was terrible, but I got used to it ... it's a different odor altogether. Whenever meat lays around for a few days it smells like that' (p. 111). Or take Conrad Swible, a gas metre reader, who just can't get the job out of his head, like a noxious jingle. 'When I get home', he says,

> I'm usually calling out numbers to myself. Usually four numbers. Like the last house I read: 2652. I'll be home and I'll be doing 2652, 2652, 2652. It'll just be going through my mind: 2652. Like a song you hear too much. (p. 277)

Or consider John Fuller, a mail carrier. 'Constantly you walk', he explains. 'You go home and put your feet in a hot basin after. That feels good. About twice a week, you give "em a good soakin"'. What John does at work determines what he does when he's not at work. 'When I'm home, I keep 'em elevated, stay off 'em as much as possible, give 'em a lot of rest. I wear out on the average three or five pairs of shoes a year' (p. 272).

Some workers garner a sense of pride from their work, like Babe Secolin, the supermarket cashier who boasts of memorizing the prices and handling the keys on the cash register so quickly and gracefully that it's 'like playing the piano' (p. 283). 'I'm a checker and I'm proud of it', she says. 'Whoever looks down on me, they're lower than I am' (p. 284). Or consider the dentist Stephen Bartlett, who likens himself not to a musician but to an artist. Dentistry, he explains, 'requires a certain skill, a certain art. If you do a good job, damn it, you're proud of it'. But, he adds, 'you want other people to appreciate it' as well and whereas 'an artist can hang his work on the wall and everybody sees it; no one sees mine except me' (p. 245).

For most, however, feelings of pride are elusive. 'Proud of my work?' Phil Stallings, a spot welder at the Ford assembly plant, ponders.

> How can I feel pride in a job where I call a foreman's attention to a mistake, a bad piece of equipment, and he'll ignore it? Pretty soon you get the idea that they don't care. You keep doing this and finally you're titled a troublemaker. So you just go about your work. You *have* to have pride. So you throw it off to something else. And that's my stamp collection. (p. 162)

Mike Lefevre, the 37-year-old steelworker featured at the start of the book, laments:

> you can't take pride any more ... It's hard to take pride in a bridge you're never gonna cross, in a door you're never gonna open. You're mass-producing things and you never see the end result

of it ... I would like to see a building, say, the Empire State, I would like to see on one side of it a foot-wide strip from top to bottom with the name of every bricklayer, the name of every electrician, with all the names. So when a guy walked by, he could say, 'See, that's me over there on the forty-fifth floor. I pull the steel beam in'. Picasso can point to a painting. What can I point to?... Everybody should have something to point to. (p. xxxii)

'In all instances', Terkel concludes, 'there is felt more than a slight ache: Ought not there be an increment, earned though not yet received, from one's daily work – an acknowledgement of man's being?' (p. xiii).

For the majority of those featured in the book, work is downright dehumanizing. This is true whether one is toiling under a hot sun or pushing paper in an air-conditioned office. 'The blue-collar blues is no more bitterly sung than the white-collar moan' (p. xi), Terkel quips. Take Steve Dubi, a lifelong steelworker living in Pullman, an industrial neighbourhood on the far south side of Chicago. 'You're not regarded', he explains.

> You're just a number out there. Just like a prisoner. When you report off you tell 'em your badge number. A lotta people don't know your name. They know you by your badge number ... Forty years of hard work and what do I have to show for it? Nothing ... I led a useless life. (pp. 554–557)

Jim Grayson, another spot welder at Ford, explains, 'you're nothing to any of them. That's why I hate the place ... There's no time for the human side in this work' (pp. 167–168). Nancy Rogers, a 28-year-old bank teller, feels similarly dehumanized. She works in what is called a 'cage'. 'It's not quite like being in prison, but I still feel very locked in'. She continues,

> I think a lot of places don't want people to be people. I think they want you to almost be the machines they're working with. They just want to dehumanize you. Just like when you walk in in the morning, you put the switch on and here you are: 'I am a robot. This is what I do. Good morning. How are you? May I help you?' (p. 261)

Workers struggle to find ways to cope with the stress and to counter the disrespect with which they are treated on the job. As Dolores Dante, a waitress, explains, 'You've got to go release your tension' after each shift.

> Really, I've been keeping it to myself. But of late, I'm beginning to spew it out. It's almost as though I sensed my body and soul had had enough. It builds and builds and builds in your guts .... It hurts and what hurts has to come out. (p. 298)

There are stories in this book of workers taking it out on themselves: too many cigarettes, excess drinking, suicide. There are even more numerous accounts of workers taking things out on each other. Mike Lefevre, introduced above, explains:

> I work so damn hard and want to come home and sit down and lay around. *But I gotta get it out.* I want to be able to turn around to somebody and say, 'Hey, fuck you'. You know? The guy sitting next to me on the bus, too. 'Cause all day I wanted to tell my foreman to go fuck himself, but I can't. So I find a guy in a tavern. To tell him that. (p. xxxiii)

Mike presses on, emphasizing both the inevitability but also the futility of the situation. 'Who you gonna sock? You can't sock General Motors, you can't sock anybody in Washington, you can't sock a system' (p. xxxii). As Studs writes in the intro, 'and look out below!' Harold Patrick, a freight elevator operator, explains it best:

> Every worker looks down at the other. Let's say he's a guy who's on top of the skyscraper and he's tossin' these things and he's walkin' out on the beam: I'm number one. Here, boy. I'm makin' the biggest buildin'. He's proud, right? The truckdriver that drives the big trailer in and out and backs it into ... he's got a certain pride. And he looks down. Now the guy who sweeps the floor in one of the shops, the elevator man can look over him, he's a little bit lower. Each one has their guy ... But what pride is there in lookin' down? (p. 570)

There is a deep sociological analysis embedded in Studs' editorial rendering: the constant put-downs and one-upmanship are a feature of the capitalist system.

Moreover, mutual derision and divisiveness are exacerbated by a set of managerial practices that have only become more entrenched in the decades since *Working* was published. The first is worker surveillance (Vargas, 2017). Nick Salerno, a garbage man, describes what it's like to be subjected to increased surveillance. 'We've got spotters now. It's new. They're riding around in unmarked cars. They'll turn you in for stopping for coffee. There's definitely more watching today'. Will Robinson, a Chicago Transit Author (CTA) bus driver, similarly identifies the increased layers of surveillance to which he's subjected throughout his daily routes. Not only does he deal with 'spotters' who board the bus to watch everything that's going on, but he also deals with 'supervisors on the street' at a series of 'checkpoints' between one terminal and another. 'If you're running a minute ahead of time', he explains,

> they write you up and you're called into the office. Sometimes they can really upset you. They'll stop you at a certain point. Some of them have the habit of wanting to bawl you out there on the street. That's one of the most upsetting parts of it.

Beryl Simpson, an airline reservationist, describes being tethered to the (then new) computer and subjected to electronic forms of surveillance:

> They monitored you and listened to your conversations. If you were a minute late for work, it went into your file. I had a horrible attendance record – ten letters in my file for lateness, a total of ten minutes. You took thirty minutes for lunch, not thirty-one. If you got a break, you took ten minutes, not eleven ... With the airline, I had no free will. I was just part of that stupid computer. (pp. 49–50)

Tipping is another practice featured prominently in these accounts that divides workers and disorganizes the workforce, as recently explored by Hanna Goldberg et al. (2024) in a piece published in the last volume of *Research in the Sociology of Work*. Consider Thomas Rush, a 57-year-old skycap who works for one of the country's major airlines. 'We have to do a lot more than the general public thinks. They think of us as a strong back and a weak mind'. Thomas' views on tipping are clearly shot through with ambiguity. On the one hand, Thomas claims that skycaps are 'grossly underpaid in salary', particularly considering that they do more than the higher-earning workers at the ticket counters. On the other hand, Thomas exclaims 'we make it on tips. Every time I walk through that door I get money'. But this reliance on tips proves problematic. For starters, it leads some skycaps to grovel to a degree that Thomas, as a Black man, views as shameful.

> I look at everybody at eye level. I neither look down nor up. The day of the shuffle is gone. I better not see any of the fellas that works for me doing it. Not ever! ... That perpetual grin I just don't dig. (p. 287)

In addition, the practice of tipped compensation generates all kinds of tension between workers. 'Don't you think these people know I'm making money?' Thomas says of his coworkers at the airline. 'I think most agents have a little animosity towards skycaps because they feel we're doing quite well' (p. 288). Same goes for the 'ramp service man', although Thomas admits that he is doing the majority of the work out in the cold while the skycap alone gets to pocket the tip. Because he feels skycaps benefit from the arrangement, Thomas rejects the idea of a union. 'We're the elite of the fleet', he proclaims.

Doc Pritchard, who works as a front desk clerk in a hotel in Manhattan, near Times Square, outlines similar workplace tensions, but from the perspective of an untipped employee:

> The clerk in a hotel is rarely tipped. The bellboys, rather, get all the tips. A fellow that comes into the hotel to do a little cheating will always tip the bellboy heavily. The boy can't help him at all, in any way, shape, or form. It's the clerk who watches his mail, watches his messages, and watches who comes in and out to see him. It's really the clerk who covers for him. But he never seems to realize that ... The clerk [is the one who] knows what's going on ... Occasionally you will get people who seem to know their way around. They will throw the clerk a couple of bucks or a five dollar bill now and then. (p. 249)

Sam Mature, a barber and owner of a barber shop in downtown Chicago, lays out an unequivocally critical view on the practice and politics of tipping. He recognizes that it is 'pretty hard to keep a person from tipping. They tip a bellhop, they tip a redcap, they tip a waiter'. But the problem, according to Sam, is that bosses of barber shops won't agree to pay the barbers more. 'They'd rather the customer help pay this barber's salary by tipping in'. As a boss himself, Sam says, 'I'm in favor of not tipping. I'd just as soon pay the man ten dollars more a week than have him depend on that customer. This way he knows that he's got that steady income' (p. 235). Tipping, Sam believes, is antithetical to the professionalism of the trade. Tipping, Sam says, 'made me feel like I was a beggar' (p. 236).

WAKING UP THE HUMAN ANIMAL

Workers draw from their jobs important lessons about the way the world works and their place within it. 'The system stinks', Studs reflects, 'was a phrase almost as recurrent as "more or less"' (p. xxii). Take Philip Da Vinci, an attorney working for Legal Aid in Chicago representing clients who are among the most marginalized in society. Philip initially stuck with the job because he 'actually felt useful', but after just a few years in, the job leaves him feeling 'emotionally sick because of [his] powerlessness'. He explains:

> You'd like to pick up a gun and get that cop who beat up that thirteen-year-old kid. You get twenty-five bucks for a kid that's had his skull split open by five police officers. You know its bullshit. Maybe the best way is to give the kid a gun and say 'Okay, square it'. But those are the depressing moments ... [The job] has helped me see a lot of things and make me aware of what's going on in our society – what the system does to people. (p. 540)

Walter Lundquist, a commercial artist and designer, also came to an epiphany of sorts via his job, realizing that 'every man, every human is a commodity to be exploited. And destroyed and cast aside'. He had wanted to be 'at the drawing board, creative, doing something [he] believed in'. Instead, he explains, 'I became a pimp' or 'commercial hack', helping companies advertise useless products. 'You begin to say 'what the fuck am I doing? I'm sitting here destroying my country' (p. 526). Walter now faces the dilemma of figuring out how to maintain his integrity, his personhood, while supporting his family:

> I'm straddling two worlds and I'm trying to move over into the sane one. But I can't make a living out of it ... I'm struggling to survive. I'm running out of funds. I may have to pimp again for survival's sake ... But I'll never again play the full-time lying dishonest role I've done most of my life. Once you wake up the human animal you can't put it back to sleep again. (p. 527)

There are countless stories in the book of workers who, like Walter, 'wake up' and draw a line. Maggie Holmes, a Black domestic worker, refuses her employer's demands that she scrub the floor on her hands and knees. 'Like you're in the fields, like people pickin' cotton. No mop or nothin''. Indignant, Maggie sneaks around the house to find the hidden mop and declares, 'There's no more getting' on their knees' (p. 116). Others take collective action, learning first-hand the value of solidarity. Phil Stallings, the spot welder at Ford, drew a line when his co-worker, Jim Grayson, was threatened by the foreman. He and his co-workers went on a wildcat strike in solidarity. Phil explains,

> The foreman was riding the guy. Damn it, it's about time we took a stand. Let's stick up for this guy. We stopped the line. Ford lost about twenty units ... That's the first time I've seen unity on that line. Now it's happened once, it'll happen again. Because everybody just sat down. Believe you me. It stopped at eight and it didn't start till twenty after eight. Everybody and his brother were down there. It was really nice to see, it really was. (p. 163)

Amidst these accounts of 'waking up', there is constant reflection on dreams: on dreams denied, dreams deferred, and dreams for a better future. Grace Clements, who toils as a felter in a sweltering luggage factory, admits to daydreaming while she's working, picturing herself on the river with her husband in their sixteen-foot boat. 'You get to be automatic in what you're doing and your mind is doing something else', she explains. Carl Murray Bates, a mason, can't help but dream of his craft. 'Stone's my life', he says.

> I daydream all the time, most times it's on stone. Oh, I'm gonna build me a stone cabin ... I'm gonna build stone cabinets ... I've got to figure out how to build a stone roof ... All my dreams, it seems like it's got to have a piece of rock mixed in it (p. xlvii).

Others dream about workplace sabotage. Frances Swenson, a hotel switchboard operator and self-described 'happy-go-lucky middle-aged woman', explains: 'We don't get respect. We don't get it from the bosses or the guests ... if they knew how hard we worked. Today communications is a big thing ... I really think we demand a little more respect'. Francis and her co-workers fantasize:

> Wouldn't it be great if we could just take this handful of plugs and just yank 'em? (Laughs) We think of it, we think of it. Like I said, you get so tense ... If we could just pull 'em. Disconnect them and see what happens. (p. 35)

But many dream of a new world altogether. They dream of abolishing the system that stinks and degrades and deprives. They envision, instead, a system in which humans can engage in creative and caretaking pursuits without concern for whether there will be food on the table or a roof over their heads.

This starts with reconsidering what we think of and recognize as work. On this point, Studs quotes Ralph Helstein, president emeritus of the United Packinghouse Workers of America.

> Learning is work. Caring for children is work. Community action is work. Once we accept the concept of work as something meaningful – not just as the source of a buck – you don't have to worry about finding enough jobs ... There's no question about our ability to feed and clothe and house everybody. (p. xxiii)

This would relieve women like Jesusita Novarro, a single mother to five children, from being made to 'feel like you're nothing'. 'I'm home and I'm working', she explains. 'I'm a working mother ... This is an all-around job, day and night .... I'm so busy all day I don't have time to daydream'. Jesusita goes on to ask, echoing the demands of the Wages for Housework movement (Federici, 1975), 'Why can't a woman just get a check in the mail: Here, this check is for you. Forget welfare. You're a mother who works' (p. 304).

Lilith Reynolds is a public-sector bureaucrat employed by the Office of Economic Opportunity, the agency responsible for administering the War on Poverty programmes. A leader in her union and advocate for the poor, Lilith, too, emphasizes the need to delink what we do for work from how we survive. She dreams of a system of universal basic income. Not only would it more adequately fulfil human needs, but it would cultivate better humans:

> I think we should have a basic security – a decent place to live, decent food, decent clothing, and all that. So people in a work situation wouldn't be so frightened. People are intimidated and the system works to emphasize that. They get what they want out of people by threatening them economically. It makes people apple polishers and ass kissers. I used to hear people say 'work needs to be redefined'. I thought they were crazy. Now I know they're not. (p. 347)

Mike Lefevre, the steelworker, shares a similar dream of human flourishing, one that he notes is increasingly within reach given advances in technology. 'Why can we send a rocket ship that's unmanned and yet send a man in a steel mill to do a mule's work?' Automation, he continues, only 'frightens me if it puts me out on the street. It doesn't frighten me if it shortens my work week ... Machines can either liberate man or enslave 'em'. For Mike, there's no question that 'the twenty-hour week is a possibility today' (p. xxxiii). Studs himself notes that 'in a world of almost runaway technology, things are increasingly making things. It is for our species, it would seem, to go on to other matters. Human matters' (p. xxii).

'Let me tell you where the grief bites you so much', says Nick Lindsay, a carpenter and poet, highlighting the absurdity of labour under capitalism and underscoring the need for attending to such 'human matters'.

> Who are you working for? If you're going to eat, you are working for the man who pays you some kind of wage. That won't be a poor man. The man who's got a big family and who's needing a house, you're not building a house for him. The only man you're working for is the man who could get along without it. You're putting a roof on the man who's got enough to pay your wage. You see over yonder, shack needs a roof. Over here you're building a $60,000 house for a man

who maybe doesn't have any children. He's not hurting and it doesn't mean much. It's a prestige house. He's gonna up-man, he's gonna be one-up on his neighbor, having something fancier. (p. 517).

As Harold Patrick quips, 'they don't get there unless the elevator man let's them up'. In other words, labour makes all wealth possible in the first place. He continues

> I believe socialism is gonna be the future. I believed that fifty years ago and I believe that today. I never lost my doubts which way the human race is gonna go. The capitalists are puttin' together cars, it's socialized, the production. But the means of returns are not socialized. It goes into a few, but it's produced by the many. You see the results in the workers around you. Some of 'em are broken at thirty, at forty, some of 'em at fifty. (p. 571)

All of these dreams endure to this day: for policy implementation of universal basic income, for shorter working weeks facilitated by technological innovation, for socialized distribution of returns. Indeed, these are not simply lofty dreams, but realistic collective demands.

CODA

'My work is trying to change this country', Bill Talcott explains. 'The daily injustices just gnaw on me a little harder than they do on other people'. As an organizer, Bill's job is to 'bring people together who are being put down by the system, left out' (p. 352). He explains that

> 'everybody's at the bottom of the barrel at this point. Ten years ago one could say the poor people suffered and the middle class got by. That's not true any more ... the middle class is fighting powerlessness too' (p. 355).

Across class, you see that 'the words are different, but it's the same script' (p. 354). One of the primary challenges of the job is that 'most people were raised to think they are not worthy'. This is why, Bill insists, 'you must listen to them and tell them again and again they are important'.

Studs Terkel was many things, although organizer was not one of them. Nevertheless, he, too, dedicated his life to listening to people and telling them again and again that they are important. I end by highlighting the striking overlap between Bill's description of his work as an organizer and what Studs Terkel has managed to accomplish with *Working*. Like Bill, Studs Terkel brought people together from different walks of life. Compiling their accounts between the covers of this best-selling book, Studs revealed that although their words may differ, everyone is drawing from the 'same script': the need for material security, the demand for dignity, the desire for recognition, the pursuit of flourishing. In an increasingly polarized and atomized world, to read *Working* is to awaken the human animal. It's solidarity-building in action.

Studs no doubt shared Bill's perspective on history. As Bill explains,

> The problem with history is that it's written by college professors about great men. That's not what history is. History's a hell of a lot of little people getting together and deciding they want a better life for themselves and their kids. (pp. 355–356)

Working – this stupendous account of a hell of a lot of little people – contributes to that history-making. Although work has changed in countless ways, *Working* remains as powerful and relevant today as when it was originally published a half of a century ago.

REFERENCES

Alvarez, M. (2022). *The work of living: Working people talk about their lives and the year the world broke*. OR Books.

Bowe, J., Bowe, M., & Streeter, S. (Eds.). (2000). *Gig: Americans talk about their jobs*. Three Rivers Press.

Cech, E. (2021). *The trouble with passion: How searching for fulfillment at work fosters inequality*. University of California Press.

Federici, S. (1975). *Wages against housework*. Power of Women Collective and Falling Wall Press.

Fink, L. (2010). Re-working Studs Terkel. *Work, Employment, and Society, 24*(2), 386–390. https://doi.org/10.1177/0950017010362160

Goldberg, H. (2024). Divided wages and divided workers: Tips and the two-employer problem. In R. Delbridge, M. Helfen, A. Pekarek, & G. Purser (Eds.), *Ethnographies of work* (Research in the Sociology of Work, Vol. 35, pp. 9–34). Emerald Publishers. https://doi.org/10.1108/S0277-283320230000035002

Graeber, D. (2018). *Bullshit jobs*. Simon & Schuster.

Hirsch, P. M., & Cornfield, D. B. (2010). When he listened, people talked. *Contexts, 9*(2), 38–43.

Purser, G. (2012). 'Still doin' time:' Clamoring for work in the day labor industry. *Working USA: The Journal of Labor and Society, 15*(3), 397–415. https://doi.org/10.1111/j.1743-4580.2012.00400.x

Purser, G. (2019). Day labor agencies, backdoor hires, and the spread of unfree labor. *Anthropology of Work Review, 40*(1), 5–14. https://doi.org/10.1111/awr.12158

Terkel, S. (1970). *Working*. The New Press.

Terkel, S. (1997). *Studs Terkel reader: My American century*. The New Press.

Vargas, T. (2017). Employees or suspects: Surveillance and scrutinization of low-wage service workers in U.S. dollar stores. *Journal of Labor and Society, 20*(2), 207–230. https://doi.org/10.1163/24714607-02002004

INDEX

Note: Page numbers followed by *n* indicate notes.

Advocacy, 30–32
Aesthetic preferences, 143, 146
Aesthetics, 150–154
Age distribution of essential workers, 137
Alienation, 178
Altruistic motivations, 7, 60, 75
Apprenticeship, 151
Armistice Day (*see* Remembrance Day)
Authentic selves, 58
Authenticity, 7, 59, 74–77

Black and Hispanic/Latinx workers, 111
Boundary work, 147–148
Breaching experiment, 59
    care work and management of emotions, 60–63
    data collection and analysis, 65–67
    emotion management and professional feeling rules during COVID-19, 67–74
    research strategy and methodology, 63–67

Capitalist production, 112
Care aides, 82, 84–85, 88
Care labour, 42
Care penalty, 16
Care philosophy, 65
Care work, 3, 5–6, 14, 41–45, 58–63
Care workers, 13, 17, 24–28, 30–32, 60, 62, 68
CareCoop, 18, 24, 27
Caregivers, 61
Center for Disease Control (CDC), 46
Centres d'hébergement de soins de longue durée (CHSLD), 88
Certified Floral Designers (CFD), 148

'CFC', 147
Civil Rights Movement, 115
Cleaning, 41
Combinatory ethnography, 150
Commercial feeling rules, 61
Commodification
    of reproductive labour, 112, 114
    of social reproduction, 112
Concept of essentiality, 133
Contestation, 98–99
COVID-19 pandemic, 2, 7–8, 13, 40, 59, 65, 82, 118
    care work, 41–45
    custodial services staff at Prairie University, 50–53
    invisibilization, 41–45
    methodology and research design, 45–47
    policy construction of custodial work as essential labour, 47–50
COVID-19 safety and cleaning labour, 51–53
'Critical infrastructure' workers, 112–113
Critical juncture, 2
Current Population Survey's Merged Outgoing Rotation Group file (CPS-MORG), 119
Custodial services
    employees, 40
    staff at Prairie University, 50–53
Custodial work
    as care labour, 43–45
    federal definitions, 47–48
    municipal definitions of essential work, 49–50
    policy construction of custodial work as essential labour, 47
    state definitions, 48–49

Custodial workers, 40
Custodians, 40
Cybersecurity and Infrastructure Security Agency (CISA), 46, 112

Deep-acting, 61
Dehumanization of work, 144
Department of State Health Services (DSHS), 49
Designations of essential *vs.* non-essential labor, 40
'Devaluation' perspective, 42, 115, 117
Dirty care work, 14, 18, 27–28, 33–34
Dirty work, 6–7, 12, 16–18, 21
  to essentiality in times of crisis, 84–85
  genuine valuation of dirty work in society, 99–101
  scholarship, 34
  studies, 14
  wound clinicians, 21–24
Discourse, 98–99
Discourses of essentiality, 82
Discrete skills, 83
Discrimination, 115–116
Division Street, 178
Dramas of Dignity (Costas), 165–166

Effective care provision, 60
Elderly care homes, 3
Emancipation, 166
Emancipatory potential, 174
  of ethnographic research, 178
Emotion management, 7, 12, 15, 60–63, 67–74
  data analysis, 20
  data collection, 18–19
  dirt y work, 16–18
  gender and, 14–16
  methods, 18–20
  performances, 64
  practices, 7, 62
  in pre-pandemic times, 67–68
  of residential care workers, 58
  stigma management, 20–32

Emotions, 14
  labour, 60–61
  work, 24
Empathizing, 17
Empirical insights, 72
Essential care occupations, 14
Essential labour, 7, 40, 54, 128
Essential work, 2, 8, 40–41, 83, 110, 164
  peculiarities, 165
  recognition and dignity to public value and reward, 4–6
Essential workers, 2–4, 8, 85, 110–115
  analytic approach, 122–123
  data and methods, 119–123
  data source and sample, 119–120
  intersectional perspective on valuation of essential work, 115–119
  results, 123–131
  variable measurement, 120–122
  wage gaps, 127–129
Essentiality, 45, 60, 111
  discourse, 92
  emergence of political and public discourse on, 92–94
  of work, 2, 6
Ethnicity, 110, 112
Ethnographers, 164
Ethnographic fieldwork, 147
Ethnographic research, 143, 146, 159, 170, 178–179
Ethnographic scholarship, 144
Ethnographic studies, 164
  contextualizing and introducing studies, 165–167
  Dramas of Dignity (Costas), 167–170
  of essential work, 143
  Grenzen aus Glas (Birke), 170–174
Ethnography, 179
Ethos, 68
Eureka database, 86
Expendable workers, 3
Expertise, 146–149

Index

Exploratory ethnography of wound healing, 18
Exposure to COVID-19, 48

Face-saving-strategies, 154–157
Fair Labor Standards Act (FLSA), 117
Feeling rules, 61
Floral culture, 151
Floral designers, 146
Floral ethics, 146
    and aesthetics, 150–154
    face-saving-strategies, 154–157
    licensing and expertise, 147–149
    methods, data, and setting, 149–150
Florist, 146
    occupation, 146–148, 151

Garfinkel's concept, 59
Gender, 14–16, 110–112
Gendered care work, 6–7, 14, 34
Gendered organizations, 15
Gendering, 15
Germany, 165
'Getting through it together', 71–74
Government policies, 7, 40
Grenzen aus Glas (Birke), 165–166
Grief in neo-natal nursing, 15

Health and social care systems, 8, 82, 100
Health system, 87
Health-related quality of life, 28–30
Healthcare professionals, 15
Healthcare workers, 87
Home care aids, 17
Hospitals, 3
Human capital, 8, 111, 115, 118, 121, 123, 127, 130

Independency, 30–32
Inequality, 42
Inessential workers, 2
Information technology (IT), 113
Institutionalised care, 31

Institutionalization, 8, 100
'Intentional initiation' of disruptive crises, 65
International Labour Office (ILO), 4
Intersectional inequality research, 115
Intersectional lens, 8, 115, 131
Intersectional perspective, 110
Intersectional wage gaps, 111, 129–131
Intersectional wage inequalities, 8, 111, 131
Interviews, 178
Invisibilization, 41–45

Jana Costas, 143, 165–166

Labour markets, 2–4, 63, 77, 99
    characteristics, 110
Labour shortage, 5
Labour studies, 144
License, 149
Licensing, 147–149
Listening, 17
Lockdown, 70–71
Low-status occupational groups, 83
Low-status workers, 8

Management by labor turnover, 172
Management practices, 84
Masculine heroism, 17
Meat processing, 3
Media, 4
'Menial' care labour, 42
Migrant workers, 167, 170
Mini job, 6
Motivations, 62
Multidimensional analysis, 61

National Labor Relations Act of 1935, 117
National Labor Relations Board (NLRB), 117–118
Necessity shield, 32, 34
Non-essential workers, 8
Non-nurturant care work, 42–43
Normative hegemony, 84

Nurturant care work, 42–43
Nurturant/non-nurturant binaries, 43

Occupational communities, 7, 12, 33, 35
Occupational group, 8, 13, 17, 86, 99, 101, 147
Occupational legitimacy, 143, 159
Occupational Safety and Health Administration (OSHA), 46
Occupational segregation, 83
Oral history, 166
Ordinary least squares (OLS), 122
Organizational feeling rules, 15, 61
Organizational model, 65

Packaging plants, 3
Pandemic challenges, 3
Parcel delivery centres, 3
Pecuniary emotion work, 15
Performativity, 8, 82–83
    of discourse, 85–86
Peter Birke, 143, 165–166, 170
Philanthropic emotional management, 16, 58
Physical taint, 13, 17–18
Policy landscape, 40, 45–47
Policymakers, 4
Political discourse on essentiality, 92–94
Political elites, 83
Politics, 83
    comparison of occupations performing care work, 89–91
    conceptual background, 83–86
    data sources, 86–87
    discourse, contestation, and social change, 98–99
    emergence of political and public discourse on essentiality, 92–94
    genuine valuation of dirty work in society, 99–101
    gradual restoration of pre-pandemic labour regime, 94–96
    methodology, 86–87
    promulgation of discourse of essentiality and signs of recognition, 97–98
    research context, 87–91
    research design, 86
Power asymmetry, 143
Prairie University, 46, 55n1
    custodial services staff at, 50–53
Pre-pandemic labour regime, gradual restoration of, 94–96
Pre-pandemic times, emotion management in, 67–68
Precarious nature of essential work, 144
Precarious work settings, 2, 4
Precarity of work, 9, 167
Prescriptive emotion management, 15, 58
Presentational emotional management, 15–16, 58
Privatization, 5
Profession, 146
Professional blunting, 29
Professional competencies, 148
Professional ethos, 59
Professional expertise, 143, 147, 155
Professional face, 63
Professional feeling rules, 15, 61–62
    of care workers, 59
    during COVID-19, 67–74
Professional groups, 17
Professional ideology, 147
Professional work, 59–60, 146
    ethos, 60
Promulgation of discourse of essentiality and signs of recognition, 97–98
Pseudonyms, 19
Public discourse on essentiality, 92–94
Public health measures, 8
Public policy implications, 4

Quebec healthcare system, 87

Race, 110, 112
Racial earnings inequality, 116

Index 193

Recalibrating, 16–17
Refocussing, 16–17
Reframing, 16–17
Relational work, 7, 32–33
Relevance of working, 3
Remembrance Day, 68, 77*n*2
Reproductive labour, 112
Residential care homes, 71
Residential care workers, 60

Sanitization, 41
Schools, 3
Segregation, 115
Sensitizing concepts, 67
Sentimental work, 61
Service relationships, 146
Service work, 168
Short-term commercial interactions, 60
Skills, 12, 25, 28–29, 118
Smiling through mask, 69–70
Social care, 12, 64
Social change, 85–86, 98–99
Social distancing, 70–71
Social fabric of exclusion within labour markets, 83–84
Social feeling rules, 15, 61
Social inequality, 111
Social processes, 67
Social stability, 111
Social stigma, 13, 28
Social stratification, 111
Social taint, 12, 17
Societal integration, 5
  implications, 5
Sociology of work, 6, 144, 146
Spiritual/menial binaries, 43
'Spiritual' care labour, 42
'Stay Home–Work Safe' order, 49–50, 55*n*3
Stigma, 12
  literature on, 14
  management, 12, 17, 20–32
  strategies, 13
Stigmatizing work roles, 143, 167
'Structure-agency' dilemma, 164
Studs Terkel, 178
Subcontracted cleaning services, 5
Surface acting, 61
Swiss apprenticeship system, 148
Swiss miracle, 147
Symbolic devaluation of women, 42
Systemic racism, 8, 110, 117

Tensions in work, 146, 158
Theory of performativity, 98
Truly caring, 17
Trust, 155

US labour market, 148

Valourization of care work, 97

Wage gap, 110
Wagner Act (*see* National Labor Relations Act of 1935)
White women, 42
Women's work, 42
Work, 12
  purpose of, 28–30
Work environment, 60
Work well done, 143, 146–147, 156–157
Workers, 13, 58
Working (book), 144, 178
  Coda, 187
  ethnographic encounters, 178–179
  on the job, 179–184
  waking up the human animal, 184–187
Wound care, 13
Wound clinicians, 21–24, 28–30
Wound stigma, 22

Printed and bound by CPI Group (UK) Ltd, Croydon, CR0 4YY
21/11/2024

14596803-0002